"Martin Keller's book combii   ing personal journey with a careful
evaluation of the theories a   e UFO world, striking a
perfect balance between   dness. His adventures
are described honestl   sifts through the
evidence the   onal thinking
about o   theories that
involve   lers will have
their

                                        iaries, and
                                        tions, and

                                   ng account of his
                                   ariencer and his
                                   Jtimately surviv-
                                   journey into the
                              one is packed with
                              sightings, lore and
                              e Space Pen Club
                                   the truth about
                                   10 owns these
                                   *rols their ob-
                                   are known to
                                   anisms and fuel
                    1el   basic needs for
              nd c

          eason 1 SNL cas,   Clues Brother, producer
       melong interest in all things psi, paranormal and saucerlogical

"I never told anyone what happened at dusk that night as my girlfriend and I cruised between cornfields on a small highway back to Minneapolis from Hutchinson, Minnesota. I did not want to hear disbelief, see the snicker forming on faces, or suffer the humiliation of telling my truth. I never told anyone, that is, until former music journalist Martin Keller shared his truth with me one afternoon over lunch and a little Prince gossip. Kudos to Keller for helping me come to grips with a series of events that happened to me so many years ago and for finally sharing his own story in this personal, page-turning epic called *The Space Pen Club*!"

Owen Husney, author of the memoir *Famous People Who've Met Me: A Memoir by the Man Who Discovered Prince*

"This book is much needed in the field of Ufology. The mix of intensely personal experiences with a chronicle of a decade's worth of colorful personalities, movements, and events is unique and absorbing. This is not just another book about UFO sightings, but rather a captivating look at how the public disclosure of UFOs has relentlessly unfolded under the pressure of dedicated activists, the ubiquity of cell phone cameras, a growing acceptance of UFO phenomena, an erosion of the government's grip on information, and an intensity of contact. Anyone interested in this topic will be captivated by this well-researched and lively written account by a true insider."

Adrian Lee, author of *Ghosts & UFOs: Connecting Paranormal Phenomena through Quantum Physics*

"*The Space Pen Club* reads like a beautifully written novel, or a perplexing mystery to solve. Or simply as the true and often funny and sometimes frightening story of one man's many attempts to find out the truth about UFOs, UAPs or 'WYWTCTs—Whatever You Want to Call Them.' Martin Keller presents the facts and the facades of this strange world we live in with a no BS attitude and a smart analysis of what's going on. And it's packed with an unforgettable cast of characters that are sometimes almost as hard to fathom as the enigmatic behavior of "the boys upstairs" – Keller's kooky shorthand for whoever—or whatever—is flying these many objects around our planet and scaring Elon Musk."

Louie Anderson, three-time Emmy Award-winning actor, comedian and best-selling *New York Times* author

THE SPACE PEN CLUB

Close Encounters of the 5th Kind—
UFO Disclosure, Consciousness
& Other Mind Zoomers

MARTIN KELLER

CALUMET EDITIONS

Minneapolis

THE SPACE PEN CLUB

Close Encounters of the 5th Kind—
UFO Disclosure, Consciousness
& Other Mind Zoomers

CALUMET
EDITIONS

Minneapolis

First Edition June 2021

THE SPACE PEN CLUB: *Close Encounters of the 5th Kind—*
UFO Disclosure, Consciousness & Other Mind Zoomers

Copyright © 2021 by Martin Keller. All rights reserved.

Printed in the United States of America.
10 9 8 7 6 5 4 3 2 1

ISBN: 978-1-950743-55-1

Cover and book design by Gary Lindberg

"Remembering speechlessly we seek the great forgotten language, the lost lane-end into heaven, a stone, a leaf, an unfound door. Where? When?"

−Look Homeward, Angel, Thomas Wolfe

*

"Who looks outside, dreams; who looks inside, awakes."

−Carl Jung

TABLE OF CONTENTS

In Loving Memory of my parents, Ted and Joyce, who showed me how the stars in the heavens and the words on the page possess their own power and light.

Dedicated to my wife, children and siblings. And to all past, present and future members of the Club.

PROLOGUE

I was "motovatin'" like Chuck Berry in "Maybellene" toward the small town of Cosmos, Minnesota, engulfed by the greater cosmos, and wondering, when did it really all begin—the strange lights and sounds in the bedroom, the unscheduled four o'clock "wake-up calls," the long nights under the stars watching the skies, waiting... waiting for something to happen?

Photo: Chuck Statler

In the early 1990s, I was stuck between jobs after working in both music journalism and public relations. But during the same period, I chanced at a side hustle I thought might take me someplace new. It was as if a strange bus had stopped to pick me up for an uncharted and often unguided tour.

Would you have gotten on?

I did.

But I forgot to check whether it was a roundtrip or a one-way ride. Somewhere in the deep winter of 1992, events began inside my home—and head—that resuscitated a buried childhood interest. An unintended journey had started traversing a subject I thought I had left behind with high-school first loves, acne and other adolescent worlds. My fleeting youthful curiosity rekindled without warning: It burst into an intense seven-year hands-on focus on unidentified flying objects and close encounters, especially Close Encounters of the Fifth Kind—human-initiated contact with "the visitors" using a systematic idea developed by Dr. Steven Greer, MD, at The Center for the Study of Extraterrestrial Intelligence (CSETI). The organization entertained the possibility that life, or what Westerners call extraterrestrial life (not the microbial-level science discoveries that always make news headlines) was a factual reality that has been staring us in the collective face for longer than we know—and that we could empower ourselves to contact it.

Through those storied seven years "on the bus," I traveled within circles of both well-defined and indecipherable reality as both an observer and the observed, an insider and an outsider. Along the way, I was forced to confront the so-called abduction phenomenon, the Byzantine secrecy puzzle, myriad other UFO groups and individuals obsessed with the truth and the lies that were out there, media skeptics, debunkers and "Birds" from "the Aviary," each with their own agendas, techniques and peccadilloes.

My life essentially split in two. The "strange" one was acted out with somewhat guarded movement, while the other one was lived in everyday sequences and activities that friends, siblings and business clients witnessed and still see today.

So, I was in the UFO closet.

But once the strange path rolled out before me, I went with it slowly, naively and, some might say, stupidly. Nothing professionally could have prepared me for such an odd track. And I was limited by how little I knew about the subject, even though I had witnessed a large, stationary UFO near the ground with three other high-school classmates our sophomore year during a time of highly recorded UFO activity in western North Dakota, an event explored in Chapter Four.

One usually goes looking for connections in such unforgettable moments, a way to comprehend the observation and place it in the conventional context of human experience and knowledge. But as I learned in the UFO field, convention is an inconvenient word and nearly inconsequential in the broader scheme of things. The other option, rooted in denial, was to just shrug the whole thing off.

Neither the PR work I had done nor my pop culture or business writing had prepared me for the events and experiences addressed in this book. The latter provided diversionary points of reference and solace. The former gave me some modest tools of mass communication with which to travel what was often a foreign and perplexing landscape, no passport required. The journey, at times akin to a long cosmic carjacking, occasionally was made comical and amusing when factoring in the unpredictability of human nature while searching for something as confounding and easily dismissible as the UFO/ET phenomenon. Plus, there was a lot of deep muck to wade through—various cultural biases, bad media reporting, sensational stories on the big screen and tired, age-old institutional thinking, along with individual prejudices.

At several points, I sensed that I should have tried to end this impossible star trek as abruptly as it had begun. In other words, just GET OFF THE BUS. Like I did that day I got a long-distance call from an inmate serving time in a Utah prison for robbery. He had found my number (most likely on the Internet) and wanted help making his prearranged connection with a mothership.

"Can you help me out?" he begged. "You know about this, right?"

He was serious—I think. I encouraged him to seek Legal Aid.

Or like that lunch when I was firmly entrenched in the "UFO ghetto," a term humorously and dismissively used by CSETI's Dr. Steve Greer, a character so maligned *and* celebrated you would think he's either the most wretched con man ever to undermine Western civilization or an enlightened visionary almost capable of tiptoeing on water. We had been eating with several esteemed UFO researchers and were ready to settle the bill. One of them weaseled out of paying his share by saying he had already kicked in his share when clearly he had not. His own cheapness and lying cast aspersions on his character and long career on the saucer circuit.

I had many other opportunities to get off the bus, but I didn't. One late afternoon, halfway through my seven-year itch, Chicken Little from The Aviary rang to check on the public disclosure process CSETI was pursuing in the mid-'90s, a large piece of which I was managing on the PR front. Chicken was one of the Aviary Birds, an ad hoc group of highly credentialed men from aerospace, government, intelligence agencies, the military, think tanks and other big-deal professions, who were all interested in the UFO subject, psi and related fields. (Psi is defined this way by Wikipedia: "In parapsychology, psi is the unknown factor in extrasensory perception and psychokinesis experiences that is not explained by known physical or biological mechanisms.") Chicken Little was especially fond of the end-of-the-world storylines that apparently emanated from his understanding of the paranormal realm in which Ufology is often lumped. Eschatology was his bag.

That afternoon, he was calling from a "gentlemen's club" somewhere in the DC area. He was at a table with Pelican, who allegedly headed the CIA "Weird Desk," and Hollywood actor Steve Seagal, who was scouting "talent" for his next film. I should have tried to turn it off right there, like the way most people just shut down stuff that no longer works for them and drop a mental wall around it. I had plenty of those opportunities including an unforgettable night when a white light outside my window struck me as I lay in bed. Suddenly, I shot straight up. This was the first time I had felt things were out of my control although I had experienced several other events just as weird and bewildering in the same room.

Many of these incidents individually or collectively should have been the last straw. Enough of trying to push the blind camel of the inexplicable through the eye of the needle of reason. But no, I didn't let it go—not then nor during the many other times when the barometric fringe factor was skyrocketing, and you needed a weatherman to find your way out of the millibars of UFO/ET craziness. I tried to mentally ditch these events as if they were some poisoned, obsessive love in a timeless country song. I tried—but I couldn't. Maybe the tenets of The Space Pen Club pulsed too strongly through my being to give it all up. Was I predisposed to the events chronicled in this book?

The Club was comprised of college classmates; it was a mostly tie-dyed collection of self-made Merry Pranksters who capriciously turned the Fisher Pen company's advanced line of Space Pens ("The first pen to write in space!") into a symbolic icon ultimately representing (at least for me, anyway) self-exploration, cosmic consciousness and communication, transcendence and the occasional quest for beer, girls, tuneage and controlled substances.

Members of that loose confederation included, among others, Cheebs, CV, Winks, Chats, Dr. K., Morris the Fallen Angel, the Queen of Hearts Mary E., the Little General, OD and Boston (both from back East), the three dogs—MurDog, GhoulDog and HairDog—and certainly der Keis and others whom you will meet in chapter five. They might tell you they belonged because of the Club's unwritten rules of conduct for personal exploration. You will have to decide for yourself.

5

Photo: Mike Schroetke

It's true that I muse about space often, but not just about the reaches of the black, star-lit world of the so-called Milky Way, now even more perceptible because of Hubble, Kepler and other advanced telescope technology. I think about deep inner space, mind space and consciousness even more these days, the real final frontier —that space between your ears and all around you, according to great past and present writers and thinkers, from Aldous Huxley and William James to Dr. Larry Dossey, MD, who has explained that "consciousness works trhough the brain, but it's not produced by the brain and cannot be explained by it: the brain is a transmissive not productive organ." This flies straight into the face of so-called conventional science and its media gurus such as Carl Sagan, from whom many of us learned about space on PBS. Sagan flatly argues that the brain's "workings—what we sometimes call mind— are a consequence of its anatomy and physiology and nothing more."

In developing this book, I tried to pinpoint when specific events started—and more importantly, why and how. The peculiar things that physically transpired in that house I shared with my future wife, Susan, now strike me as even more troubling and perplexing than when they began. My recurring dreams (if they were indeed "dreams") in retrospect seem like part of a much longer seven-year period of cryptic learning from teachers both seen and unseen.

When was the real starting point for that mercurial period between 1992 and the new millennium when I tried to make sense of it all? How long could this tale possibly last, populated by a seemingly endless parade of informed UFO experts and well-dressed hucksters peddling far-ranging stories and unvarnished theories at weekend expos, on TV, in the tabloid press or on dense websites spidering across the planet?

Even before a totally unexpected *New York Times* story in December 2017 about a secret Pentagon study of UFOs (termed UAPs, unidentified aerial phenomena followed by subsequent *Times'* news stories in 2019, 2020 and 2021, *and* opinion pieces in 2021—the subject has been heavily marginalized to a nonstarter level in major media, a glaring untouchable. But then, in May 2021, the bolts flew off the news cycle machine and it became choked with such stories: an in-depth piece in *The New Yorker* (most likely a first-time subject for the high-grade media bastion) plus *60 Minutes, CBS This Morning, The Hill* (a Washington, DC, paper about the House, Senate and Supreme Court), MSNBC, Fox News, CNN… you name it. If your favorite media outlet didn't have a story, it was missing the party.

So now the topic has become increasingly mainstreamed on everything from *The Huffington Post* to *The Wall Street Journal*, which is a broader topic explored in Chapter Seven. That chapter was prompted by the totally shitty (there's no finer word) reporting by CBS and its program *48 Hours* about a research mission in the Mexican "volcano zone" by a Close Encounters of the Fifth Kind/Rapid Mobilization Investigative Team (RMIT) of which I was member. There, after I was embarrassed on national TV, I had another opportunity to flee the arena, to abandon the bus and everyone on it. And yet, I remained and dug in more deeply.

I never had any strong intentions to write about unidentified flying objects, ETs, or anything of the sort. Nor was I interested in the search for interstellar life using radio signals a la the research organization, SETI (Search for Extra-Terrestrial Intelligence), an exercise that seems futile and has consumed decades of searching and loads of Microsoft money from the late Paul Allen, a SETI donor, as well as the time and money of many others. If anything, this book is a farewell to it all, a kiss-off, a "Hey, hey, goodbye."

When the weird stuff started in the house, my assumptions were simple, or maybe simplistic. I allowed for ETs in whatever form(s) they might take. I had always thought "they" were out there biding their time, doing what they do, maybe keeping an eye on the small blue planet. But what would be the point of writing about "them?" The universe is still a vast unknown, and the comprehension of it is a slowly unfolding process within the current limits of human understanding and its various channels of study. "Reality" has always been a fluid construct but was made to appear like hardened cement.

Besides, the pool containing the topic was polluted and occasionally toxic if one swam too far into the deep end. This whole subject could swallow up mountains of bandwidth and human mindshare. And it was a lunatic magnet of the first order, feeding the groupthink of cults like Heaven's Gate, the California-based sect whose members drank badly concocted vodka Kool-Aid in anticipation of rendezvousing with a space ship they believed was tailgating comet Hale Bop as it made an approach in 1997.

I never bought the idea that human beings are the high point on the evolutionary scale: Our history of wars and the ways we deal with resources, different populations, race, ideologically driven economic models and nation-states good, bad and catastrophic, argues against it. In writing this book, I had to lay aside judgment and my assumptions, then later re-gather and re-access them. Who was I to pass sentence on someone else's wild UFO or paranormal story when I carried one as good or better in my back pocket, trusting only a few friends with my experiences?

I am not sure whether some of the unusual events that make up this incomplete puzzle have anything to do with the UFO facts that longtime UFO researcher and Project Blue Book contributor Dr. J. Allen Hynek once called "the embarrassment of riches." That was then. Today he could have been referring to more than 3,000 documented military and commercial-pilot sightings, reams of declassified documents and astonishing statements by US presidents, high-ranking military officials and others over the past sixty years.

Even "conservative" mainstream science and official sources assume that conditions are ripe for ET homelands on other planets and allow for interaction with this one. The Rand Corporation, a think tank on the Tucker Carlson (Fox News) side of the universe, publicly released a non-peer-reviewed paper titled "UFOs: What to Do?" in 1997. The paper tracks UFO sightings from the 1500s to the modern era, including "the large number" of UFOs spotted near atomic and military installations. The report speculates there could be 200–600 million intergalactic civilizations more advanced than our own. But could "they" get here from there?

In early 2011, the old gray lady of journalism, *The New York Times*, set the table for establishing plausible next steps or implications when reporting on the discoveries of the Kepler planet-hunting satellite, "which identified 1,235 possible planets orbiting other stars, potentially tripling the number of known planets… Of the new candidates, 68 are one and a quarter times the size of the Earth or smaller—smaller, that is, than any previously discovered planets outside the solar system, which are known as exoplanets. Fifty-four of the possible exoplanets are in the so-called habitable zones of stars dimmer and cooler than the Sun, where temperatures should be moderate enough for liquid water." That number has risen even more significantly since then, as has the number of Earth-like planets.

Of course, that doesn't mean ET has filled its canteen from these distant liquid basins and somehow shot off to this tiny exoplanet that is orbiting a big star. But it might, if you accept the alleged comments by former US President Harry Truman: "I can assure you the flying saucers, given that they exist, are not constructed by any power on Earth." Or, if you dug up this once-classified Canadian document from 1950:

> To: Doctor Solant, Chairman of the Canadian Defense Research Board, the Controller of Telecommunications
>
> From: Walter B. Smith, Senior Radio Engineer, U.S. Dept. of Transportation
>
> November 21, 1950.
>
> I made some discreet inquiries through the Canadian Embassy staff in Washington who were able to obtain for me the following information:
>
> > a. The matter [ET issue] is the most highly classified subject in the United States Government, rating higher than even the H-bomb.
> >
> > b. Flying saucers exist.
> >
> > c. Their modus operandi is unknown but concentrated effort is being made by a small group headed by Doctor Vannevar Bush.
> >
> > d. The entire matter is considered by United States authorities to be of tremendous significance."

As I write this prologue, more than fifteen countries have opened their UFO files, providing a flood of information that establishes if nothing else that the planet's air traffic includes quite a few objects that have not filed mandatory flight plans and are potentially a serious safety hazard in conventional air space, especially around airports in Mexico, Russia, China, Scotland and the US where critical UFO incidents have made the mainstream news, and in some cases, closed the airports. Thousands of witnesses have had encounters at a distance or up close with indiscernible aerial vehicles (Unknowns, or "Ovnis" as the Mexican media calls them) and with beings that don't appear to be from our planet.

Write about what you know, isn't that what writers are told? Up until that point in the early '90s, I had nothing to show or tell. My interest in the subject was DOA until the quiet awakening began. There were unsold screenplays and a couple of novels among my various writing projects, mere works in progress:

- A "running from age" novel about a young heartsick Midwesterner who is hired by a family back east to be a "manny" for its kids.
- Another novel set in the brewing chaos of a small town caught in the chokehold of the North Dakota oil fields, where the blind ambitions of a 30-year-old woman returning home to her family of livestock barons—and her brother's complicity in an illegal oil play—is disrupted even more by her friendship with a motley bunch of oil workers, one of whom she falls in love with.
- An autobiography project tentatively called "Some Get the Chair" with Larry Kegan, one of Bob Dylan's lifelong friends, helping him write, edit and package his life story lived mostly in a wheelchair but lived in ways that were always inspiring, instructive and full of surprising adventures and revelations.

These and other projects seemed more deserving of my time than poking around in what many believe is nothing more than odd atmospheric or weather phenomena, Mylar balloons escaping beyond your vision field, Elon Musk's Starlink satellites, Chinese lanterns, drones, swamp gas, Venus setting or rising, experimental or stealth aircraft not yet in the public domain, lenticular clouds that only look like a mothership coming into Utah to pick up a prisoner, and objects that seem foreign or go down as simply misidentified.

At the time it all started, the UFO topic was still way out in the boondocks—untouchable, out of mind and out of step with where I was going or hoped to go... until I could ignore it no longer—until it continued to tap me with its incremental signal breaking through noise and I set forth with this written testimony, my witness to—and withdrawal from UFOlogy—call it what you like.

What was the big deal anyway? Aerial anomalies, longwalkers, flying saucers, uncorrelated targets, bogeys, Foo fighters (not the band), you could rattle off a half dozen or more names for these things coined by the military that regularly tracked them and the people and organizations all across the world that regularly reported on and researched the objects and them.

You know, *Them!* Your garden variety star travelers and assorted ETs from the twilight zone regions who had come here, most of which I had read about or heard from other humans:

- The nefarious "Grays" who were reportedly hustling people off-planet in the night; the ultimate blind date that ends very badly the second it begins.
- The "Nordics," very tall blondes allegedly benign, friendly and helpful to those they seek to aid; like super-svelte, interstellar Swedish welfare workers from parts unknown.
- The enigmatic "Pleidians" transiting from the seven sisters formation overhead; the apparent merry tricksters of the cosmos.
- The "Space Brothers," talked about by the classic ET contactees from the '50s like George Adamski; harbingers of peace, love and understanding (like the hippies from the '60s).
- Little green men from underground cities on Mars—or from general casting in Hollywood.
- The more spiritually defined ethereal creatures like "The Watchers," or the "Nephilim," the "Fallen Ones," the Bad Angel demon seed who got it on in the Good Book with the fair daughters of men in Genesis.
- Or the more scientifically named "EBEs" (extraterrestrial biological entities), and all the other nomenclature on the topic: "The Visitors," "Ancient Astronauts," "Ancient Aliens" as that History Channel show is called (aren't there any Modern Aliens we could pick on?)

Eventually, as I tried to discern what was happening (discernment is often lacking in the UFO ghetto), I started chauvinistically referring

12

to the phenomenon, aka "the visitors" and the Ovnis, as "the boys upstairs."

In my personal search for answers to such common Big Questions such as why we are here, I invariably have favored the ideas that allow for alternate explanations of "reality" such as String Theory. According to celebrated physicist Michio Kaku, String Theory suggests that we live in a multiverse, and that our universe could be thought of as a three-dimensional bubble floating inside a larger eleven-dimension realm. If String Theory were true, wouldn't bleed-throughs be possible now and then from the 5th or 10th Dimension Stringers, their A-team pushing the envelope from their side of the bubble, like Matthew McConaughey pushing the books out of the shelves in *Interstellar*?

Space science in general—like the shifting search in Earth-bound anthropology for the missing link—is just a widely accepted but unacknowledged work in progress too. But what if evolving consciousness itself is the link? And what if that higher consciousness spirals upwards exponentially among other more advanced beings on other much older planets and on unseen dimensional planes, giving them capabilities that would seem fantastic and unbelievable, like magic? What then?

It seems that every time a 400,000-year-old tooth is found in the Israeli desert, or new carbon-dated bones are uncovered in an archeological dig somewhere on the planet, volumes of well-established science are suddenly up for grabs again. These little watershed moments never quite fill the reservoirs of truth or satisfy the thirst we have for where we came from—or where we might be bound.

* * *

Maybe there is no real beginning to my story. This memoir appears to begin in an *unconscious state*—in bed, asleep and dreaming. All the characters in this story, with their unique assumptions and circumstances, and all the various realities that may have informed this beginning, now belong to memory, a house made of darkness, shadow, light.

The time is the second week in February 1992, roughly twenty-three years ago, that I experienced my first UFO sighting during halftime at a basketball game near the North Dakota Badlands. This evening, my girlfriend and I are asleep in our south Minneapolis home. It is extremely cold with subzero temperatures outside. Unknown to me, a strange process is about to unfold over the next eight months, much of it while I'm awake but some of it while I'm asleep—in that altered state of being in a parallel world in which life is thought to be acted out in the unconscious.

But the unconscious, as I soon would discover, is occasionally interrupted and illuminated by some instructive lamp of lucidity even while dreaming... even while undergoing an installment of many dreams that comes innocently enough, or not, stacked like stones into an ethereal cairn on a densely wooded trail, pointing the way out of the forest of the unconscious into the waking mystery of experience.

CHAPTER ONE:
THE BURNING PIER, THE QUIET AWAKENING

Thinking of a series of dreams
Where the time and the tempo drag,
And there's no exit in any direction
'Cept the one that you can't see with your eyes.
Wasn't making any great connections,
Wasn't falling for any intricate schemes.
Nothing that would pass inspection,
Just thinking of a series of dreams.

Dreams where the umbrella is folded,
And into the path you are hurled,
And the cards are no good that you're holding
Unless they're from another world.

–Bob Dylan, "A Series of Dreams"

In the dream that may anchor a starting point or doorway for this story, a small dark-haired woman who looks like Linda Hunt surveys the cards on a table. She cries out in an unfamiliar language, throwing her head back and gesturing to the overturned Tarot images. Her surroundings suggest a medieval fair, but I'm fixated on her visage, the ageless look and dark olive skin, that drastically foreign voice and the portents of the illustrated cards at her fingertips. Suddenly, her delivery becomes strident, her tongue speaking in an ancient Mideastern language—or perhaps the gibberish of dream time. Is she warning me?

While I can't understand her words in my vivid dream state, I'm intuiting their meaning. Something about strangers. And then her im-

15

age vanishes, and I am in a small room opening a door in an unfamiliar, semi-darkened house, a cottage that seems to be circular, like a Hobbit hut. There are five or six figures lined up at the doorway, all long in form, bald and fit, except for the one closest to me who is the size of a child. He studies me.

Circus people, I surmise, perhaps keying off the Tarot reader's setting. The several figures in the rear are completely shadowed. The next two, behind the small figure, wear blank expressions and dark clothing. But the smallish one wears a tunic or gown. Looking like an eight- or nine-year-old boy, he raises his hands and holds them inches apart, one slightly ahead of the other with the fingers curling inward as if he were about to catch a ball.

An energy field is created with his hands, and suddenly silver dollars come spilling out of it onto the floor. In my dream, I think, *What a cool conjuring trick, unlike anything I've seen at any circus or carnival!*

"Can you teach me how to do it?" I ask.

The others in his group are silent. They passively watch with no expression, as if "the kid" is the only one who can perform this feat.

The young one does not audibly speak but I understand his answer: "You can do this, but you have to take this first."

He produces a white tablet the size of a baby aspirin. I pop it in my mouth, more eager to create the force field than to see the silver coins, and I raise my hands like his, as if I, too, were going catch a ball. The others, silent as ever, watch off to the side.

I feel a slight force at my fingertips but nothing dramatic—and no coinage, not even one thin penny. A message comes from the kid that simply says, "You can you do it, in time, with practice." Then, the strange dream comes to an end. But in fact, it does not "end."

I feel the "circus people dream"—or the ramifications of this unforgettable nighttime imagery—plays forward into the weeks ahead leading from winter to spring and summer with a subtle, rarefied trajectory, the intensity and meaning of which I did not or could not grasp for many months.

Upon waking the next morning, I scribbled key images into a notebook and set my hands apart again to create the energy field I'd seen in my dream, wondering about this unusual episode. I've always been a power dreamer, remembering at least one or two of them every morning. I can even remember dreams from childhood, good and bad. But this one was a first of its kind.

Dreams, as I've read and learned firsthand, often hold keys to waking reality. In fact, it was a dream I had—after years of on-again, off-again therapy to explore on-again off-again issues like depression and relationships—that fostered the big breakthrough that anyone "on the couch" strives for. It specifically came in a dream, but metaphorically. And even though my shrink wasn't trained in this school of analysis, he immediately knew what the dream signified, and we took things from there. He would have had a much harder time, though, with this new one and those that followed.

My pedestrian interpretation of the dream visitors was quite simple. At the time, my work load was manageable—several business stories for the *Minneapolis-St. Paul Business Journal*, music reviews for a now-defunct magazine called *Request* where Susan worked, and talk of developing a public-relations campaign for the city's first green retail store, Restore the Earth (only the second one in the country). But I also had been working on a synopsis for a screenplay about Indian gaming.

I rationalized that the Tarot reader was the elderly Jewish woman, Hilda, who wanted me to explore a film story about the growing number of Native American casinos across the country and the tension it was causing in select communities. Hilda had been part of a Twin Cities investment group that helped finance the first Coen Brothers' film, *Blood Simple*. The silver dollars were right out of the casino that Hilda and I visited near Mille Lacs, a popular fishing lake a couple hours north of the Twin Cities where one of the earliest Native American casinos was built by the Mille Lacs Band of Ojibwa. Dream solved—no shrink co-pay required.

But not so fast…

17

* * *

The quiet of the next few days led to more reflection about the circus dream, but the matter seemed entirely over—until, on consecutive evenings, lights started coming on while we were both asleep. At first, neither of us paid any attention. Each night, we went to bed, often indulging in the books and magazines on our nightstands. Her's was stacked with fiction or the occasional music biography, as she was always looking for review material for *Request*, a national music rag like *Spin* and *Rolling Stone* read by music fans and record buyers to prolong adolescence, guild our passion and indulge our music fixes.

My nightstand, next to a window that looks out onto Minnehaha Creek, mostly featured books by Christian mystics and seers like Rudolph Steiner and Edgar Cayce. It was a phase I was in, it seemed, exploring knowledge about Rosicrucians, the Gnostics and other esoteric sects of Christianity, which I had been striving to reconcile with my birth faith.

A handful of those books lay on the nightstand, including The *Autobiography of a Yogi* by Paramahansa Yogananda, and two more obscure works published by The International Society for Krishna Consciousness that I'd found at Present Moment, a funky used bookstore in south Minneapolis. The titles were long, such as this one: *Chant and Be Happy: The Power of Mantra Meditation "Featuring Exclusive Interviews with John Lennon and George Harrison," and "Based on the Teachings of His Divine Grace A.C. Bhaktivedanta Swami Prabhupada."*

Another one, entitled *Lennon 69: Search for Liberation* "Featuring a Conversation Between A.C. Bhaktivedanta Swami Prabhupada and John Lennon," revealed an alleged past life of Lennon's in India as a wealthy but generous man prior to his birth in England and into Beatledom. The swami had learned of this in a dream, underscoring his status as a true holy man: "The Vedas confirm that a spiritual master who is a pure devotee of Krishna is empowered by the Lord with mystic perfection - - *tri-kala-jna,* the ability to know the past, present and

18

future lives of every human being."

I found other references to such seer realities in *The Little Book of Saints*, based on a larger hardcover volume my parents kept in our North Dakota home when we were kids getting heavily dosed with Catholicism. And I have fond memories of a scene read in college from *Be Here Now*, the book by Ram Dass, aka Richard Alpert, the former acid consciousness researcher with Dr. Tim Leary at Harvard, whose guru "saw" him coming to India long before Alpert arrived at the ashram. Those East and West texts made up much of my night reading and stoked my preoccupations. I also had the big idea that screenplay work might be fulfilling.

Two How-To books about screenwriting and a slew of magazines were also in the holy pile, including a new copy of *UFO Magazine*. I picked that up mostly to see how UFO rags had changed since my best friend, Jim, and I once read them in the drugstore aisle when we had nothing better to do in western North Dakota, or until we got chased out by an angry pharmacist. This issue focused on abduction experiences along with the usual sightings chatter and speculation from the trenches of UFOland.

The lights thing in the house, however, was perplexing. Neither Susan nor I knew how long they had been coming on, but it seemed to begin right after the circus dream. I didn't pay it much mind until one night during that cold February. Our bedroom was upstairs, and it was about the fifth time I'd been awakened by the lights switching on throughout the second floor after we had turned them all off.

This was now a puzzling part of our morning conversations that invariably went like this:

"Didn't you turn the lights out in the upstairs hallway and that other bedroom before you went to sleep," I asked.

"Yes," she always answered. "Did you get up in the night and forget to turn them off?"

"No, I didn't."

"Oh, you probably did and just forgot about it."

"Yeah, you're probably right."

Then we'd forget about it until the next time it happened.

A few weeks later, at four in the morning, the upstairs hallway light was on again. But this time there were sounds—seemingly a recording of someone, or possibly two someones, speaking backward in an animal-like squeal. I also heard what sounded like our two bearded collies, Nellie and Sophie, racing across the hardwood floors, their claws—at least I thought it was their claws—tapping across the wood. Then I fell back to sleep. As was custom, the Beardies would get me up for their morning walk two or three hours later.

On this morning, after the noise event I clearly remembered the sounds and could rationalize the noise on the hardwood floors. But that piercing, high-pitched sound? I had no idea. I filed it away in what would become my mental tinfoil folder.

Four in the morning was becoming a special time for me. An old, now-departed college friend told me that was the time when the veil was thinnest between the natural realm and the other world. But was this "other world" something I was stepping into? Or was it something else—not a world at all, but a hidden destination, a shrouded moment in time, a lost or newly found path?

As the days moved forward, I began having a different style of dream, recurring images I dubbed "newspaper vision." They never varied and went like this: I would see an image of the newspaper on the front step. Then I immediately began reading its contents before the paper hit the front step. After several seconds, my gatekeeping rational mind would switch on and intrude, as if to say, "No, the paper isn't even here yet, how can you be reading the news of the day?" Then the dream would cease.

Between March and June of that year of dreaming crazily, I must have had 30 or more of these dreams, always the same, always reading the news before the paper hit the doorstep, only to be shut down by my overbearing rational gatekeeper.

In my waking moments, it occurred to me that the newspaper

was a kind of marker from my past intruding on my recent reality. As a kid, I used to get up every morning and deliver *The Dickinson Press* before sunup to over thirty customers. Why now was my mind seizing on reading the newspaper over and over again? Was the simple opening and reading of the daily news a metaphor for expanding one's daily consciousness about reality?

It's not like I relished that delivery job and now my unconscious was spewing it back at me for some reason. In those cold long winters, the newspaper route was almost unbearable, especially if the papers were late off the presses and we had to walk to the plant to pick them up, then do the route and get home in time to leave for school. In the summer, of course, I just wanted to sleep in. The news most of it bad, was about Vietnam, civil rights riots, car wrecks, stolen laundry, lost pets and quaint small-town gossip in the editor's column.

But wasn't the role of the daily paper to raise awareness and provide information about one's environment, one's reality? Was my recurring dream teaching me a new way to "read reality," to raise the frequency of consciousness and glimpse aspects of it before it had occurred? Was this even possible?

The spiritually-oriented books on my nightstand said it was. Even in the so-called pagan world of the Australian nomads or the druid-filled realm of the Irish Celts, dream states played a major role in waking reality. Author John O'Donohue wrote in his compelling book, *Anam Cara, A Book of Celtic Wisdom*: "In the Celtic world... there was a wonderful sense of how the visible and the invisible moved in and out of each other... For the Celts, the visible and the invisible are one."

But I wasn't a Celt. Or an aborigine in the outback. I was just a guy trying to figure out what to do with his life.

In my focused waking hours, however, when dreams were clearly dreams and conscious reality was what it was (the line drawn in the mind), I was beginning to wonder if the obsessive-compulsive newspaper dreaming was a reflection of degrading mental health. I knew from the cautionary 1973 Nicholas Roeg film *Don't Look Now* about the danger of following images foretold in dreams or by psychics into the waking world, especially if the subject gets interpreted fatally wrong! Nonetheless, I went about my work with no problems, and made mental and physical notes of this curious chain of ephemeral events. My psyche, it seems, was slipping into some strange turf at night, which for now was OK. But could that make the lights come on? And what about the clatter on the hardwood floor?

I didn't know it then, but I already had boarded that bus.

* * *

In the "real world" following the Tarot and newspaper dreams, the Indian gaming movie idea had faded to black. Hilda decided she didn't want to fundraise for such a movie, and I was getting too old in my late thirties to be writing more than one thing at a time on spec, which I was already doing with comedian Tom Frykman. This goofy comedy set during the St. Paul Winter Carnival medallion hunt was intended to be like the movie farces I enjoyed as a kid—*The Wrong Box*, *It's a Mad Mad Mad Mad World* and many others. I mostly kept my nighttime sleep (mis)adventures to myself. And then the fabric of reality suddenly frayed and reassembled itself in an astonishing way.

In late May, I had a dream so real it barely seemed like a dream at all. It seemed physically "present" minus one element—a flying school bus. I was standing on the shore of a bay in a city I didn't recognize. Skyscrapers surrounded the waterfront and cast long shadows. The sky was clear and Seattle blue. I looked down and spied parts of an old pier that had collapsed into the water. A few pieces of it still stuck up above the water. One exposed plank was smoldering, giving off white smoke. Suddenly, the flying school bus came into view and "flew" away!

Upon awakening, I made notes about the dream and went back to the real world of chasing business stories or the stray record review and trying to win a few more PR clients. This dream went into the Tinfoil file with the rest of them.

In mid-June, a friend told me of a lecture/workshop concerning UFOs taking place in Wyoming and mentioned something called Close Encounters of the Fifth Kind.

"Oh, yeah, I was into UFOs in grade school and high school," I noted, and let the matter drop.

I had my own travel plans anyway. The first week of July, I flew with my parents to Boston and took in a weekend of baseball at Fenway Park (the Minnesota Twins versus the Red Sox). Fenway is the promised land for any diehard BoSox devotee like my father, who had been a lifelong fan but had never made the pilgrimage to honor the Green Monster. My siblings and I pitched in to send him and my mother on the trip as part of a big wedding anniversary. I tagged along, only later to take the train down to visit friends in Hadelyme, Connecticut, and New York City.

After almost six hours of flying, including a long connection in St. Louis, we arrived in Boston in the late afternoon. The skies were densely overcast and it was cold. As we took a cab to a Marriott near Faneuil Hall, we all agreed it didn't bode well for outdoor baseball.

At the hotel, I got my parents settled and met up with Kathy Chapman, a photographer friend from Minneapolis living in Boston. She had photographed a lot of rock groups I covered and had begun shooting broader subject material in her newly adopted city. To save me a few bucks, she was going to let me stay in her loft just up the harbor while she was house sitting for a professor in Cambridge.

While we drove through a light drizzle, we quickly caught up with each other and yakked about mutual friends back in the Twin Cities. At her place in the Ft. Point Channel area, she unlocked the door and it flew open onto a straightaway-view into the kitchen in which a large oil painting, at least five by three-and-half feet, hung on one wall.

More silent synchronicities: The *Ezekiel's Wheels* painting in Boston.
(Photo: Kathy Chapman)

The painting, dominated by Boston buildings against a dark char-treuse sky, was filled with sinister little flying saucers. On top of each saucer were tiny, winged creatures that looked like figures from the Hieronymus Bosch painting "The Last Judgment."

"Wow, flying saucers!" I said with a laugh. "Kinda crazy."

"It's my friend's painting. He calls it 'Ezekiel's Wheels,'" she said. "Magnus Johnstone," she added, explaining that he was an underground artist and celeb of sorts and had pioneered hip hop or rap records early on at the MIT radio station. She showed me the rest of the loft, handed me the keys and said she would see me tomorrow for drinks after the game. I threw my stuff in the bedroom and took one more look at the

24

painting. It looked like a freakin' invasion of Beantown. I hit the sack and slept soundly till morning.

The sunlight was already filling the loft as I got ready to walk over for breakfast at my parents' hotel less than half a mile away. The Boston air was crisp and refreshing. The rain had cleared out all the muck, the clouds had vanished and it was going to be a beautiful day. Play ball!

I could see the Marriott in the near distance as I crossed a tiny foot bridge over the bay. But I stopped in my tracks at the peak of the bridge. The rising skyscrapers, the morning light, the waterfront—it all looked too familiar. It was the harbor city I had seen several weeks earlier while sound asleep in my Minneapolis bed!

I looked down into the water for the collapsed and smoking pier. A couple of planks were exposed all right, stacked above the remaining ones submerged below. But unlike in the dream, they were not smoking. The water was just gently lapping against them. Nevertheless, this was the same view I had seen minus the white smoke—and minus the flying bus. I looked over my shoulder at the Boston World Trade Center, then back at the downtown harbor and those water-logged piers.

I leaned against the rail and took a deep breath. My mind was racing. What was happening? I had better start paying attention, or else start looking for help. Somehow, standing in the exact location I had "previewed" while asleep earlier in May, I felt that the newspaper dreams and this dream, and maybe even the strangers foretold in the Tarot dream, were somehow connected. But how? And more importantly, why? And what about the flying-saucer painting? Was it a colossal coincidence—or a fitting synchronicity?

My good friend Tom, a charter member of The Space Pen Club, had once joked after college that I was always expecting the universe to give me clues. But this was the universe—or something *inside* my personal universe—banging on my door with an anvil to get my attention.

Standing on the bridge, replaying the synchronicities bombarding me, I thought about one of the real pioneers of the interior cosmos, Carl Jung, and his lifelong interest in synchronicities and UFOs.

25

In fact, he coined the term "synchronicity." Oddly enough when I first opened *The Portable Jung* in a park in Basel, Switzerland, while backpacking around Europe the summer after my junior year in college, I discovered on the first pages that Jung was from Basel. Basel was also where chemist Albert Hoffman, working for Sandoz, accidentally invented LSD and took his famous acid bicycle trip through the city on April 16, 1943, an event still commemorated there with proponents from all over the world. Space Pen Club members were not unaware.

Hoffman, on his 100th birthday, made a revealing comment about his discovery to the Berlin online newspaper, *Taz Cooperative*: "All I can say is that the LSD called me, I did not look for it. It came to me, it reported."

* * *

By the time I interviewed Donovan about his album *Sutras* in 1996, the self-described "Celtic Buddhist" and minstrel rock poet mentioned something that seemed to underscore the Jungian view. Besides talking about new songs, he had provided insight into an earlier period of his. He'd said synchronicities were really moments that create greater spiritual awareness and affirmations of sorts.

Jung wrote eloquently and persuasively about the subject in his 1920s work, *Synchronicity—An Acausal Connecting Principle*. But I later stumbled on an article published on the internet that seemed to update those ideas. According to Peter Fotis Kapnistos, an American journalist now living in Greece who had turned his attention to the paranormal, Jung bridged the invisible mechanics of the real world with early quantum thinking. Kapnistos wrote: "After discussions with both Einstein and [Wolfgang] Pauli, Jung believed that there were similarities between synchronicity and quantum mechanics."

Kapnistos noted that "Quantum entanglement or superposition is a phenomenon in which the quantum states of two or more objects are linked together even though the specific objects may be spatially separated. Since quantum entanglement implies faster than light-speed interactions, it creates an experience of non-locality, or what Albert Einstein called 'spooky action at a distance' that defies classical and relativistic concepts of space and time…

"His synchronicity concept reflected a mysterious effect very similar to quantum entanglement," the expatriot continued. "Sigmund Freud observed this line of reasoning in his essay 'Dreams and Telepathy' (1922) pertaining to synchronicity… Jung was fascinated by the idea that life was not a series of random events but rather an expression of a deeper order, and that the realization of this was a spiritual awakening."

I didn't know much about this Kapnistos person who was writing from the Mediterranean, but he was good material for the club. Now living on the isle of Patmos, where John the Revelator, one of the apostles of Jesus, allegedly wrote the harrowing and incomprehensible "Book of Revelation," Kapnistos went on to quote David Robson in a 2010 piece in *New Scientist* when making the case for such quantum entanglements in the human mind as the basis for memories: "Subatomic particles do it. Now the observation that groups of brain cells seem to have their own version of quantum entanglement, or 'spooky action at a distance,' could help explain how our minds combine experiences from many different senses into one memory. Previous experiments have shown that the electrical activity of neurons in separate parts of the brain can oscillate simultaneously at the same frequency—a process known as phase locking. The frequency seems to be a signature that marks out neurons working on the same task, allowing them to identify each other."

I didn't know from neuron oscillation and phase locking, but it sounded plausible and worth thinking about. And so there it was… maybe: A dream of a place while in Minneapolis, then several weeks later standing in that place in Boston, may have illustrated quantum entanglement. And it was kind of spooky—if you let it be framed that way. But the club allowed for such thinking, even if it was proved wrong, even if it was, to use a popular expression of the tie-dyed era, too far out.

Jung also believed that UFOs were projections from the collective human unconscious even though he had never seen one. He may have been shocked to learn that in 1976, an Iranian Air Force General named Parviz Jafari in an F-4 jet chased what appeared to be a solid-state aerial vehicle "comparable to that of a 707 tanker" with flashing red, green, orange and blue lights, according to Leslie Kean's first- rate book *UFOs: Generals, Pilots, and Government Officials Go on the Record* from 2010. This was a celebrated case in the UFO ghetto that even members of the Aviary, often given to scientific debunking, allowed. The now-retired Iranian general even had the air ship on his radar and was about to fire on it when his weapons system jammed. Perhaps one of the most famous and well documented cases of the past 30 years, this and other incidents readily challenged Jung's notion of UFPs—Unidentified Flying Projections. Plus, that acronym just didn't parse too well.

As I stood on that Boston bridge, I may have been reading too much into this moment on the waterfront, but I could not let it go. I stood in that spot for about fifteen minutes. As I slowly moved off the site, I replayed the dreams and tried to make rationalizations for them. But if I didn't hurry, I would be late for breakfast. Still, there was no time to be anyplace except at the ballpark by one o'clock.

The rest of the harbor scenery faded as I slipped into heavy reflection. I started with the Tarot dream. Within my Catholic grade-school upbringing, trying to divine the future or to understand the present with Tarot or believing in psychics and other gray areas was considered "dark behavior" and strictly *verboten*.

But later, as a college student of literature where understanding symbols often provided the key to perceiving a book's larger meaning, I also learned to love the rich symbolism of the Tarot as much as I did such metaphysical symbolism as William Blake's densely written and painterly work. Later, I thought of the Tarot as an intuitive tool, however primitive, to get in touch with the seen and unseen, or the Noetic realm of human experience.

Over time, I had several Tarot readings, usually from Reanna, a Botticelli-like blonde from Texas who moved to Minneapolis many years ago and was a scenester during my music-writing period. To me, these readings were like watching a scientifically-based weather report. They were an interpersonal forecast of probable intuitive outcomes with elements of unpredictability sprinkled in based on the science of chance and unseen circumstances. Here, it was the turn of symbolic cards and a speculative interpretation of same that may or may not be on the money.

I had read a couple of books about the Tarot and its origin, chiefly, P.D. Ouspensky's *The Symbolism of the Tarot: Philosophy of Occultism in Pictures and Numbers*. The book is almost shorter than its title but is worth reading more than once. Ouspensky writes, "There are many methods for developing the sense of symbols in those who are striving to understand the hidden forces of Nature and Man, and for teaching the fundamental principles as well as the elements of esoteric language. The most synthetic, and one of the most interesting of these methods, is the Tarot."

Even Ouspensky—the early 20th century Russian philosopher who helped promote the work of George Gurdjieff, whom I had interest in as well during this period in which dreams were becoming increasingly more, ah, "manifest"—was hard pressed to pin down its origins: "The history of the Tarot is a great puzzle," although it seems to have surfaced at the end of the 14th century in Europe. And, according to Ouspensky, it had ties to Egyptian hieroglyphics and is associated with "the Hermetic Sciences of the Kabala, Alchemy, Astrology and Magic.

"The Kabala, Alchemy, Astrology, Magic are parallel symbolical systems of psychology and metaphysics. Any alchemical sentence may be read in a Kabalistic or astrological way, but the meaning will always be psychological and metaphysical… The Tarot in its turn is quite analogous to the Kabala, Alchemy and Magic, and, as it were, includes them."

As I hurried to meet my parents and bumped into shopkeepers and clerks heading to work around the square, my mind tried to add it up. What did I have? A dream-state fortune teller and odd visitors offering energy portals and a strange tablet, lights on in the house with weird noises, pre-read newspapers repeatedly, and the burning/not-burning pier. Oh yes, and that big-assed UFO painting in the Boston loft. Synchronicities were killing me softly. At least the painting and the pier were "real." Of course, I would later discover, this was a dimmer view of things.

"We are surrounded by a wall built of our conceptions of the world, and are unable to look over this wall at the real world," writes the erudite Ouspensky of the Tarot. I knew as I entered the lobby where my parents stood waiting that my wall was crumbling fast. But understanding the how and why would have to wait for the big green wall of Red Sox baseball, and then some.

The proverbial Zen notion that a teacher arises when the pupil is ready seemed apropos. But there was no human teacher yet, just unconscious and conscious imagery in play. I tried not to look distracted as a Red Sox fan snapped a photo of my parents and me standing outside Fenway. And while we enjoyed the game together and an early dinner afterward, I was often lost in thought. That night, after my parents had gone to bed, Kathy and I hit the local bar in South Boston near the neighborhood where I was staying. It was a working-class 'hood mostly made up of new Irish immigrants that she had resolutely captured in intimate black-and-white photographs of young mothers and their children, which she later exhibited. Her boyfriend was playing with his garage rock band, the Classic Ruins, at a packed joint near her loft. The accents of the emerald mother country were detectable above the fiery rock the Ruins cranked out, and we partook of Guinness and a shot or two of Jameson, getting caught up in the spirit of the night.

Afterward, we went back to the apartment and I put on the 1989 Bob Dylan record *Oh Mercy!* that had been leaning against a stack of records by the stereo. I played the track "What Was It You Wanted?," a piercingly understated slow-stomping tune that seemed to express Dylan's trademark exasperation with the world. It also packed some hilarious one-liners. In retrospect, I felt it was the appropriate soundtrack to the behavior of my subconscious for the past six months: "What was it you wanted?"

Dylan has always loomed large in my life. The first record review I tried to write as a teenager was about *John Wesley Harding*, and I got my first break publishing a story in *The Twin Cities Reader* (an alternative weekly) after I'd had a chance encounter with Dylan and a friend of his at a Luther Allison blues show at the Cabooze Bar. Later, at the peak of my pop-culture writing career, I was fortunate enough to meet him again and interview him after the 1983 release of *Infidels* and make a weeklong swing through the Midwest with his entourage on his Never-Ending Tour in 1990. Long before I met him, however, he too was there in a parade of repeated dreams many years before I started covering music, scrutinizing my sleep life or thinking about quantum entanglement.

The recurring Dylan dreams, perhaps motivated by the power of his music and lyrics as well as a desire to land a rare interview with him, always struck me as representing something bigger than just the jingle-jangle representations of Robert Zimmerman in the phantasmagoria of the mind. Maybe he was a personalized Jungian archetype for creativity. My 1983 interview with him was published first in *City Pages* (another Twin Cities weekly) and then around the world. But it seemed like I had been somehow interacting with him "in dreams," as Roy Orbison (and one of Bob's fellow Traveling Wilburys) sang, for a long time prior to the reality of our actual meetings.

Mind is the builder. So Edgar Cayce, "the sleeping prophet," writes again and again in his work. The Christian-believing man gave thousands of readings about individual's health, past lives, personal struggles and historical events past and future, while he was in a trance or sleeplike state. But could mind pave the way to a backstage pass with one of the greatest songwriters of the 20th and 21st centuries?

The Dylan dreams, though, were nothing like these latest ones which were tangled up in UFO imagery. The flying bus, I learned later, was really a masked image of a UFO or flying saucer. Now I had an esoteric clue to throw into my pot of stewing strangeness. Back in that Boston loft, as I pieced together my tale for my obliging host including the pier just down the road, I played that Dylan track at least five times until she stopped me.

To get me away from the stereo, she said, "Come on, let's go up on the roof. I've got something to tell you about that pier."

Sitting on beat-up folding chairs under the stars above the Boston harbor on a lovely midsummer night, she took a swig of beer and said matter-of-factly, "You know, that pier catches on fire a lot. People flick their cigarettes butts on it and the old creosote catches fire and they start to burn again. Sometimes the fire department even has to come and put it out, and it smokes like what you described seeing in your dream. You just happened to catch it on a day when that didn't happen, when it didn't catch on fire and smolder."

I rocked back on my chair and sat quietly for what seemed longer than necessary. "What do you think it all means?" I finally asked.

"Who knows," she said, shrugging in the dark, "but keep me posted. I mean, if you ever figure it out." She smiled, and we clinked bottles.

The next day, the Minnesota Twins played two with the Sox. The late singer-songwriter Bill Morrissey joined us and helped me nurse a wee hangover by sharing a brew at Fenway. Bill was an accomplished Boston-based folkie from New Hampshire who recorded sides for Rounder Records and other labels. He would later write two well-received novels. The pained weight of the world seeped out of his serious tunes, but Bill was always friendly and intellectually engaging, especially about writing of any kind. He was casually funny, and he went fishing often, sometimes with a songwriter from Iowa that I admired greatly, Greg Brown. The two of them were nominated in '94 for a record they made together, *Friend of Mine,* about fishing and a lot more.

In a moving obit for Bill, *Chicago Sun Times* music writer David Hoekstra ranked him with John Prine, Tom Waits and Bob Dylan as "America's best contemporary male singer-songwriters." Studs Terkel said of Morrissey, "His songs haunt me." But Morrissey was under the radar. He was so far under the radar that his sudden death on July 23, 2011, did not make national news. "The worst thing Bill did in his life was die on the same day Amy Winehouse died," his friend Chicago singer-songwriter Fred Koller quipped earlier that week. "It blew him off the charts." Koller noted that Bill was "kind, sensitive, rare and doomed."

I never sensed the doom part about Bill, and I have no idea how he would have reacted to this flying-saucer journey I'd stumbled into. Probably with a show of his dark humor and that warm smile. But like my old man, he was a true, never-flagging Red Sox fan, living with the curse of the Bambino, its own kind of long-suffering doom. I'd gotten friendly with him when I gave him a ride to Minneapolis from the Winnipeg Folk Festival one summer, and we'd stayed in touch.

All smiles and funny remarks to my parents, he came for the first game, disparaging the home team a bit as he would his own experience with Catholicism from the stage. He went home after the first nine innings to rest for his coffeehouse gig later that evening. After dinner following game two, the folks were tired and wanted to turn in. I took in Bill's set, momentarily losing myself in his goofy tunes like "Grizzly Bear," and his more serious, emotional numbers such as "Standing Eight," "These Cold Fingers" and many others. With his impossibly rugged deep voice and the wry sense of humor and irony he tossed off between songs, his set was a good antidote to the burning-pier episode and the questions blazing inside my head.

My East coast summer swing, "The Quiet Awakening" tour I now call it, took me next to Connecticut. There, I told my friend Rob, with whom I'd worked during college, the whole story, looking perhaps for validation that I wasn't losing my mind. An avid birder, bird carver and illustrator whose work had appeared in the Audubon Society magazine, select books and other bird publications, Rob was caretaking a lovely estate for an elderly couple. We sat on two lousy lawn chairs under the night sky and watched the stars as we talked. Or as I talked, mostly about what was happening.

"Geez, nothing like that's ever happened to me," he said with a hint of envy and derisive humor in his voice.

"Maybe I'm suddenly pre-cognitive," I added matter-of-factly.

"Pre-what?" he laughed.

"You know, you can see or know things in advance of them actually happening."

"Is there a cure for it?" he snickered. But neither of us were really laughing about it now.

When I got back to Minneapolis, I quickly resumed my schedule with paid assignments and spec work on that "Medallion" screenplay. A fresh message was waiting on my answering machine from that friend who'd gone to Wyoming in search of ET. It had been potentially a life-changing event, the friend said, and this guy Steven Greer was doing groundbreaking work in the UFO research field, and "we saw two ships"—as if I could swallow this—"and now [Greer] was looking for someone to write a story about his organization and philosophy and might I be interested?" The machine clicked off.

I reasoned that I would be. Soon, I would indeed be interested, not knowing but rather feeling that it was the right thing to do. And suddenly, I was drawn further into the territory to meet someone I would discover was another pioneer of the cosmos and consciousness. Oddly, the long series of midnight-special newspaper dreams abruptly came to an end. They ended, it seemed, while I was standing on that Boston foot bridge, one lesson about the pliable nature of reality learned—or at least glimpsed—on the way to the Green Monster.

CHAPTER TWO:
CLOSE ENCOUNTERS OF THE FIFTH KIND

"We agree that at times hard, physical craft exist, but there is much more to the phenomena. Unfortunately the true boundaries are unknown. It seems certain that human consciousness is at least part of the formula."

—John B. Alexander, PhD, UFOs: Myths, Conspiracies, and Realities

Soon after meeting Dr. Steven Greer of the Center for the Study of Extraterrestrial Intelligence (CSETI), it became clear that traditional UFO researchers fell basically into three camps: hunters, gatherers and signal spotters. The first group, the data hunters, retroactively collect data—witness observations, photographic evidence, interviews with authorities tasked with policing the sky and protecting public safety, radar readings, ground measurements, or traces of a craft if something had landed and left impressions. Among the bland UFO shows on cable and satellite TV in 2012, one even had "Hunter" in its title. The hunters also include interviews with anyone having Close Encounters of a Third or Fourth Kind—observations of humanoids and on-board interaction of same, sometimes gathered through hypnotic regression and formal "conscious" dialog, and so on.

Contemporary groups like the Mutual UFO Network (MUFON), Peter Davenport's National UFO Reporting Center, CUFOS (Center for UFO Studies) and NARCAP (the National Aviation Reporting Center on Anomalous Phenomena) were prominent in this area. They were part of a storied line of alphabet-soup organizations that stretched back into the 1950s, all trying to investigate the phenomenon, although many believed the best cases indicated ET at work.

The paper gatherers in the second group chase down documents, usually through the painstakingly bureaucratic process of filing Freedom of Information Act (FOIA) requests with various government and military agencies. (Often there were transcriptions of interviews with witnesses.) Then the waiting and waiting for FOIA responses, which, when eventually arriving, would have large portions blacked out to protect sources and—as those in the UFO ghetto believed—to blind the reader to the more relevant "good stuff."

The late nuclear physicist Stanton Freidman is one such researcher who has made a career of writing and lecturing about the ET reality and the so-called cover-up of the facts, which he calls a "Cosmic Watergate," even though he has never seen a UFO. (His comeback is that he has never seen a proton in a nucleus, but he knows it's there! Protons, however, will never show up in anything, unlike UFO images, which seem to be everywhere since cameras and now cell phones have been able to record them, give or take a few thousand fakes.) Kevin Randle and Don Schmidt, celebrated Roswell investigators, and others have toiled in the pursuit of documents and worked tirelessly on researching and vetting reams of paper along with valuable witness testimony. The ghetto was rife with both hunters and gatherers, and they were important for creating a foundation of research knowledge in the literature.

The third group, the signal spotters, often seemed like the first group, but its efforts were based more in the realm of established or accepted academic science, including the belief in empiricism and its demands for trial-and-error methodology to prove claims.

NASA's Search for Extraterrestrial Intelligence (SETI) program initially searched hoped-for ET radio signals blasted from interstellar space toward Earth-based radio telescopic locations. In some cases, during the life of the storied program with numerous affiliations and funding sources, SETI also sent out similar signals toward targeted star systems thought to be most like ours. These expensive, primitive radio-grams were eventually lost, found, discarded or ignored in space.

It was not hard to imagine the radio-signal sending arm of SETI—or the Earth itself off-gassing its mixture of radio and electromagnetic energy—as one big cosmic deejay. The hope was that ET was dialing in on that frequency, perhaps after stumbling upon Voyager I in deep space. Launched in 1977, Voyager I is now so far away that it started leaving our solar system late in 2012 after passing through an area of decreasing solar winds in a frontier known as "termination shock," which is the sun's way of giving such objects a pink slip as they head into the greater Milky Way.

Voyager I was loaded with images and information about Earth on the spacecraft's own "gold records." The musical portion of one of the gold discs contains snippets of music from classical music giants such as Beethoven and Stravinsky and a token pop tune by the father of rock 'n' roll, Chuck Berry and other recorded works from the planet.

Voyager I also contained a rather somber greeting from then-President Jimmy Carter, whose personal UFO sighting is well documented and now legendary: "This is a present from a small, distant world, a token of our sounds, our science, our images, our music, our thoughts and our feelings. We are attempting to survive our time so we may live into yours."

If you've seen the 1997 movie *Contact* (adapted from Carl Sagan's novel), you get a sense of how the radio messaging scenario might look and sound from the film's powerful opening sequence. Radio waves from Earth flush out into the galaxy mixed with SETI signals in an audio greeting card from Earth of a dubious but distinguished pedigree. The waves include all sorts of mostly bad-news tidbits from the 20th century layered with recognizable fragments from popular television and radio shows, plus *Billboard* hits like "Itsy Bitsy Teeny Weeny Polka Dot Bikini" from 1960 and "Funkytown," the 1980 smash. (I have a long history with that one, since it was written in Minneapolis by Steven Greenberg and became a global hit on my pop-culture watch.

Years later, Greenberg became a PR client of mine for his various post-"Funkytown" projects.)

Once the federal space agency abandoned the SETI program, the private sector attempted to pick it up until it suddenly ran out of money in the spring of 2011. Then SETI, the Energizer Bunny of private space exploration, found yet more scratch to somehow bounce back again into limited operation. Prior to going dark in recent time—and with no significant results to show from previous decades—the SETI Institute shifted to deep-space assays looking for ET in "the Goldilocks' regions" (i.e., those most friendly to harboring life) uncovered by the Kepler telescope by using digital signal processing to scan greater numbers of microwave channels under the assumption that these channels were viable modes of communication.

In Paul Davies' 2012 book about SETI, *The Eerie Silence: Renewing Our Search for Alien Intelligence,* the author demolishes the basic assumption of SETI's research, that radio frequencies are where it's at. A review in *The New York Times,* written by Dwight Garner, makes the case: "The problem with SETI as it's currently conceived, in Mr. Davies' view, is that it has been blinkered by anthropocentrism, the assumption that alien beings will be anything like us. He quotes the British biologist J. B. S. Haldane, who remarked that 'the universe is not only queerer than we suppose, but queerer than we can suppose.'

"We must jettison as much mental baggage as possible," Davies advises. "Forget little green men, gray dwarfs, flying saucers with portholes, crop circles, glowing balls and scary nocturnal abductions… Drop those *X Files* DVDs and walk slowly away." It's mildly batty to search for radio signals, sent intentionally or not, from what may be a very advanced civilization, he writes, because even Earth's own radio output is already beginning to fade. "Radio signals are outdated technology, nearly as sun-bleached as an old issue of *Omni* magazine. (E.T. surely has cable by now.) And because even a nearby alien civilization would probably be some 1,000 light-years away, conversation is likely to be impossible. Even if this distant civilization could spy on us, here's what they'd see right now: Earth about 1010, long before the Industrial Revolution."

I would learn in the early '90s that Greer's view at CSETI also strongly held that this was a futile mode of communication based on the fact that if you sent a radio signal to Alpha Centuri or vice versa, it would take far too many light years to arrive and return, not tenable for establishing a sustained dialog, let alone set the foundation for a meaningful exchange or relationship. Even the SETI Institute's website offers a rather glaring caveat about its signaling work: "If the nearest civilization is 100 light-years away, we will have to wait 200 years for a reply." Good luck with that.

Greer acknowledged the activities of the hunters and gatherers as vital to forming a public record about the phenomenon, although he was completely distrustful and disdainful of abduction research. He was extremely well read in the volumes of vetted material that amounted to the observation of ET spacecraft and documented close-encounter cases. He had less—or almost no time—for the SETI dead-letter radio signal paradigm. He averred that nearly instantaneous subluminal thought between two parties was the ultimate cosmic smartphone and protocol for communication.

As he notes, "If you have a civilization based, for example, in Zeta Reticuli, which is 37 light years from Earth, how are you going to communicate with your home base if you're restricted by the speed of light? What transcends the speed of light? Consciousness. Mind. It is instantaneous because it is non-local and is not bound by the time-space continuum. The linear progression of radio waves at the speed of light to Zeta Reticuli to say, 'Hello, how are you doing?' and to get a response, 'Fine, thank you,' takes 72 years at the speed of light."

What intrigued those who learned about his views and organization is that Greer took the established research models and tried to merge the database with real-time research. He did so by forming Working Groups across the country and in England, and the groups tried to make contact in areas where there had been sightings as well as in "de novo" areas where there hadn't been. Who needed the government to make a disclosure announcement (although he would rigorously push for that a few years later, as explained in Chapter Nine) when your group might make contact on its own?

Using high-beam lights to signal, along with the playing of looped audio tones allegedly recorded during a close encounter in New Hampshire and a loop of sounds from the British crop circles, the CSETI teams began a simplistic form of communication: signaling to acknowledge the presence of an ET vehicle as well as indicating the intention of the Working Group to take things a step further—or possibly *many* steps further in the event of an on-board and/or off-planet encounter.

The heart of CSETI's contact exercise was complex remote viewing (RV) techniques learned—or not learned—in weekend crash courses (a kind of Remote Viewing 101.) Greer's RV style has its roots as much in his work in transcendental meditation as in the 50-plus-years-old psychic programs at Stanford University led by the late Ingo Swann and others. RV has been employed in various military programs, such as those mentioned in books by Joseph McMoneagle, who was part of the U.S. Army's Stargate intelligence team. Remote viewing was, to borrow from a Library Journal trade press entry about McMoneagle's work, "the ability to perceive psychically and describe unknown objects, people, places, or events."

The Stargaters used RV to spy on enemies and look at probable future events, but leading advocate McMoneagle was adamant that anyone could learn to remote view. As part of the Cold War, the Russians had their RV teams and systems in play as well. I prefer George Harrison's definition of it in his raga rock song "Inner Light" on the flipside of the *Lady Madonna* 45 rpm: "Without going out of my door/I can know all things on Earth/Without looking out of my window/I could know the ways of heaven." I would soon learn my own precognitive dream of the Boston harbor one month before meeting Greer was a form of RV.

40

Armed with assumptions based on the literature and Greer's strongly held personal beliefs and experiences that the visitors were non-hostile, early teams used only videotape, audio recorders and paper debriefs to document any Close Encounter of the Fifth Kind event, or CE-5. The CSETI members were trained to view the CE-5 process as both a diplomatic and scientific effort—and above all, an experiment.

The good country doctor likened Working Group participants as "ambassadors to the stars or the universe," a phrase that became the (marketing) title of hundreds of lectures, seminars and real-time events he has conducted over the past 30 years. His path dramatically and controversially diverged from those of the hunters, gatherers and signalers of the UFO ghetto through the key element of his contact process, using mind and the engagement of the science of consciousness in what he called "full-spectrum reality."

Group members not only send affirmative and intentional "mental signals" to any object spotted in a Working Group area but also try to facilitate a landing and subsequent meet-and-greet. These intergalactic spaceships and occupants, Greer reasoned, could pick up these mental texts, much like a radar signal reads its object at a distance if the mental imaging or messaging was highly focused and done in repetitive series (what he called Coherent Thought Sequencing, or CTS). It was simultaneously the most outlandish and visionary idea I had ever heard. And the implications of it—if even remotely true or workable—reeled me in for a time.

Although it had been almost two decades since I had read the UFO tabloid press and mainstream media about sightings and related events, or consumed the popular-culture servings of films like *Close Encounters of the Third Kind* and *Communion* or television movies like *The Intruders* (based on the abduction-related work of Budd Hopkins), I instinctively felt that Greer's assessment of mind or consciousness may have been the missing link in the UFO/ET discussion. I was eager to learn more about it and see if CSETI was a pioneering initiative worth exploring, if only to determine that its mind-bending theories and methods worked or were just a lot of complicated thinking and acting out.

Greer's interstellar brain-to-brain interface seemed almost cosmically comical at first glance, promoting contact in part through thought power directed intensely at other conscious and sentient beings. Yet, in 2000, applied medical science that targets paralysis was already harnessing cerebral power as a viable means of restoring movement to paralyzed individuals and those with artificial limbs.

According to WebMD's site, "Duke University Medical Center scientists implanted electrodes in the brains of two owl monkeys that enabled the animals to use brain signals to control a robot arm. The brain signals were even transmitted over the internet, remotely controlling a robot arm 600 miles away at the Massachusetts Institute of Technology in Boston. Findings from the studies were reported in the Nov. 16, 2000 issue of *Nature*. Researchers say their computerized system could be an important step toward what they call a 'brain-machine interface,' that would allow paralyzed patients to control prosthetic limbs. Their research could also provide a clearer understanding of how the brain works."

Less than ten years later, as reported in the July 13, 2006 *New York Times*, monkey testing had given way to human trials wherein an implanted sensor system called "BrainGate" in the motor cortex allows a paralyzed individual "to control a computer, a television set and a robot using only his thoughts, scientists reported. In a variety of experiments, the first person to receive the implant, Matthew Nagle, moved a cursor, opened e-mail, played a simple video game called Pong and drew a crude circle on the screen. He could change the channel or volume on a television set, move a robot arm somewhat, and open and close a prosthetic hand."

Greer's exploratory mind work was light-years ahead of these contemporary medical achievements of the brain-machine-interface. Still, it seems both were well grounded in the use of the billions of neurons required by mind-produced conscious thought to communicate and accomplish objectives. If ETs and/or their vehicles were wired in a similar fashion and had hyper-acute space receptors to track such thought power through or around the vastness of time-space, what were the implications?

Greer spoke often of the boys upstairs having "consciousness-assisted technology, or technology-assisted consciousness." At the time, I had almost no point of reference for these CSETI's contact techniques and concepts using human consciousness. But on two separate but distinct occasions years before I met Steve Greer, I may have had relevant and prescient notions about them. My recent precognitive experience in Boston seemed to lend itself to, or be a part of, the larger mind or psi component that was part of the full-spectrum-awareness mode.

The other occasion was in the late '80s on a trip to Glacier Park with my brother. It was a particularly despairing time for me after a breakup of a serious two-year relationship that resulted in a mid-life crisis at thirty-five. Long before knowing about Close Encounters of the Fifth Kind, which broke down the line in the mind, I had toyed with the same methodology, although I would have never characterized it as such then.

Even though I enjoy rejuvenation in the serene comfort of hiking the majestic woods and alpine reaches of the Rocky Mountains, this trip wasn't as successful in getting me through the lovesick blues. It was "raining in my heart," to borrow a line from a '60s blues tune by Slim Harpo, and it seemed the storm clouds would never break.

Even after a beautiful day of fishing Cameron Lake on the Canadian side of the range, where I caught a nice 10-inch trout that the Prince of Wales Hotel in Waterton, Alberta, deliciously prepared for dinner, I couldn't shake the disease of separation. After my brother went to bed, I sat outside under one of the most pervasive and engaging star fields anywhere on earth. The Victorian-era hotel faces the grandeur of the Rockies, while behind it sprawls the vast open prairie of Alberta, which looks as if someone has completely erased the mountains from the landscape. But under a clear night, the stars blanket both prairie and peak and you feel, gazing into the black and light-pointed heavens, that the Earth really is just another large mass in the unfathomable pool of space, and the entire planet is on a blind journey through the universe, or many universes.

On this lonesome night, I ridiculously felt that if I focused my attention long enough into the stars, hopefully, fantastically, I could be rescued from my terrestrial misery by being lifted into a traversing spaceship like so many in popular UFO culture. The Who's Pete Townsend had a line for that reasoning from "Naked Eye," one of the band's lesser efforts. "The stars are all connected to the brain."

So, I spiked out Morse code lines of desperate, anxious thought, feeling self-conscious and quite stupid while quietly in awe of the vastness of the stars and the limitless possibilities overhead. After about a half-hour, I was both embarrassed and enthralled by such an idea, as if I could cure my low-down circumstances by getting even further out into deep space—someplace else with a couple of ET copilots or a robotic AI machine.

But years later in 1992, with my world view in serious flux and this Montana experience my only other loose connection to Greer's thinking, I needed to satisfy my curiosity and herd the unexplained events in my home and in my head into a cognitive place of knowing and understanding—at least so I could move forward with greater clarity and maybe even closure.

* * *

Einstein once was asked, "What is the most important question?" to which he then replied, "Is the universe friendly?"

Greer had quickly built a controversial reputation while simultaneously building an entire organization on the assumption that at least the conscious beings visiting the planet posed "no net hostile intentions." Their "right stuff" was perhaps as good as or better than the men and women who had the "right stuff" for our US space programs. In more recent times, Einstein's heir apparent, Stephen Hawking, mused that aliens might be hostile, an opinion that seems naively dangerous from one of the great scientific thinkers of the early 21st century. Such a comment also belied his lack of knowledge of the verifiable UFO data, or at least demonstrated a willingness to play to the fear base.

I met the good country doctor Greer in mid-August 1992 in Woodland Hills, California, a suburb of Los Angeles. It was a month after my trip to Boston and the quiet awakening. Without sharing much information about Greer, my friend had told me he was a medical doctor and father of four children from Asheville, North Carolina, also the home of writer Thomas Wolfe (*Look Homeward, Angel* and other novels.) I didn't yet know or understand Greer's MO.

Prior to the trip, I phoned him to introduce myself. We talked briefly about his work and his interest in getting a writer to tell his story. I assured him the story was a good one, but also cautioned that it might simply be too hard to believe for many readers. He acknowledged that suggestion with a carefree chuckle. He wanted me to fly out to LA and shadow him during a weekend lecture and workshop, squeezing in interviews when we could.

Before our meeting, Greer had sent a fifty-five-page CSETI document about its assessment of UFO/ET phenomena plus related essays about the CE-5 Initiative ("The Next Generation of UFO Research") and field reports from Gulf Breeze, Florida and the 1989 Belgium UFO wave, which was witnessed by thousands, from generals to farmers, and is well documented in Kean's book and other reliable sources. He also sent a recording of a recent lecture full of significant ideas and acute observations about the UFO ghetto. I played the tape first and was struck by one particularly significant comment he had made about the clichéd question one hears constantly about why ET doesn't land on the White House lawn.

He left no doubt about the terrain he traveled and those many others who walked it. "Most Ufology is wastebasket Ufology," he said. "It's loaded with some of the most paranoid people you'll ever run into. The field is full of conspiracy buffs, people with very low self-esteem, people with very little stability and their own ill-conceived agendas." He went out of his way to dis the UFO cottage industry at large, which he estimated at being worth hundreds of millions of dollars annually.

He continued, "Frankly, I'm worried more about the *meshuganas* in the UFO community than I am about the bogeyman at the NSA [National Security Agency]. The government has done a lot more research into this area [UFOs] than they've publicly admitted and a hell of lot less than most UFO investigators give them credit for." He also claimed that the self-interest in the UFO community has been ghettoized, making it easier to discredit either by people who don't care about the topic or by government agencies with "black budgets and billions of dollars," who for reasons of national security need to manage the information and/or debunk it when the so-called national interest is threatened.

As to why the ETs he believed were coming provided no open contact, he turned philosophical: "These visitors, ETs or UFOs, have been knocking on our front door and on our back door and on our side door and up from the basement for about fifty years or more in a very serious way." But, he stressed, our responses and our history of intra-planetary warfare have demonstrated a hostile intent on our part in response to an ET presence.

He surmised that if we continued to spurn these overtures, we do so at our own possible peril and expose our collective ignorance as a planetary civilization regularly divided by warring nation states over power struggles, extremist religious ideologies, natural resources and monetary systems. With the current capability of atomic weapons being deployed in space, we may pose an even bigger threat to ourselves—and to them.

I had never heard anyone take such a reasoned view of all things ET, especially one that accounted for a plausible extraterrestrial perspective. I wanted to know more, I wanted to hear more and I wanted to see some action under the stars. At the very least and very best, I owed it to the members of the club and the spirit of the pen.

* * *

Before I got my rental car to go meet the good doctor, I hit the men's room to splash cold water on my face after flying for three hours. In the image-conscious matrix of LA, the city of show business, two Hispanic men employed as valets were filling empty Evian bottles with the city's finest tap water and hustling back to their jobs pretending to have the expensive French stuff. My strange dream life has not really let up (although I am not retaining as much information from my dreams), and as I dried my hands and face, I debated how much if anything I should share with Dr. Greer once we meet.

A month before landing, I had finally read Greer's report from crop-circle country "Close Encounters of the Fifth Kind: Contact in Southern England" detailing a close encounter with a handful of people who were part of a larger group that had disbanded before the event.

The larger group included Linda Moulton Howe, who is well-known for her work in everything paranormal-plus, had written about cattle mutilations in *Harvest of Fear* and is heard today on the popular radio program *Coast to Coast*. British researcher Collin Andrews was also on hand and was an early crop-circle investigator who had established Circles Phenomenon Research. English writer Peter Russell (*A White Hole in Time*,) and British painter and instructor Chris Mansell and a friend from the Netherlands, Annick Nevejan, were also in the group. A doctor of psychology from Cincinnati, Dr. S., who didn't want to be identified, and various CSETI members from America and England such as Maria Ward and the late Reg Presley, the former lead singer of the group The Troggs ("Wild Thing") rounded out those in the gathering, along with a few hangers-on from the media and some locals.

On the night of the close encounter, the group had witnessed four amber-colored UFOs to the east followed by strange lights in the woods nearby. An unmarked helicopter—alleged to be military—interrupted things long enough for the group to shut down its activities and a bank of black clouds to roll in. Suspecting rain, many left the area. Greer, Dr. S, Mansell and his Belgium friend soon decided to change locations, each pair leaving in a separate vehicle. Then, things got downright "Spielbergian."

In Greer's report, he wrote that at first a "carouselling" [sic] white light shone down on top of the cloud bank, "big, hundreds of yards and seen by all of us." But as the foursome vacated along the muddied farm roads, something else showed up. Mansell was the first to see the lighted object and started beating on Greer's car window, yelling that there was something coming through the field. Soon, all four were out watching what Greer described as a "structured metallic craft, maybe 80-to-150 feet in diameter, 20 feet over the ground at eye level, about 400 yards away, floating over the field."

"Chris used the word 'gobsmacked' to describe his excitement," Dr. S. later said of the incident. "It's a northern English expression. We were all gobsmacked by what we saw." What they saw was a bank of contiguous red-to-white-to-green lights moving counterclockwise at the base of the craft, which had a cone-shaped top with three or four amber lights spinning more slowly than the ones at the bottom. Mansell and Dr. S admitted the structure seemed to change shape from circular to triangular or "a Christmas tree-like formation with red, blue and orange lights in this shape," Mansell recalled. "It was pretty spectacular. I've never seen anything like it in my life!"

The event lasted around fifteen minutes and included several light exchanges between the craft and the four humans. Led by Greer, the group blinked their high-powered flashlights at the object, which would respond in kind with the same number of light bursts, a primitive, wild-thing hoedown between those in the farm field and the lit-up shape-shifter from parts unknown.

Maria Ward, who earlier had departed from the foursome and was about a hundred meters from the event, said she saw the same object and could see the signaling by Greer's group, although she did not know it was them at the time. She also saw one of the amber lights detach from the flying structure.

Others on a hill away from the event also witnessed one of the amber lights detach from the main craft and float off into the mist, confirming the information provided by Greer's group and Ward. It was a spectacular sighting. As I made notes in the margins of the report, I felt incredulous about the report but also anxious to meet this man.

CSETI 1993 publicity photo of Dr. Steven Greer, MD

I took brief stock of my Tinfoil file as I climbed into the rental car to head for the hotel. While the newspaper vision dreams were over, in other dreams there now seemed to be interactions and conversations with people I didn't know but who were trying to tell me something.

I can't remember the dialog, which is lost to time. The lights-on phenomena in the bedroom also had subsided, but there would be more serious hoohah inside that house.

After shaking hands, Greer and I sat in the lobby of the hotel at which the CSETI Friday night lecture and all-day Saturday workshop were to take place. Studious-looking and well-dressed in a sport coat, slacks and tie, Steve Greer appeared to be a polite, bespectacled southern gentleman, sandy-haired, fair-skinned and freckled. As we began talking, I admitted that I wanted to share a couple "strange things" that had been happening in my life.

I told Greer about the redundant newspaper dreams, the awakenings with the lights on and the sounds in the house, and the burning pier episode. I basically spilled all the cosmic beans to this stranger from North Carolina, hoping he wouldn't think I was some kind of nutter and a mismatch for the writing gig.

A small smile creased his face.

"In my lecture, I describe how consciousness, or awareness, is non-local," he said emphatically. "You'll get a better understanding of what I mean by that, which may help explain your experience in Boston. Non-locality of consciousness also forms the bases of the CSETI protocols and the CE-5 Initiative. Of course," he hastened to add, "the people in the UFO ghetto think this is utter bunk and that I'm some kind of *crackpot*." He put heavy emphasis with his slight Carolina drawl on the word and smiled again. "I always find that amusing. But we are continually affirming these methods can work. You'll hear about the CE-5 in England earlier this summer and also in Gulf Breeze."

I told him I'd read the reports. He then mentioned a man, "Chicken Little," who was allegedly spreading falsehoods throughout the ghetto—and maybe even to people in media—that he wasn't really a medical doctor. He wondered aloud if a cease-and-desist letter from an attorney would shut him up.

"Why would he do that?" I asked naively.

"To discredit me basically, and my whole approach to real-time research with the CE-5 Initiative. But that's life in the ghetto, it's full of this type of malicious and back-stabbing stuff. You have no *idea!*" He put the same weight on the word "idea" as he had on "crackpot." We talked for an hour about his upbringing, his family life and the general interview subjects that writers use to soften up their subjects and get on familiar ground.

I learned of Greer's growing up in a middle-class family, having some Native American blood on his mother's side, and that his father was an alcoholic. Both parents were atheists: "If you couldn't put something in a test tube and measure it, it didn't exist," he said. We talked about his medical studies and impressive career as a doctor, and about his four daughters. He and his wife were of the Bahá'í Faith, a relatively new religion founded in 19th century Persia by Bahá'u'lláh, an Arabic word that translates to "Glory of God." It was a monotheistic faith that believed, he explained, that the cosmos was resplendent with life and that "every fixed star had its habitable planets."

The Bahá'í religion emphasized oneness and the unity of all humans on Earth. The oneness note echoed something that the mystic Edgar Cayce had often referenced among his thousands of readings given in an unconscious state. Information and insights poured out of him through a channel to a higher source Cayce believed was tied to his Christian faith. He predicted in such a somnolent mode that humanity at a point in the future would experience universal oneness for a long reign of peace on Earth.

Ahh. The great oneness, I thought. It could not come quickly enough.

In a telling moment, Greer added that he was "first shown" his wife, Emily, in a dream. Quantum entanglement as Cupid's arrow? The concept, it seemed, knew no boundaries or religious barriers. The doc was also a student and teacher of transcendental meditation, the Eastern technique popularized in the global mind by the Beatles and their guru Maharishi Mahesh and later embraced and promoted by people like singular filmmaker David Lynch, madcap comic and recovering addict Russell Brand and others. Greer quickly ran up points with his interviewer, given my interest in transcendental ideas exposed by the 19th school of New England transcendentalist poets and the mystical practices from the East that have attracted many people from the music world. Even Mike Love of the Beach Boys embraced TM, a point he made to audiences during the group's 50th anniversary reunion tour in 2012 by introducing an old song he'd written about it.

I also liked the way Greer set himself apart from those in "the UFO field." Some of my favorite artists, musicians, writers and social change agents—I sensed Greer considered himself more in this social-agents camp than the UFO arena—were, as a variation on the old Groucho Marx expression went, not willing to be in a club that would accept them as members. During the next few years I was in Greer's company, he always made a point of quoting a line from cultural anthropologist Margaret Mead during lectures and interviews: "Never doubt that a small group of thoughtful, committed people can change the world. Indeed, it is the only thing that ever has." And he always strove to keep his distance from the fringe elements.

Asked about what he believed the government knew—the big money question for those in and out of the ghetto—Greer said he thought the alleged Majestic or MAJIK-12 (aka MJ-12) group that managed the UFO issue since the late '40s was no longer the body in charge. According to the Wikipedia entry on the Majestic group of 12 individuals, "The organization is claimed to be the code name of an alleged secret committee of scientists, military leaders, and government officials, formed in 1947 by an executive order by US President Harry S. Truman to facilitate recovery and investigation of alien spacecraft. The concept originated in a series of supposedly leaked secret government documents first circulated by ufologists in 1984."

Any discussion of that group leads to a Ufological dead end: There have been numerous debates, books, affirmations and denunciations of the MJ-12 claims, plus heated denials about its documents that have surfaced over the years as being elaborate hoaxes, disinformation (another prized ghetto term) or propaganda (traceable, or not, to obscure Pentagon offices).

How the secrecy works or has worked through the decades is explored in greater depth in Chapter 9 about the CSETI Disclosure initiatives that took place in later years. But during our first meeting, Greer allowed that close sources had told him that the key players now in charge of the UFO issue belonged to a group called PI-40. He didn't know what the P or I stood for and assumed 40 referred to the number of individuals involved. It probably was made up of current and former government and military officials plus others in academia and the corporate world. Its secrecy was maintained along the conventional lines used by the military: Sensitive information or knowledge was compartmentalized and on a need-to-know basis, possibly with other security safeguards built in. He also noted that his insiders described a split within the group—old-guard members were totally against declassifying and disclosing, while younger members were pushing for it. The prevailing arguments against disclosure were outdated, this younger faction believed. The idea of disclosing an other-world, off-planet civilization would create a panic in all religions and disrupt the educational, governmental, economic and other institutions. These fears were no longer realistic expectations.

Listening to him, I realized Greer might be climbing treacherously steep terrain and wondered about his safety.

With the first leg of our interview completed, Greer invited me to a television producer's office for a viewing of the show "Sightings," which aired in the early '90s. Sean Morton drove us to someplace in West Hollywood. Morton was a radio and TV producer who also had a colorful if checkered history as a psychic, astrologer and investment advisor (which would later get him in serious trouble with the SEC.) He haphazardly tossed opinions and comments around in the car while navigating traffic, touching on everything from impending earthquakes and other rumblings from psychics he knew to the latest gossip about longtime players in UFO-ology and meeting some of the early astronauts during parties at his parents' home. His dad, he said, was a PR guy at NASA.

"Great job," I offered.

Sitting in the back seat, I felt ignored and more than a little out of place. I had nothing to contribute to this bucket of scuttlebutt as cars littered the freeway on all sides. I was curious about which astronauts he'd met. I was a longtime "fan" of the early space program and had autographed pictures of the Mercury, Gemini, and Apollo crews, as if they were pop stars to be posted on a bedroom wall. In my world, they were pop stars, after a fashion. I grew up having a collection of tear-out magazine articles and covers about space exploration that rivaled my stack of 45 rpms and long-playing rock, pop and R&B albums, two passions that my parents didn't fully understand but approved of none-theless.

Greer indulged Morton until we got to the production office where four of us, including the show's producer, watched a videotape of a CSETI event near Gulf Breeze in mid-March of 1992. Four objects had interacted with Greer's group on the ground in what he described as "a conscious lock on" with ET occupants and an ensuing "photon dialogue" between the CSETI group and one of the airborne objects, which responded in kind to the flashing of a 500,000 candle-power light "in intelligent sequences."

In the course of the video, Greer drew a triangle in the sky with his light to continue the "light conversation." Three of the objects moved into a triangular formation and hovered about a half mile over the CSETI team's location. The surprised sounds on the audio were distinct and genuine, and the written report offers that a fair amount of "pandemonium" ensued, as a landing was anticipated.

"A CE-5!" exclaimed one man.

While the footage was mind-blowing, I found the doctor's next statements even more so. Greer relayed that on his flight to Gulf Breeze the day before, he had experienced a premonition about an encounter that would take place the night before the Working Group's interaction with the multiple-light objects. He sensed that it would occur at or around midnight and involve a single object. He conveyed this information to the group during the day. That night, almost precisely at midnight, a "deep glowing cherry orange-red object which throbbed in pulsatile (sic) fashion" appeared in what Dr. UFO deemed "a First Degree CE-5."

That night, Dr. Joe Burkes, who worked in the Kaiser Medical organization in the Los Angeles area, introduced Greer to a room of about a hundred people. Bearded, with modified long hair down his collar and around his ears, the affable Burkes was a self-described red-diaper baby raised during the commie scare following WWII, and the wars in Korea and Vietnam. His interest in the ET/UFO subject matter was relatively new, he confessed, and his animated introduction of a fellow medical colleague who was blazing a courageous new path in UFO research pumped up the audience.

Greer did not disappoint. I filled more than half my notebook during the Friday lecture with notes on such highlights as Greer coining the CE-5 category after reviewing several prominent cases in the literature where "second degree" Close Encounters of the Fifth Kind had taken place. Those included the widely reported incident at a mission in Papua, New Guinea, where on June 26, 1959 a Catholic priest, Father Melchior Gill, and thirty-eight people witnessed over a three-hour period a disc with four humanoids on the outside, followed the next night by a larger, mothership-like craft, that was again in the area with four humanoids visible. The priest waved to these humanoids and they waved back. Light signaling with a flashlight ensued on the ground, which caused the object to move forward toward the group.

Greer cited several other "first degree CE-5s" cherry-picked from the gatherers. These were compelling cases in which human-initiated actions brought a response from the visitors and/or their craft, including a 1978 incident near Indianapolis in which a caravan of trucks was engulfed in a blue light that caused their engines and radios to falter. One driver shouted into his CB radio, "Hey UFO, if you have your ears on, I want to go with you," and then the blue light briefly returned and was witnessed by other drivers on the highway. This was a CE-5 over a CB channel (there could have been a kick-ass Merle Haggard song there, I am certain). Greer also predicted an international landing event of the visitors someplace in the four-corners of the US that would be televised, probably within the next ten years.

Many years since then, that hasn't happened.

In the introductory CSETI booklet, Greer lists a number of similar encounters from across the world including a 1981 event in Uruguay where a police chief flashed his car lights at "a huge UFO" that stopped suddenly and "zigzagged in response," only to follow the chief's car and the automobiles of several others for ninety minutes or more and hover closely "at 50-100 yards" at one point, giving a clear view of "a disc-shaped object with a dome on top."

In the same CSETI materials, Greer seems to obliquely cloak an experience of a "college student" in 1972 hiking near Boone, North Carolina. This "student" appears to be Greer himself. The student encounters a craft and humanoids outside of it, and experiences missing time. But he realizes afterward how to conduct telepathic interactions through "a specific series of thought projections"—what CSETI groups subsequently called Coherent Thought Sequencing—all of which "precipitated numerous UFO sightings in the area" and were reported in the media once the student started experimenting with the technique.

When I read this and learned of other historic incidents of alleged Close Encounters of the Fifth Kind, it triggered memories of my Prince of Wales thought projections under the powerful night sky while heartbroken and star-longing in the Rockies. I wasn't the only one to believe such things were possible—even if way out on the ledge.

I made small talk with Dr. Burkes after the speech while other participants crowded around Dr. Greer with questions and friendly comments. Greer asked how I liked the lecture. I said it was compelling, with the caveat that "I'm kind of a neophyte these days, despite an early interest as a kid." Joe said he, too, was a complete neophyte before consuming mass quantities of UFO/ET literature and media to get up to speed.

"I'll send you some things you might be interested in," he added. "It might help with your story."

Following the Friday lecture, the Saturday morning CSETI workshop nearly filled the hotel ballroom. Chairs were set in a long, squeezed, oblong circle, with Greer at a center point. The crowd ranged from teenagers to those in their 70s. Each participant in turn gave their name and why they had come, including me. I informed the circle that I was "just a participating observer, here to write about Dr. Greer and his organization."

"So watch out," Greer said, "he's with the *media*," using the same personalized intonation he'd used earlier with the words "crackpot" and "you have no idea." The crowd laughed. "And you know they can't be trusted on this topic!" he added. A bunch of people hooted. I thought his was a prejudiced view of things, but my attitude about his opinion of media was soon to change.

I was surprised by the number of psychologists in the group—six or seven—who each said basically the same thing. They were there to learn more about the subject of ETs and/or other beings because some of their patients had reported nighttime interactions, many in dreams, with what seemed to be other life-forms, and both patients and shrinks were struggling with that. That dreams comment landed hard: Had their clients' consciousness been hacked somehow?

By the time everyone had been introduced, I'd noted a number who confessed, "I'm a contactee," and wondered what that meant. What were they being contacted for? And who was contacting them? These individuals ranged from a couple of the teenagers to middle-aged, middle-class men and women who seemed to be rational. I wondered for a second, was I a contactee? Not a club I wanted to be in, I thought.

While Greer ended the niceties and began with a recap of his Friday night lecture, I surveyed the self-confessed contactees. I started thinking about an old tune Dan Hicks had written and recorded called "Hell, I'd Go," a wry song about going off with ET, given the sorry state of the world. Hicks was a favorite among certain music-lovin' members of the club. Walking down the college dorm hallway of third or fourth floor Tommy, where most of the Space Pen members roomed, you could often hear verses of "I Scare Myself (Thinking About You..." sailing through the air.

Thinking about the Hicks tune, I recalled the number of times I'd heard friends briefly bring up the UFO/ET discussion in which someone would say, "If I had the opportunity, I'd go." Or, "Honey, if I came home and you were gone and had left a message about going off into space, I would completely understand—and approve." For these people and those sitting in the hotel that day, "Hell, I'd Go" was their soundtrack. Or maybe their swan song.

The day-long lecture covered a wide range of CSETI issues—its philosophy and assumptions; the purpose of establishing Working Groups in different parts of the country and in other countries; basic training about remote viewing and the non-locality of consciousness as a key contact protocol; the REMIT groups (Rapid Mobilization Investigative Teams) comprised of four to five seasoned CSETI members that dispatch to hot spots where ongoing sightings provide an ideal setting for initiating contact, like the hot spot in crop circle country a month earlier; and other topics like those covered in the CSETI handbook, including "Developing Appropriate Collective Self-Esteem." It sounds funny and corny on paper, but within the canon of Greer's encompassing thoughts and research, it was right in the pocket.

The Doc was emphatic that regardless of how advanced visiting ETs might be, humans must not perceive them as superior or themselves as inferior. In his visionary view, what leveled the playing field was simply "conscious intelligence… Our equality as beings is founded in the fact that both humans and extraterrestrial beings are conscious, intelligent sentient creatures. Conscious Intelligence is both our point of equality and our point of unity; it is the basis for relationship itself."

Tied closely to this CSETI platform was "The Imperative of Consciousness" discussion, in which he took on, in part, the prevailing media and popular culture notions of ET. "Of almost equal importance is the question of how we view ETI intentions and motives," he said. "If the tabloids, sensationalistic books and rumor mills are to be believed, ETI are either gurulike space gods or Darth Vader space conquerors!

"Our tendency to polarize either side of this issue is both premature and unwarranted—and it is dangerous. It is unlikely that they are either perfect gods or evil-empire operatives, yet these views of their motives have influenced and will continue to influence our attitudes and actions unless consciously addressed. A review of the cases to date would indicate that while some actions are enigmatic and even disturbing to some human sensibilities, no evidence of net hostile intentions exists."

All told, it was a challenging day of material, occasionally infused by a shared thought by someone with a personal reckoning or belief about the subject. That night, most of those gathered for the event traveled to a desert location out of town for three hours of Working Group activity, trying to "vector in spacecraft" by remote viewing means, or watching for non-conventional aircraft that might have originated off-planet.

The desert was cold and windy as we formed a circle under a partly cloudy sky. The stars peered down across our location. A young woman next to me named Joyce, who was a waitress but really wanted to be an actress like so many in the Mecca of show business, started shivering. I gave her my thick sweater, zipped up a heavy jacket I'd brought along and asked what she thought of the day's proceedings.

"What do you think?" she deflected.

"I don't know yet. I'm taking it all in."

"Is that what you're going to write?" she asked with a laugh.

While the larger group scanned the dark skies and a smaller group broke off to do the remote-viewing exercise, others created light patterns with high-beam flashlights. The weird, ricocheting tones of the alleged downed spacecraft could be heard playing repeatedly on a cassette recorder, each tone sounding like it might have originated in a Hollywood sound studio—or someplace else beyond the Milky Way.

The sounds became hypnotic (and later, down the road a piece in my own Working Group in Minneapolis, I would find them soothing.) As the tones played in the background, I wanted to tell the young thespian that I hoped this whole thing wasn't going to prove to be just a lot of bad LA tap water flushed into fancy Evian bottles. But instead I just shrugged.

"I think it's the future," Joyce said, finally answering my question. An hour later she gave the sweater back with a thank you and headed for her ride home. I went back to looking at the night sky, peering into the infinite blackness, wondering and waiting. A couple of lights in the southern distance appeared and momentarily caused a small stir in the group. It was in the direction of where part of the International Space Station was being built, and Greer reiterated a point he had made during the lecture/workshop—that sightings were common around military and space installations and maybe "they" were checking out the progress of this component part. Still, the lights were too distant to be discernable and eventually veered out of view.

In the years since this first CSETI skywatch in LA, besides the aforementioned Rand report outlining nuclear site incursions, other events have reached my radar, including one of the more famous incidents at Malmstrom Air Force Base in Montana that indicates the relative ease with which our elite missile systems could be tampered with by unknown aerial objects.

Richard Dolan's account of this November 7, 1975, event in the second of two must-read volumes, *UFOs and the National Security State,* provides a disturbing view of the Malmstrom base struggling to deal with "a brightly glowing orange disc, as large as a football field, hovering over the missile site" at three in the afternoon at the restricted location K-7, triggering alarms and sending a Sabotage Alert Team (SAT) to investigate, which "surprisingly" refuses to do so.

The object had risen from the missile area and appeared on NORAD radar. "F-106 interceptors were promptly scrambled" from the base. Eventually, the hundred-yard-long disc reached 200,000 feet, Dolan writes, and disappeared from radar. "Afterwards, members of the SAT received a psychological examination which indicated that they had been through a traumatic experience."

But the missile launch system had been traumatized too: "The missile at K-7 showed indications that its computer targeting systems had been tampered with, and it had to be removed. It was later revealed that six other Launch Control centers reported UFOs that day." And the following night they returned! "Throughout November 1975, UFOs continued to enter US military air space with impunity," Dolan wrote.

My reaction to this information raised more questions. Were these hostile acts on behalf of the Ovni's (the Mexican word for "The Unknowns?") Or were they messages being sent of one sort or another to say, "Your defenses are inadequate to deal with us," or, perhaps, "You are trudging on the wrong path." Or both? Perhaps they were just probing the quality of our defense systems and the psychological reactions of those caught up in the event.

Back in the desert after the mild excitement of seeing the distant lights, the group went back to its assigned duties—remote viewers in one place, the beacons just outside the circle, and sky watchers primarily in the main loop.

"Be sure to cover the zenith," Greer and Burkes stressed now and then. "Cover the zenith!" Apparently the space directly overhead was prime ET real estate for approaches. I imagined a night owl swooping down on a rodent that neglected to cover its zenith. But I thought better of the image in light of everything I'd heard over the past two days.

In the morning, I met the two doctors and went to brunch at the house of a real-estate businessperson who had attended the workshop and wanted some personal face time with Dr. Greer. On the way, Greer invited me to meet other members of CSETI and some of his peers who supported his work, including Brian Leary, the "Marsonaut" who was part of NASA's astronaut corps assigned to the Mars mission until it was scrubbed. They would be available and eager to talk at the annual IANS (International Association of New Science) meeting in Ft. Collins, Colorado. I wasn't sure what New Science was, but if it was like CSETI, it was going to be a strange new world. I agreed it was a good idea and would help flesh out the story.

Over a friendly brunch, I listened to the first of many ET stories I would hear in such gatherings. This one came from the real-estate guy whose wife and two adolescent children seemed pretty in tune with the overall discussion. He'd heard that at an exclusive meeting between Mikhail Gorbachev, then leading the Soviet Union, and his generals in Russia, an ET had suddenly materialized in the room and warned them to pursue the goals of détente with the West.

I might have swallowed my OJ hard at that point. I looked at the two docs to see their reactions. Dr. Joe listened politely while Greer replied that he had heard this story too but had no way of knowing if it were true. But it made sense, at least from his view of things, that such a thing might be conveyed given how likely and devastating an all-out nuclear war between superpowers would be to the countries and the planet—and probably to the ETs themselves.

I put it in the Tinfoil file and flew home later that day. My mind was racing. Part of it was saying, "This is too far out for any mainstream publication." But the broad, free-form thinking of the Space Pen Club shouted back, "It's no stranger than what you've been through to this point. Just go with it."

Once home, I made plans to travel to IANS in a month. I had no way of knowing what it would be like. And I could never have predicted what unpleasant events would follow it. Still, I had signed on for this gig, and the strange events in my house and head somehow seemed to fit into its trajectory. Or was I conflating things that seemed to be related in order to find a convenient category for them? I didn't have that answer yet. The journey was on. I would play it as best I knew how, although I knew now that all the metrics for determining best to worst seemed to have been thrown out the window.

Gearing up for another trip West with the radio on, I heard the 1966 hit that Smokey Robinson wrote for the Marvelettes called "The Hunter Gets Captured by the Game." Back in my youth, it was a clever, fun song about love, passion and pursuit. Now, twenty-five years later, it sounded like the cautionary tale it really was.

CHAPTER THREE:
PSYCHOTRONIC NIGHTMARES AND THE
ALIEN ABDUCTION BLUES?

"Technologies exist, which are ready, off-the-shelf capable, and which can fit in a panel truck or on an antenna in a city, which can totally induce an experience. If it is desired, a targeted person—or group of people—can be made to have a conversation with their personal God, and they will believe it is real, and they will pass a lie detector that it is real, because for them it is real."

—Abductions: Not All That Glitters Is Gold, by Dr. Steven Greer, MD

IANS—the science conference Greer urged me to attend—was lousy with "New Age" vendors, visionary individuals and far-out ideas looking for a fan base. It brought out the old, younger rock-critic cynic in me at first blush. The merchandise tables were the first thing I saw entering the conference. They were covered with pamphlets for this healing issue and that herbal use, product demos, books autographed by presenting authors, info for other "Paradigm-Shifting" conferences and IANS swag. The event drew people from all over the states, Canada and Europe, and its organizational founders had impressive if not impeccable credentials.

One was cofounder of the Peace Corps, Dr. Maurice Albertson, Ph.D., who was then a civil-engineering professor at Colorado State

University. "Maury," as everyone called him at the event, had also been involved in two International Conferences on Paranormal Research at CSU and the International Forums on New Science. A fellow cofounder was Brian O'Leary, Ph.D., a former Apollo astronaut and professor of astronomy/physics at Princeton University, the University of California at Berkeley and Cornell University.

Looking a little like Roger Daltrey from The Who, O'Leary had a twinkle in his eye under a head of curly locks and had penned *Mars 1999* and other books including *Exploring Inner and Outer Space* and *The Second Coming of Science*. My first impression when talking to him about Greer was that this guy, for all of his academic credentials and solid ties to the US space program and its Mars mission, which he had been slated for until the program was cancelled, had really gone native in woo-woo land. And I wondered what had triggered it, woo increasingly becoming the new normal, it seemed.

Bob Siblerud completed the IANS leadership troika. He was an optometrist and environmental-physiology researcher at the Rocky Mountain Research Institute who had done quite a bit of work in mercury poisoning from dental fillings. He was also president and cofounder of the Society for PSI Research and Education and past president of Rocky Mountain Research Institute. He gave CSETI glowing reviews for its pioneering contact initiative with ET.

Although only a year old, the non-profit organization, according to its charter, fostered "the promotion of a new science that will help the evolvement of mankind in a manner that will complement and preserve the natural order of the universe. The goal is to unite individuals of a New Science philosophy and initiate a paradigm shift in science and health care... The IANS believes that man [what about all the women, guys?!] should be using science for unselfish purposes with special regard for the welfare of humanity and the planet Earth. We believe there is an inter-connectedness among all things and the IANS will promote a science whose main consideration is the welfare of the whole."

Presenters at the event, including Dr. Greer, came from across the fields of medicine and health, science and physics, agriculture, psychology, environmental sciences, new energy and something called the nonphysical sciences, which the IANS charter described as "near-death experiences, out-of-body experiences, intuition, ghosts, UFOs, extraterrestrials, crop circles, possessing spirits, channeling, psychometry, clairvoyance, mysticism and spiritual realm." New Science, I surmised while walking the row of books and gewgaws, was a catch basin for all things out on the ledge. It starkly contrasted with Old Science, which has given us miraculous life-saving drugs and procedures alongside bio-weapons and bio warfare, new technologies and understandings of how things work, along with horrific weapon systems, MAD models of "peacekeeping" and nearly insurmountable environmental problems caused by systems enabled by the Old Scientific thinking that produced towering achievements and unmitigated disasters.

Underlying these non-mainstream realms was the IANS rationale that many of these "non-physical" disciplines were not or could not be explained by traditional science and that "quantum physics principles may help provide answers." I sensed more than a whiff of patchouli-oiled hippie idealism at the IANS core and wondered how it might have played with the members of the club, some who had gone on to train in the hardcore sciences as pre-med and environmental science students. A good example might be B'log, who lived across the dorm hall from me one year and looked like Frank Zappa, or CV from St. Louis who insisted on eating salad with his fingers, even in front of his new girlfriend's parents. I'm fairly sure, though, that all of them would have readily embraced "the welfare of humanity and the planet Earth"—the signature platform of IANS. After all, that let-the-sunshine trope was the flowery Zeitgeist of the age. And The Space Pen Club embodied the big Z, and in many ways it was similar to Ken Kesey's Merry Pranksters from a decade earlier.

* * *

I was dragging physically and mentally the first day of the conference. I'd worked long and late to finish writing assignments and other business to make the trip. Greer had invited me to attend a CSETI organizational member meeting scheduled during the conference. I had a couple hours to kill before that and hung out briefly with people from Minneapolis that I vaguely knew and who in turn introduced me to others. One was a young woman from a Twin Cities suburb who weeks earlier had spontaneously started "drawing" people's names in a long hieroglyphic manner that incorporated symbols from the natural world along with the oddly shaped glyphs and strokes.

A young woman, who suddenly started writing people's names in strange exotic scripts two weeks before the IANS conference, riffs on mine

I talked to her at length and had her do my name as well, trying to figure out what she was doing and why. Mine was packed with doodled imagery that included Indian iconography, planets, stars and writerly tools (a pen quill and paper.) It also had a fragment of what looked like Hebrew or Arabic. Another part of it looked uncannily like what Prince would create when he changed his written name to a symbol during his dispute with his record label in the early '90s.

She explained that she *thought* she was channeling names into another language, but she didn't know what it was. Maybe it was an ET script. She knew little about IANS, had never seen a UFO, flying saucer or anything "out of the ordinary" and could not shut off her newfound ability. A friend had recommended she go to the conference and see if she could make connections and gain some insights. Aside from her weird transcriptions, she seemed perfectly "normal," whatever that meant.

The other person I met was Howard, a transpersonal psychologist from Ontario and avid CSETI member of a year or so. We hit it off instantly. He insisted on introducing me to Dr. Richard Haines, who was loosely affiliated with CSETI and might provide insights for the story I was going to write. He came with solid credentials, among them NASA Ames. Since Haines wasn't yet there, we briefly ducked into Greer's morning lecture, the same one I had seen in Los Angeles three weeks earlier. The room was packed.

I noticed a petite Asian woman in the back of the room meditating on a folding chair, her legs tucked into the lotus position, her eyes closed. The last time I had seen anyone meditating in an enclosed public space was in 1977 at a SOHO loft in New York City during a Phillip Glass Ensemble concert. The audience also included the influential *New York Times* music critic, Robert Rockwell, an early champion of Glass' mesmerizing minimalist works for keyboards, voice and horns. Glass prefers to call his work "music with repetitive structures." To me, it was comparable to Greer's Coherent Thought Sequencing method, oft-repeated and concise musical sequences that were as hypnotic as they were transcendent. I later came to love Glass' bigger works, the operas like "Einstein on the Beach" and numerous film scores including *Koyaanisqatsi.*

I was also intrigued by a Glass Ensemble performance of "10,000 Airplanes on the Roof" in the Twin Cities many years later. The collaborative music-theater piece with David Henry Wang, is described on Glass' website as "science fiction music drama." The synopsis, however, reads: *The character "M" recalls encounters with extra-terrestrial life forms, including their message, "It is better to forget, it is pointless to remember. No one will believe you." Are the surrealistic details an accurate recollection of a voyage through space, part of a drug-induced nightmare, or the beginning of a mental breakdown?"* Maybe *Airplanes* was a preview of coming attractions for me, though two decades removed from events described thus far.

Howard acknowledged the CSETI people he knew, including a man next to the meditating woman, whom he said was Wayne. His wife, Grace, and he were from Atlanta and early members of CSETI, like himself. He pointed out Shari Adamiak up near the lectern, "Steve's right–hand person," and Ron Russell near the front row, older with a long graying ponytail. He looked like George Carlin.

"Ron's very well known for his paintings of space. Great guy, too," Howard said in hushed tones. I whispered that I had just heard this lecture and would meet him in his room later.

I walked back to the hallway where the vendors grazed and examined the Maitreyan literature laid out by a thirty-something British gent, possibly of descent from India. Apparently, Maitreya was already in the world and being acknowledged as a kind of universal spiritual Master, the second Christ for Christians, the Imam Mahdi for the Moslem faith, the Maitreya Buddha for Buddhists, the Messiah for Jews and Krishna for Hindus. Man, this guy had it covered! I read quickly through the pamphlet, noting that Maitreya simply wanted to be known as "The Teacher."

The International Association of New Science IANS logo and brochure.

I moved down the line to someone selling an assortment of crystals that held or generated frequencies for various health maladies and mental states. My jury was still out on their value. I hung around briefly in front of the crystal mart to overhear a UFO conversation between a young man and woman who were talking about the Grays, how they were organized like a hive and found human individuality curious and worth studying, maybe to get some individuation back. More Foil for the folder.

I moved on to a nicely dressed woman in a boho chic outfit with a colorful silk scarf around the top of her head. She held some kind of pen-sized flashlight apparatus. Behind her was a banner that said that thing "could open the third eye."

"Would you like to try it," she asked, holding it up at eye level. Why not? A third-eye opening was a positive thing, I rationalized from the little I'd read about this inner spiritual periscope.

"Sure, go ahead."

She placed the device where my third eye should be and pushed a little switch, which produced a flash of red light strong enough to make me quickly blink and close eyes one and two but hopefully open number three. I blinked a few times and heard her say as I tried to focus my two good eyes again, "You need to do it several times over the course of a few weeks for the full effect."

"I bet you do," I said, moving away from the merch tables, blinking madly like a certified fool and heading toward a room in which a man was giving a talk about where the Holy Grail was. Using a projector, the authority on the Grail laid out a grid with various points plotted on it and proceeded to mix historical relevancy of this sacred item (allegedly a cup or similar utensil used by Jesus at the last supper) with Celtic mythology and his own inferences.

Lots of dates or data points pinged onto the screen. I listened politely and tried hard to absorb even a sip of information. But after twenty minutes, that train ran off the track into a haystack where no needle was ever detected. I quietly dashed out (feeling more at home with the Monty Python interpretation of the Holy Grail) and into another talk down the hall.

A sixty-something woman was halfway through her spiel about the last day of Atlantis. She was big-boned and her shock of hair was dramatically combed back, creating an open bouffant that was falling around her, not unlike a helmet. Several times she made note that she was a former Catholic nun, and I believed her. She was loud, like Sister Gerald from my sixth grade, the cracked nun who used to make bad kids pray to a clock on the hardwood floor of her classroom after school. "Gerry" wore the old-fashioned full-on nun habit and had a bad habit during bathroom breaks of busting into the boy's john and pulling guys in line for the urinals away from those already going at the trough, yelling, "Give these boys some room!"

The ex-nun at IANS had learned she had lived a former life in the time of Atlantis with her son, who was a leading scientist for the

71

vanished civilization that went under the sea. She had been regressed hypnotically several times, gaining more insights into the mythical lost continent each time until she was confident enough to share her story at such gatherings of gilded new-age sages.

As the ex-nun carried on, I realized I was glad my girlfriend had decided not to come. I would have had no way of defending what I was hearing and seeing. I made a mental note to finish this CSETI story and get the hell out of cosmic Dodge for good.

The sistah from Atlantis started building to a good lather in the homestretch. Ten or so people sat staring at her, perhaps too terrified to leave the room before the finish. She walked down the aisle and glanced at me, her perplexed student, like nuns have been doing since convents were convened, her voice rising to an even higher decibel.

She pivoted and walked back to the front of the room, saying, "We knew the volcano was going to blow and we knew it was the end! We knew it was the end. So, my son took charge and exercised his responsibility as the leading scientist. We knew it was the end!! He blew the volcano up by pressing the button. He blew it up! He blew it up! He blew the volcano."

In my head, I could hear batty old Sister Gerald shrieking, "Give that boy some room."

* * *

Dr. Haines was in Howard's room when I called, and he invited me up to meet him. Haines' considerable credentials were impressive—a retired NASA scientist, former Chief of the Space Human Factors Office at Ames Research Space and author of several books. Later, I couldn't understand why he'd come to IANS. But he seemed to support Greer's work in an advisory capacity, and he knew a lot about the UFO issue, abductions and the deeply investigated UFO photographs and 3,400 pilot sightings, especially those cases that he had documented over the years going back to the beginning of aviation and including foreign and commercial air flights.

In our official "on the record" interview for the CSETI story, Haines said, "There's a great deal of denial within the scientific community about UFOs. They're afraid of them. Admitting they exist would put a lot of people out of work. But then there's a great deal of denial about everything throughout our present society." He also said Greer was a "man of integrity," and his approaches to making contact "are about as good as it could for a group like this." He did worry the fledging organization would be torn apart by petty in-fighting, become too cult-like or, more probable, be co-opted as the research group NICAP was "by certain government agencies."

Many years later, Haines was instrumental in creating a national organization called the National Aviation Reporting Center on Anomalous Phenomena (NARCAP). A group of scientists, researchers and other professionals that spurns the use of the UFO term, NARCAP calls them UAP or unidentified aerial phenomenon. Haines' organization has made an ongoing public cause about UAP as a real threat to aviation safety based on a number of publicly reported incidents in the past few years in the US, Mexico, China and elsewhere.

In a 2000 web interview with Richard Thiemes, a speaker, consultant and author, Haines is self-described as "an experimental psychologist by training and experience at NASA." With his erudite manner, Haines offered poignant insights into the CE-5 realm aligning with my experiences described in *The Quiet Awakening*. Our man from Ames liked researcher Leo Sprinkle's idea that the sighting of a UFO or UAP and the interaction of so-called abductees with their abductors was often an initiation. Sprinkle called it a "cosmic consciousness conditioning. It's a one-way change that seems to be going on." Sprinkle, who was also at IANS that weekend, was a Ph.D emeritus professor of Counseling Services at the University of Wyoming and was an early pioneer in the use of hypnotic regression in so-called abduction cases.

In the Thiemes interview, Haines talked about abductions and Close Encounters of the Fifth Kind with an intellectual lucidity that rivaled only Greer's. "I have interviewed a lot of people who claim to be abducted and, in those cases, the rubric of recruitment is much more valid. There's something else going on that these people did not ask for, mostly. In CE-5, it's people who voluntarily go out and try to establish communication themselves and bring the phenomenon under their control. In those 200 cases, they claim a reply or closing of the loop which I interpret as a sign of intelligence. The case is quite strong for an intelligence of some form—a programmed robot or actual localized intelligence. The evidence speaks for it."

He also nicely framed why mainstream science has failed so miserably in addressing this topic. Eventually, such a person gets a "maze effect" the longer one is around the subject, which requires strong grounding. Hanes seemed to suggest that you lose your way inside the big ball of cosmic twine spread throughout your cerebral cortex and fall into the numbing UFO/ET plot lines running through mainstream culture—like some Halloween cornfield sliced and diced with a hundred blind passages and dead-end stops. Christianity seemed to be Haines' anchor, a point he would occasionally remind me of in the years ahead. On at least two occasions, he seemed like he wanted me to come to Jesus. He regularly blessed his food and prayed over it like my parents made us do when we were practicing Catholics, even in public.

Haines agreed with and responded to Thiemes' view that the phenomenon is "extremely multidimensional, so much so [that] traditional science is really not up to the task. Now, that's an insight that has come slowly over the years, because I clung to science as a method, a technique to tease out these fine points and eventually get to the bottom of it, but the longer I am looking at the evidence, the less I am convinced that that's the way to go. There certainly is part of the phenomenon that will yield to science—but there is a whole other psychic or psychological dimension that not even psychology is going to come close to. I can see why a lot of my colleagues are in denial about this."

This published discussion reminds me of a written comment made by C.D.D. Bryan in his *Close Encounters of the Fourth Kind: Alien Abductions, UFOs, and the Conference at M.I.T.* in which he wrote in

1995: "During the days immediately following the [MIT]conference, I am struck by how my perception of the abduction phenomenon has changed: I no longer think it a joke. This is not to say I now believe UFOs and alien abduction are real—"real" in the sense of a reality subject to the physical laws of the universe as we know them—but rather that I feel something very mysterious is going on. And based as much on what has been presented at the conference as on the intelligence, dedication, and sanity of the majority of the presenters, I cannot reject out-of-hand the possibility that what is taking place isn't exactly what the abductees are saying is happening to them. And if that is so, the fact that no one has been able to pick up a tailpipe from a UFO does not mean UFOs do not exist. It means only that UFOs might not have tailpipes. As Boston University astronomer Michael Papagiannis insisted, 'The absence of evidence is not evidence of absence.'"

One of Haines' later statements in the online article leapt off Thiemes' web page with clear and fresh thinking on a topic that I had never seen elsewhere: He reasoned that encoded photic bacteria from space—or other dimensions—travels to Earth through "vast interstellar distances at the speed of light, but when it arrives—the host is the human eyeball, the aperture of the iris, the pupil of the eye, so that its entry into the nervous system is immediate—in fact, that's one of the prominent characteristics, how fast the phenomenon affects a person, it's almost instantaneous, so that in a viral sense, it has a cognitive impact that is almost immediate. So, if you don't shut your eyes almost immediately and then deny it, close it out and turn your head, you will be affected. Then, how does it encode itself in the nervous system? How does it gain further meaning, if you will, within the nervous system, to gain the great complexity that we know it has? I'm still working on that part, that's the challenge."

As much as I liked such theoretical solutions and alternative explanations as to what "this" was all about, it still had the ring of science-fiction rather than scientific fact, a compelling theory in search of proof. Perhaps naively at this point, I had somehow experienced what Dr. Sprinkle called a cosmic initiation. But I wanted some real-ity-based, three-dimensional evidence—even a memento, a token, an autograph... *anything* would do. The kind of human terms, in other words, that also demanded that my space travelers, my boys upstairs, be traveling in hardware I could rap my knuckles on like a Toyota I might buy. And I wanted them benign. Or at least opposed to the vio-lence prone, Ramboesque tendencies humans exhibited on any given scale or occasion and regularly projected onto the ETs in films and other fictions.

Nevertheless, the deep-thinking Haines was in a more guarded mind frame at the New Science confab. Right after the introductions, Howard told him I was writing about CSETI. Without missing a beat, Haines glanced at me and said he hoped anything I wrote about him wouldn't end up in *The National Enquirer,* which for many years had run outrageous tales about ET and Earthlings. In fact, for a long time the UFO subject was a best-selling trope for the *Enquirer* brand. I thought it was an odd comment and assured him that the *Enquirer* was not a publication I intended to pitch with story. An early cellphone adopter, Haines took a call on one and whispered that it was his Rus-sian friend, and they had some UFO business to discuss. He excused himself and headed to his room, warbling in Rooskie.

By now, fatigue was really setting in and I told Howard I should head to my room before attending the CSETI meeting and grab a short nap. He appreciated my appraisal of the IANS event as "some kind of new age fair." Sitting on one of two beds in the room, he acknowledged that one had to use discretion in weeding out the kooky stuff from the legit players and information. Then we proceeded to bullshit about our work, his wife and family.

Howard was likeable. We shared a lot of the same interests in non-UFO/ET matters, although we invariably returned to the topic in our discussions. He even indulged me as I waxed on about what con-tact—and more importantly, disclosure—could mean, although I still considered myself just a peeping Tom at the party. Still, I blathered on, talking in the kind of ebb-and-flow stream of consciousness that tiredness brings on and the mind's personal filter slows way down.

"You wonder what another life form might find attractive in human culture," I offered. "What passed for art in their civilization? How would a public acknowledgement affect the balance of power, the arms race... Would they like our music—would they like the blues?"

He laughed at that one. "These are all good questions, my friend."

"I mean, I'm fairly new to this subject," I said, "and you've probably read a lot more about it than I have, but these are the things I'm thinking about now that I've met Greer and read some of his stuff... And I'm very tired and running at the mouth."

"No, you're on a roll," he said with a chuckle.

I fell back on the bed, propping my head up as I talked. "You know, I grew up in a small town in the middle of nowhere in North Dakota and my younger brother had a slight clubbed foot that required special shoes. But we couldn't get them where we lived, so we had to drive a hundred miles to Bismarck and get them from some podiatrist, and we always used to go along 'cuz it was a much bigger place, twice the size or more of the population where we lived. And it was usually a fun day trip away from Nowhereville to Someplace, even though not really that far away, or unique.

"And as we would drive through the state capitol streets to the 'shoe clinic,' I would marvel at the number of parked cars everywhere and how many more people there were and how would you change their thinking about everything, or anything? How would you begin to change their minds about something important? Every time I made this trip, I would wonder the same thing. What would it take? How would you do it? And looking back, I think it would take something like the discovery of life or a civilization on another planet to make people start thinking differently about everything. Everything!"

I fell silent.

"You are absolutely right," Howard said firmly without a trace of judgment or condescension.

"Jesuz, I'm starting to sound like somebody at this conference! Thanks for listening to my tripe. I'll see you later." I got up and went to my room, grabbed forty minutes of shuteye and got ready to meet the inner circle of CSETI.

* * *

Thinking about Greer's assistant Shari, as I often have since meeting her, she seems even more enigmatic to me now because of the range of activities she was involved with inside CSETI. Paralegal by day, sky watcher by night, she was about my age, like most of the CSETI members I would meet at IANS and later. She had a gentle look in her big doe eyes, but she could quickly go from green to red if mad. Shari was passionate about the CSETI vision and contact protocols.

She and Ron Russell were close Rocky Mountain friends, both living in Denver. Ron had an impish gleam and could articulate what he called "inter-species/interstellar communication" in perfect sound bites, especially the few times he was interviewed about CSETI's Close Encounters of the Fifth Kind (or CE 5) Initiative. Ron's "space paintings" would later adorn select covers of Greer's self-published books. Howard, Haines, a woman named Mary and a married couple with the names Steve and Mary were all from Asheville, and together with Wayne and Grace, the Atlanteans, this group seemed to form CSETI's inner circle.

The CSETI meeting itself at IANS was attended by 20–30 people from all over the country and fairly mundane, consisting mostly of organizational business issues and upcoming events to be scheduled, including the First "Ambassadors to the Universe" event in Arizona the next spring. Greer asked me to say a few words about what I was doing. I briefly explained how I was interviewing people, but then began talking about my work in public relations after someone asked me about my background. I pointed out that CSETI would have significant challenges once in the public arena, especially in its positioning.

"You raised a few eyebrows," Howard said after the meeting. "Really, it was good. People needed to hear it. You know, especially the die-hards." Before we all headed out to our homes in the morning, he and I and a woman who did "energy work" from Minneapolis strolled away from the IANS setting and jabbered into the night. We approached a street light and Howard said, "Let's try to make it blink out." Oooo-kay.

The three of us standing there intensely fixated on the light would have made for a really dumb picture. But it was all in good fun. Years later I learned that Scientologists often claim this ability during completion of their early training once they got their L. Ron Hubbard mojo working.

In the morning we headed back to Denver to fly out. Ron Russell packed five of us into his car, including Shari and Greer, who sat quietly most of the drive while the rest of us talked at length about the conference and the map just released by Gordon Michael Scallion. Scallion was an electronic consultant who was "normal" one day—whatever "normal" was—but suddenly lost his voice and hospitalized himself in 1979. In the hospital, apparently, he had a profound psychic experience with a female apparition—his own cosmic initiation—and then regained his voice. In subsequent years, he had a series of visions in which he was shown a dramatically changed geography of the planet.

Scallion's map showed a disturbing image of North America after severe "Earth Changes." The continent was reduced drastically, and the US was broken up. The west coast was now Utah, and the Mississippi River was much wider, with many adjoining states almost completely inundated. Someone had purchased the map at the conference. Greer's single contribution to the discussion of Scallion's map was a passing comment about potential winds of 120 miles per hour or higher for this part of Colorado. No one followed up on it. We had all heard a lot more outrageous things in the past 48 hours.

* * *

Late Sunday afternoon I returned home to happy dogs and a hungry girlfriend. We went to eat nearby and thankfully didn't talk much about the past two-and-half days. I was still processing my experience and eager to get the CSETI story done and move on. "It was kinda New Agey, but some very brilliant people were there, and I discovered a lost brother from Canada!" I told her about Howard, and she talked about work. A deadline was always looming in her magazine world. Even more exhausted now from the trip, I opted for an early bedtime and went down around nine.

I slept soundly until four in the morning, again—4:03 to be precise. I know because I had to look twice at the clock to make sure I was awake and not dreaming. In the room were five ping pong ball-sized objects that were cherry red and completely silent. I blinked a couple times to make sure I was awake. There were two at the foot of the bed about six inches off the mattress, one at eye level and the other just below it about four inches. To the left of those was another one maybe two-and-half-feet and down a bit toward the end of the bed at the same level. Another one stood about two feet away from me and almost over the window that looked out onto the street.

The fifth one, the closest to me, was a foot or less from my head, and when I saw it, it made me quickly glance at the clock again because this one seemed to be inside and outside simultaneously, as if the wall had dissolved. This dire strangeness—which I did not have time to mentally process—made me catch the time once more for a reality check. Still 4:03 a.m. And when I checked, I noticed the first two objects I had seen at the foot of the bed were now moving very slowly in straight lines but in opposite directions and completely synchronized. Then, BAM! I was back asleep, the "event" no more than 10–15 seconds in duration—at least the conscious portion. Susan never stirred the whole time.

With daylight, I awoke perplexed and bewildered by the incident now barely two-and-a-half hours old. As I started walking the dogs toward the lake at six-thirty, the top of my scalp at the crown began to feel like it had goose bumps around it. The feeling intensified as I walked and did not seem to affect any mental activity or mobility or anything physical. I put my hand to the spot, feeling for anything that would cause this sensation. Nothing was there. The tingling seemed to fade. Then it intensified again, and then diminished until I reached the lake and a large sports field four blocks from the house.

I don't remember that daily walk, usually a fifty-minute brisk stroll. I do remember the five little red orbs, dense and well-defined and seemingly *inserted* into the bedroom, especially that fifth one, which looked like it was inhabiting space both inside and outside the bedroom. How was I going to explain this to my girlfriend who had slept through it all?

"Uh, can I make you breakfast, how did you sleep and, by the way, did you happen to see five little red spheres in our bedroom at 4:03 a.m.? I didn't think so. But I did…"

No, that would definitely not work.

I kept quiet about it that day. She went to work while I tried to write on the third floor, a large finished attic space that served as my office. But I realized as the day progressed that I had no energy and felt bulldozed by something. And then the flaring would start at the top of my head again. It happened at least five times that day and continued through the next two days. But it lessened in the number of times it occurred each day. Did I have some kind of seizure, some frontal-lobe epilepsy event? Was I hallucinating? Or was this the result of that third eye opening thing that had been flashed into my middle forehead forty-eight hours earlier in Colorado? I had a lot of questions in search of an elusive or most likely unknowable answer.

Nonetheless, I was completely shot. The incident seemed to zap my will, like it had suddenly been suspended and sucked into a void and replaced with a sensation at the top of the head. I had no appetite, and I felt a true, deep nothingness inside that didn't make sense. I summoned what energy I could for help.

My first call was to Howard.

* * *

Howard listened politely, but I could hear excitement in his voice when he asked me to describe the "five little red balls," then the sensations I felt later, then what I had told Susan. He laughed when I said I was looking for the right words before telling her.

"You at a loss for words? I don't know you really well yet, but you don't strike me as the type."

"I'm generally pretty tight-lipped," I replied. "Except when I'm tired and running at the mouth, like in Fort Collins."

"You know what? I think they installed their radar in your crown chakra. That's what I think."

"My crown chakra?"

"You know, the spiritual portal at the top of your..."

"Howard, I know where and what the crown chakra is, and..."

"That's what I think. You asked me, that's what I think."

"Who are *they*?" I asked, and answered myself with a question. "The boys upstairs?"

"Uh-huh."

How could he be so sure? I wondered, then laughed.

"Look, call Greer, call Dick Haines. Run it by them. See what they say." I took Howard's advice reluctantly. I was on the precipice of exiting this weird period that I had been in for less than a year, and yet I was being drawn further into it searching for answers, or at least some understanding.

The phone rang in Asheville and Mrs. Greer answered. Anyone who's ever spent ten minutes with Emily Greer, Dr. UFO's devoted wife, knows how kind and understanding she is. But I had yet to get to know her, so my cold call to their house caught her off guard. Plus, she had talked with me only once about Steve's schedule in LA and wasn't ready to discuss what I had seen at four in the morning when most people are slumbering toward dawn.

"We see balls of light around here all the time," she said glibly with a dismissive wave of her hand. (At least that's how I pictured it.) "I'll tell Steven you called."

Dick Haines listened politely and surmised that I'd had a "hypnogogic experience." I asked him to explain. He described it as a relatively new-found state of consciousness between sleep and wakefulness—was this the line in the mind? It could involve both audio and visual hallucinations and other sensory phenomena. I listened politely and said I would think about what he'd said, but I wasn't sure this explained my experience, especially the residual effects.

I later poked around this subject a bit and discovered that Dr. Andreas Mavromatis had done work in the '80s, calling it "well-trodden and yet unmapped territory." Just what the student-patient ordered. More unmapped but well-mapped territory. WTF! Could you have it both ways in this strange new world? The visual imagery associated with hypnogogic experience as described in the Wikipedia entry does include images potentially like those of the five red spheres seen in my bedroom. The entry reads: "Among the more commonly reported, and more thoroughly researched sensory features of hypnagogia are phosphenes, which can manifest as seemingly random speckles, lines or geometrical patterns, including form constants, or as figurative (representational) images. They may be monochromatic or richly colored, still or moving, flat or three-dimensional (offering an impression of perspective)."

Most of the information I discovered about hypnagogia detailed states of consciousness going *into* sleep, not coming out of it. My view of the five little red blobs was more in the domain of a hypnopompic state, I learned long after the conversation with Haines.

I changed the subject with him, perhaps on a whim or at a subconscious level, and asked if he could recommend any books about the so-called abduction experience. From what little I had read, I surmised that the number of escalating incidents of high strangeness might constitute a run-up to such an abduction event, a handful of gateway experiences leading to what Greer called a "close encounter of the fourth kind (CE-4)"—face-to-face contact, often on board a craft, rather than an "alien abduction." In fact, in subsequent years, Greer abhorred the alien abduction word usage and often, with a show of defensiveness, dismissed such accounts as "ghost stories," similar to how the late Carl

Sagan, once the patron saint of mainstream science, equated abduction stories to sexual-abuse theories.

The only solid mainstream literature I had read about what an abduction might be—if it wasn't in fact a CE-4 or some other inexplicable phenomenon—was in *The Atlantic Monthly*. And the writer did, in fact, explain it as a psychological response to repressed early childhood sexual abuse. That sounded viable to me. I packed the idea away, as my side-hustle bus had somehow wandered off the main roads and driven—or maybe flew—onto the cosmic highway in the early '90s.

The first book Haines suggested was Edith Fiore's *Encounters*. I added it to the list of ET/UFO books I wanted to read, which included Jacques Vallee's *Passport to Magonia*, and Whitley Strieber's *Communion*, which I owned but had never read after seeing what I thought was a fairly bad movie version of same. The French researcher in Spielberg's *Close Encounters of the Third Kind* was allegedly modeled on Vallee. Depending on who you talked to in the ghetto, Vallee was rumored to be a member of The Aviary under the handle Partridge.

Haines asked if my wife had experienced anything, and I told him she had remained sound asleep. I added guiltily that I had not yet told her about my experience.

Fast forward a week. The sensation atop my crown chakra, where Howard said the ETs had installed their technology, was almost non-detectable. My energy and will power had returned. I heard from Greer, who said my bedroom experience was very interesting and described other balls of light he and CSETI Working Groups had seen in the field—mostly blue orbs, but occasionally orange too. He was at a loss, though, to definitively state what they were, or weren't. And no, I still had not told Susan about the event, but maybe I'd get an opening.

One night in mid-September, as Susan and I were debating whether to watch the presidential debates featuring Ross Perot, the third-party candidate finally allowed into the electoral process, she mentioned that there was mail for me, a package near the front door. I retrieved it and noticed it was from Dr. Burkes, a care package to help me with my article. Maybe this was the time to lay it all out for Susan. I imagined how I would do it. I'd open the package and exclaim, "Oh, it's that stuff from Joe Burkes in LA, the other doctor involved in CSETI. You know, the weirdest thing happened to me the other night while you were dead to the world..." I would convey everything I had experienced.

Instead, I bailed. I quietly moved to the living room and opened the package from Burkes. The contents included a friendly note, one narrative indie movie about the ET topic, a tape of some recent UFO TV shows he had compiled, and a white paper written in very small type called *THE CONTROLLERS: A New Hypothesis of Alien Abduction* by Martin Cannon. The white paper was fifty-seven brain-chewing, intoxicating and repulsive pages long. I read it for the first time over the next two hours, not fully realizing what a slippery-slope-suddenly-turned-into-a-frozen-mile-high-alpine-plunge I was gliding down on freshly waxed skis. And I didn't ski.

The Cannon monograph was released around 1990 and later turned into a 300-page book, now out of print. It was heavily annotated so it seemed not to be the work of a crank. However, its implications were frightening, despite the fact it was well written, had a droll sense of humor and knew well the audiences for all matters saucerological.

A strange but telling caveat about Cannon's work is that in March of 1997, a personal request was posted to the ufomind.com website asking that his name be removed from the site's list of ufologists: "I have disavowed the theory outlined in my work 'The Controllers,' and have requested everyone carrying the piece on the web to remove it. That damned thing has caused nothing but trouble." But after reading it—and finding corroborating support for the position elsewhere— methinks the man doth protest too much!

"Both Believer and Skeptic, in my opinion, miss the real story," Cannon writes early on in the work. "Both make the same mistake: They connect the abduction phenomenon to the forty-year history of UFO sightings, and they apply their prejudices about the latter to the controversy about the former." Granted, there have been UFO sightings for far longer than forty years, but I present his thoughts and research here because the abduction piece of the puzzle often stymies a serious discussion of the well-documented cases and evidence that do exist and points to visitors of some "sort" from some "where" doing some "thing" with the human population and its planet.

Arguing that abductions and UFOs "may well be separate issues," Cannon lays out a strong historical and self-admitted "bizarre" case that the abduction phenomenon is largely an insidious man-made event, manufactured for whatever reason. In my opinion, perhaps to create another strategic propaganda meme in the Ufological realm, and/or as a memory-scramble device to pollute the veracity of a real CE-4? Or simply because a manipulated abduction/CE-4 event can be carried out as part of the evolution and long legacy of mind-control and behavior modification experiments or programs carried out by various intel agencies, the most famous being the MK-ULTRA program. That fairly well publicized brain-fuck platform briefly got the CIA in hot water with Congress in the '70s when it came to light that LSD and other mind-bending techniques had been used on unsuspecting servicemen.

Early in his assessment, Cannon asserts that "UFO abductions and mind control have more in common than their mutual ostracization. The data overlap. If we could chart these phenomena on a Venn diagram, we would see a surprisingly large intersection between the two circles of information."

Cannon lists four conclusions about mind control as an alternative explanation to the abduction story, emphasizing that the '70s MK-ULTRA congressional hearings were blatantly misleading, and that clandestine research into thought manipulation "has not stopped... As CIA veteran Miles Copeland once admitted to a reporter, 'The congressional subcommittee which went into this sort of thing got only the barest glimpse.'" In conclusion three he noted that the CIA was not the only agency involved: "Indeed, many branches of our government took part in these studies—including NASA, the Atomic Energy Commission as well as branches of the Defense Department."

Yippees co-founder, the father of the underground or alt press, Paul Krassner: UFOs as a government mind control program?! (Photo: Laura Levine)

Cannon's research intrigued me because it fit the thought patterns of select people I respected who were well informed about covert government heavy-handedness, like the late Paul Krassner, the so-called "father of the underground, or alternative press, comedian, the biographer of Lenny Bruce, a co-founder of the Yippee and the Merriest of Pranksters. Krassner occasionally published well researched articles about covert ops in *The Realist*. And he believed that the UFO subject was a mind-control operation, or used in part as such, although I never believed it when he shared the idea in a 1981 interview that I had done with him for the monthly Twin Cities music newspaper *Sweet Potato*, which later became the alt weekly *City Pages*. When asked what he thought was the mother of all conspiracies at the dawn of the '80s, he replied, "My current fantasy is that these alien abductions are really a cover-up for government experiments in mind control."

> MK: You're not alone in that. The use of psycho-tronic – or "non-lethal" – weapons to manufacture alien abduction scenarios in order to spin control the issue when it's finally revealed that the ET's have been here all along and voila! We have a great new evil empire here to eat us for dinner and so we need to raise another trillion dollars for the military industrial complex.

> KRASSNER (laughing): They may be here to eat us for dinner, but why do they need anal probes as an appetizer?!

Predictable butt probe jokes aside, through subsequent friendly correspondence over several years, Krassner admitted he had never seen a saucer and maintained it was quite possible the subject had its roots in the kinds of nefarious dark things Cannon's paper outlined in hard detail ten years later.

As I was working on the CSETI I story, the abduction card increasingly became a polarizing one to play in the story. And it was like fly paper to hand to the press, and vice versa. At the time, I was becoming vaguely aware of the published work of Dr. David Jacobs, Associate Professor of History at Temple University, who passionately warned of a human-ET hybrid breeding program and the ultimate bad intentions of the ETs—more like the stuff from the goofy front pages of *The National Enquirer* and *Weekly World News,* tall tales sold from the supermarket point-of purchase aisles. That said, Jacobs had also written in 1975 one of the finest "histories" of the UFO phenomenon to date: *The UFO Controversy in America.* How, I wondered after reading it many years later, could the professor move from outstanding research and scholarship to making outlandish claims that ET was infiltrating the human gene pool?

I also knew that Budd Hopkins had been doing hypnotic regressions with alleged abduction subjects in New York City through his Intruders Foundation. But I didn't want my story about CSETI, which I was now writing, to suddenly become an argument for or against whether "alien abductions" were a reality. The reality and critical thinking Greer had presented was more interesting and fresh at the time. The abduction talk sometimes seemed too much like inside baseball despite the fact that a suspicious baseball, seemingly, kept slamming though my bedroom window, rolling around the floor, flipping on our lights and making cat-rutting noises.

But Cannon's litany of research drew me in, especially those issues he studied in the MK-ULTRA programs. Perhaps they had been applied in the field to unsuspecting targets, or, more precisely, had been applied to individuals who had experienced a real encounter?

What did the MK-ULTRA program entail?

"Everything," writes Cannon, "including hypnosis, conditioning, sensory deprivation, drugs, religious cults, microwaves, psychosurgery, brain implants, and even ESP... Mystery still shrouds another area of study, the area which seems to have most interested ORD: psychoelectronics"—or psychotronics as I've seen it called.

Cannon poses the possibility that radio hypnotic intracerebral electronic dissolution of memory (RHIC-EDM) technology has been perfected to the point that it can induce a hypnotic state into which false memories are implanted and lost time is experienced. Like some of the best in the ghetto, Cannon remains at a loss for hard evidence, writing early in the monogram, "I cannot claim conclusively that RHIC-EDM is real," while adamantly calling for more research and real transparency into the "behavioral effects of microwaves, extra-low-frequencies (ELF) and ultra-sonics" and those who wield these weapons of mass mind induction. However he demonstrated that other kinds of mind-control devices capable of altering brain waves, among them microwaves, long have been a tool in the "spy-chiatirsts" black bag.

"In 1970," Cannon notes, "a RAND Corporation scientist reported that electromagnetic microwaves could be used to promote insomnia, fatigue, irritability, memory loss, and hallucinations. Using black humor, he allows that such microwaving of victims might also "cook the target before it got the chance to launder his thoughts," an ideal scenario for a *New Yorker* cartoon, or at least one to rival the cartoon in which two ETs are standing with a bewildered abductee and one says to the other, "You abducted him, you feed him!"

"You abducted him—you feed him."

A *New Yorker* cartoon takes an easy shot at the "abduction" issue years before it would run a serious piece about UFO's – along with most of the media – in the spring of 2021

Cannon states that "once an 'abductee' has been implanted [with a chip or similar receiving device somewhere on his or her body]—and if we are to trust hypnotic regression accounts of abductees at all, the first implanting session may occur in childhood—the chip-in-the-brain would act as an intensifier of the signal. Such an individual could have any number of 'UFO' experiences while his or her bed partner dozes comfortably."

A chip in the brain. Or elsewhere? Really? Well, that could explain Susan's slumber—she hadn't had her chip!

Though I joke here, I took very seriously what Cannon wrote, noting that much of the seminal work on such mind-robbery technology and its applications were as old as the '50s, or even earlier. Neuroscientist Dr. Jose "Bob" Delgado, who invented the "stimoceiver," did some of the key psycho work. It was "a miniature depth electrode which can receive and transmit electronic signals over FM radio waves."

Cannon writes that "abductees' implants strongly suggest a technological lineage which can be traced" to the stimoceiver and that their activation could account for the classic "missing time" and "floating sensations" and lay the ground work for implanting false memories of any sort, including a CE-4. He supports his hypothesis in part by quoting Delgado's book from 1969, *Physical Control of the Mind: Toward a Psychocivilised Society*, which argues for a kind of filthy George Orwell-meets-Philip K. Dick sadist's world in which, as Cannon suggests, "the experimenter can electronically induce emotions and behavior. Under certain conditions, the extremes of temperament—rage, lust, fatigue, etc.—can be elicited by an outside operator as easily as an organist might call forth a C-major chord."

Delgado wrote, "Radio stimulation of different points in the amygdala and hippocampus in the four patients produced a variety of effects, including pleasant sensations, elation, deep, thoughtful concentration, odd feelings, super relaxation, colored visions, and other responses. The evocative phrase 'colored vision' clearly indicates remotely-induced hallucination; we will detail later how these hallucinations may be 'controlled' by an outside operator."

It doesn't take long in the Cannon canon to learn how these brain-seeking signals could be delivered. Targets of this mad manipulation could even be remotely hypnotized—and then offered false or screened post-hypnotic memories full of the stuff vividly described in UFO/ET literature and movies.

How would this be accomplished? Somehow through "implanted" chips into or onto a person—just like in the abduction scenarios available in the mass market wherein the "Grays" do all the dirty work and leave tell-tale "scoop marks" or scars on a shin, arm or other body area. And their subjects experience "missing time." Only these aliens are turning out to be twisted, sociopathic humans, psychotronically gaming fellow human beings.

Notes Cannon as he explores the evolution of this odious technology application, "Certain journalists have asserted that the CIA has mastered a technology call RHIC-EDOM.... Together, these techniques can—allegedly—remotely induce hypnotic trance, deliver suggestions to the subject, and erase all memory for both the instruction period and the act which the subject is asked to perform." It sounded like the recurring plots in the Jason Bourne films.

"EDOM is nothing more than missing time itself," Cannon writes, "the erasure of memory from consciousness through the blockage of synaptic transmission in certain areas of the brain. By jamming the brain's synapses through a surfeit of acetocholine, neural transmission along selected pathways can be effectively stilled. According to the proponents of RHIC-EDOM, acetocholine production can be affected by electromagnetic means. (Modern research in the psycho-physiological effects of microwaves confirm this proposition.)"

Cannon also quotes from a 1966 speaking engagement during which the dark lord Delgado "asserted that his experiments 'support the *distasteful* [italics mine] conclusion that motion, emotion, and behavior can be directed by electrical forces and that humans can be controlled like robots by push buttons.' He even prophesied a day when brain control could be turned over to non-human operators, by establishing two-way radio communication between the implanted brain and a computer."

Distasteful? Imagine how advanced such post-Orwellian techniques might be today if they had been developed fifty and sixty years ago and had obscene piles of research money allocated annually in the so-rightly-called "black budget." The mind—the first and last bastion of freedom—reels. I did find in Cannon's research more information that made me doubtful that our entire house might be a staging ground for the boys upstairs. But was it a potential reality that the house might indeed be a staging area, or part of a pilot program, for mind games? If given a choice, I would opt for the former; the latter was even more frightening to consider.

And neither would play well in the town square, as I recalled again the synopsis and mantralike quality of an expression in the notes for Phillip Glass' *One Hundred Airplanes on the Roof*: "It is better to forget, it is pointless to remember. No one will believe you." And yet, here it is considered.

One piece from Cannon's work, however, was an attempt to explain brain wave states—or in this sad case, perhaps, brain waive states—as they pertain to hypnogogic states.

"The brain has a 'beat' of its own," Cannon writes early in his exhaustive research. "This rhythm was first discovered in 1924 by the German psychiatrist Hans Berger, who recorded cerebral voltages as part of a telepathy study. He noted two distinct frequencies: alpha (8-13 cycles per second), associated with a relaxed, alert state, and beta (14-30 cycles per second), produced during states of agitation and intense mental concentration. Later, other rhythms were noted, which are particularly important for our present purposes: theta (4-7 cycles per second), a hypnogogic state, and delta (.5 to 3.5 cycles per second), generally found in sleeping subjects."

* * *

It was clear after trying to digest the Cannon material—a bitter pill indeed—that I was getting a strong dose of "The Alien Abduction Blues" (a song I could imagine my old friend Bill Morrissey writing, or the Black Keys, or Steve Earle). Talk about Dick Haines' "Maze Effect." Even as I write this many years later, the little-red-balls episode of this chapter seems unreal, not even plausible, and yet it's an experience as "perceptively real" as the words on this paper or screen.

And still, in late 2012, I continued to encounter stories or references about it, like this one from James Donahue's eclectic blog I read from time to time: "The Finnish journal *Spekula* published a report in 1999 by Dr. Rauni-Leena Luukanen-Kilde that warned that scientists not only had developed the technology but were using it in the United States and Sweden, without the knowledge of the people. In the '50s and '60s, electrical implants were inserted into the brains of animals and humans, especially in the U.S., during research into behavior modification and brain and body functioning. Mind control methods were used in attempt to change human behavior and attitudes. Influencing brain functions became an important goal of military and intelligence services."

The report continues, "Thirty years ago brain implants showed up in X-rays the size of one centimeter. Subsequent implants shrunk to the size of a grain of rice. They were made of silicon, later still of gallium arsenide. Today they are small enough to be inserted into the neck or back, and also intravenously in different parts of the body using surgical operations, with or without the consent of the subject. It is now almost impossible to detect or remove them. It is technically possible for every newborn to be injected with a microchip, which could then function to identify the person for the rest of his or her life. Such plans are secretly being discussed in the U.S. without any public airing of the privacy issues involved."

Donahue asks, "His story was published in 1999. How far have military and government 'leaders' allowed this weapon against human freedom of thought and action to go since that date?"

Cannon's earlier work, like this Swedish update, was so disturbing that when Dr. Helmut's book *Preliminary Findings of Project MILAB:*

Evidence for Military Kidnappings of Alleged UFO Abductees came out in the mid-'90s concerning MIL-ABS (military abductions of alleged alien abductees), I deliberately avoided it. But after years of following this piece of narrative, is it prudent to assume that most, some or many "abductions" are hoaxed human events, and Close Encounters of the Fourth Kind (CE-4) are those legit episodes conducted by the boys upstairs?

I did agree with one premise that I'd read online about Helmut's book—that some branch of the military/intel matrix would intervene with a reported experiencer or contactee. That made sense from a "Controllers" point of view—pollute the original experience with a manufactured one to make the issue even muddier or more sinister, in a sense to manipulate an original CE-4 so that the subject and his or her story becomes compromised. Then, if set free in the public square, the controlled abductee's wild tale would continue to be a nonstarter for the majority who have no such experiences or points of reference. "Just move along, nothing to see here." Of course, the implication for Manchurian-style candidates to carry out any number of acts while being manipulated in these types of mind-boggling, mind-breaking maneuvers should be obvious, as Cannon imparts frequently in his work.

According to an oft-cited Roper Poll of 6,000 people conducted in 1991—the period in which I fell into full-spectrum strangeness in my house and with CSETI—roughly two percent of the American public believed they had had possible abduction-like experiences. In the poll, 119 people answered "Yes" to four out of five "key indicator questions" rather than report actual alien abductions. Other estimates put abductions at 0.3% of the population.

Did that mean, as Cannon's work implied, that while some encounters may have been real, the rest were mind-control projects delivered to your head while you slept, courtesy of covert counter-intel operatives who went bump in the night? It was almost too preposterous to consider. And yet, clandestine "black" projects take place all the time (a subject explored more in Chapter Nine) and we are generally none the wiser, either in knowing about them (and what their intentions are based on), or what the desired outcomes are. US history is littered with secret activities carried out in the name of national security, defense and "scientific study."

Well known now are the secret bombings of Cambodia and the Iran Contra saga starring a host of federal executive-level people including Ronald Reagan and George H.W. Bush, Oliver North and prosecutor Daniel Sheehan. Lesser known are the attacks, or "experiments," on US civilian populations in military- or government-sanctioned tests. Like the odious and virulently racist 40-year Tuskegee "study" conducted by the Public Health Service on poor African-Americans in the South. Between 1932 and 1972, these unsuspecting victims thought they were getting free health care when they were really being studied for untreated syphilis.

More recently, Professor Lisa Martino-Taylor, a sociologist at St. Louis Community College, claimed in a September 29, 2012 story published in the British paper *The Daily Mail* and reported widely in this county that "the United States Military conducted top secret experiments on the citizens of St. Louis, Missouri for years, exposing them to radioactive compounds, a researcher has claimed." Her research is based on hundreds of pages of de-classified documents.

The story claims, "[Martino-Taylor] has accrued detailed descriptions as well as photographs of the spraying, which exposed the unwitting public, predominantly in low-income and minority communities, to radioactive particles." Professor Martino-Taylor said to KSDK, a St. Louis TV station that as with Tuskegee, "…the study was secretive for a reason. They didn't have volunteers stepping up and saying, 'Yeah, I'll breathe zinc cadmium sulfide with radioactive particles.'"

"Through her research," the *Daily Mail* article continues, "she found photographs of how the particles were distributed from 1953–1954 and 1963–1965." And we learn a few paragraphs later that, "In Corpus Christi, the chemical was dropped from airplanes over large swaths of the city. In St Louis, the Army put chemical sprayers on buildings, like schools and public housing projects, and mounted them in station wagons for mobile use… Despite the extent of the experiment, local politicians were not notified about the content of the testing. The people of St. Louis were told that the Army was testing smoke screens to protect cities from a Russian attack."

A similar incident occurred in Minneapolis in 1953, at St. Stephen's Church, a community-based center for the impoverished. According to an Associated Press story of February 27, 2011, these types of practices were nearly routine over many decades: "Shocking as it may seem, U.S. government doctors once thought it was fine to experiment on disabled people and prison inmates. Such experiments included giving hepatitis to mental patients in Connecticut, squirting a pandemic flu virus up the noses of prisoners in Maryland, and injecting cancer cells into chronically ill people at a New York hospital."

* * *

Not long after discovering the Cannon work, I ploughed through my notes trying to finish the CSETI profile with a self-imposed deadline at the end of September. I liked what Greer had to say about the so-called abduction phenomenon, that these "CE-4 events" most likely were not happening at the rate or frequency that was being reported in the early-'90s media, and that many were probably another kind of paranormal experience being mistaken for an ET encounter, perhaps poltergeists or other ethereal interference. He also made two declarative assessments that repudiated the MOs of the abduction camp.

First, as an ER doctor, he frequently did things for patients that they may have objected to or disliked. But if in the end the procedures saved lives, such patient concerns were irrelevant. Imagine, he would say in lectures, that a highly advanced civilization from another part of the galaxy, or even more distant, was visiting and needed to obtain critical medical data about a planet's inhabitants. A so-called abduction might be the only way to obtain that information if our planet's people were perceived as hostile and both sides were at risk of self-destruction through nuclear annihilation, environmental catastrophe, plagues, and so on.

Secondly, Greer's analysis continued, if the abductions were in fact all ET-initiated and had ominous connotations like those discussed in the abduction literature, then it was even more imperative to create a bilateral relationship that was open and conducive to ending such actions, or at least to understanding them to chart a more beneficial course for both parties. These tenets, of course, underscored the whole CE-5 Initiative, which was framed as a visionary project that embraced the foundations of science and diplomacy, the latter sorely lacking in the official space quests.

Greer also wrote insightfully about this in a 1996 piece called, "Abductions: Not All That Glitters is Gold," which is still available on the CSETI website. In it, Greer expressed his belief that an induced false reality about the ET abduction experience was very possible, if not already an abject circumstance at play in the larger discussion. He writes, "I realize that this information is harder to accept than [even] the idea that we are being visited by extraterrestrial life forms. *But that is the point* [italics mine]. *These secret projects are so bizarre and sociopathic, that they are their own best cover.* Who would believe it? And by manipulating the images and ideas in the public domain on this subject, we are led to either disgust and rejection of the entire phenomenon, or to anger and hate toward the visitors. How convenient..."

Besides offering the sources at the new science symposium for my story, Greer also recommended that I talk to Colin Andrews, a longtime and respected crop-circle investigator from England. Andrews had been working with CSETI abroad and was aware of the unusual events that had taken place in the summer of 1992 near the Oliver Cromwell Castle in Southern England in a wheat field beneath Woodborough Hill owned by Tim and Polly Carson. Events included the spaceship that materialized on the rainy night discussed in Chapter Two.

However, another incident the night before had taken place that involved a CSETI team and Andrews. Members of the group had put themselves in a meditative state and employed the rest of the CSETI contact protocols. Earlier in the evening, they had drawn an equilateral triangle on paper with circles at its points. The members had then "drawn" the image in the field below them as best they could with high-powered lights.

At one point during the experiment, a spinning amber-colored disc appeared but vanished when a military helicopter flew into view. "Then," as Greer described it in my story that I'd almost completed, "a brilliant silver-white streak came again from the same direction and appeared nearly overhead, which 50 people saw."

The next morning, a "pristine crop circle precisely the shape that we had visualized to the crop circle makers [had appeared]," according to Greer. "It was as if the equilateral triangle with the circles at each point had been lifted right off our minds and put into the field. People were absolutely stultified."

The cryptic crop formation bearing the same preplanned image was proclaimed by Greer to be another step in making contact with the intelligence that had made the circle. He never said it was ET, but some intelligent source that had interacted with the group (hence the "I" for Intelligence in the CSETI moniker). The triangle design—the CSETI crop icon—soon became the CSETI logo, and the photo of it eventually went into the CSET Media Kit.

The CSETI crop icon publicity photo: "It was as if the equilateral triangle with the circles at each point had been lifted right off our minds and put into the field," said Greer

99

I made advance arrangements for a phone interview with Andrews about a week after getting that care package from Joe Burkes. The "croppie"—as the crop circle investigators and watchers call themselves with some healthy self-effacement—would be my last interview for the story. I would simply drop in Andrews' comments where appropriate and it would be finished.

Then radical "reality" intervened a couple times before the call. The first incident allowed me to finally tell Susan about the five little red spheres.

As morning dawned one day in the run-up to the Andrews interview, I hooked up the Beardies to their leashes for a run around the lake. About a block away, I stopped abruptly at a neighbor's property on the corner. There, across several slabs of sidewalk, his young kids, all under age ten— at least I guessed they were his kids—had drawn several perfect flying saucers in various chalk colors on the concrete.

My God! I thought. Was it happening all over the neighborhood?

Fixated on the coincidental chalk work of saucers, I ran back to the house as Susan was getting ready for work. "Did you see what the neighbor kids drew on the sidewalk?" I asked.

She gave me a reluctant look that said, "Yes."

"Do you think this weird shit is happening all over the neighborhood?" It was a rhetorical question, since she didn't answer. So, I calmly laid out the 4:03 a.m. incident with the five little cherry bombs in our bedroom a couple weeks earlier, complete with the aftereffects and Howard's explanation about them as well as Haines' hypnogogic theory.

She looked at me as if I had started to put bad voodoo on her morning ritual. Finally, after a long pause, she offered, "I believe there is other life in the universe. I even believe there are ETs or whatever you want to call them that have visited Earth. I just don't want them in my house."

Fair enough. But what should we do—hang out a warning sign? I started worrying that this Andromeda strain on our relationship might become a hindrance at some point. But I was at a loss about what to do.

I had told her I wanted to get away from all this "stuff" once my story was finished. Maybe that would be the end of it.

We both went off to work. I had a couple of business stories to work on through mid-afternoon, at which time I would return to the CSETI story and get it in final shape.

Andrews' studies of crop circles were the best one could find, and his online bio claimed he had coined the term "crop circle." I'd seen images of crop circles in the press, and as a rock fan, my first awareness of a circle was on the cover of Led Zeppelin's 1990 *Remasters* box set, a collection of favorites digitized for compact disc. The image of the now-famous "Key" crop circle (with the shadow of a zeppelin over it) had virtually no impact on me until later years when I started seeing pictures of these gigantic formations that someone romantically dubbed cosmic mandalas. Crop circles existed prior to 1990, though, and not just in England. This point is often missed by those who ignorantly believe that two UK guys, Doug and Dave, hoaxed all the circles back to the '80s as they claimed in 1991. End of story, right? These jokers did them all?

Even today, I'm not sure what the cereal instagrain-grams are, who makes them, or why. I'm not in the mind to discern if they are "extraterrestrial," multidimensional, or—as one of the Birds in the AVIARY has suggested—intricate imprints beamed in from a microwave source like HAARP (The High-frequency Active Auroral Research Program was initiated as an ionospheric research program jointly funded by the US Air Force, the US Navy, the University of Alaska Fairbanks and the Defense Advanced Research Projects Agency.) I don't know if crop circles are vortex insignias burned into crops from hovering spaceships or swift-moving orbs that you can google for videos. Maybe they are created by Doug and Dave adherents creating enigmatic patterns, or perhaps they're made by wonderfully weird, worrisome and wacky meteorological effects.

I am more interested in how to tell real ones from the fakes—testing them the way the late Dr. W.C. Levingood, a biophysicist, has done: Look for telltale signs or anomalies such as unbroken nodes on the grain stem; a swelling of the cell walls of the plants that have been "branded," revealing that a rapid healing and cooling process has transpired; and soil samples that contain larger and anomalous radio nucleotides and similar chemical alternations.

Andrews was trained as a British electrical engineer and was an early pioneer in "cerealology," as some have called his work in the fields of southern England going back to the late '70s. I was looking forward to my upcoming conversation with him, even though these grain glyphs didn't personally interest me the way the larger UFO/ET discussion did.

The most elaborate circles were nearly a mile long. Who made them? Was it done by plank-board—by hops-inspired homo sapiens cereal-stomping their way around in the dark? Or were they elegantly realized by some unknown force or consciousness with a celestially exotic or earthily magnificent imprint method? Whatever the source, they remain a kind of found cosmic folk art either hoaxed by humans or freshly minted by unknowns.

But as noted once by the acerbic Brit writer Rupert Sheldrake (the controversial science philosopher/ provocateur whose "Morphic Resonance" theory is brilliantly stimulating and lies squarely on the doorstep of so-called new science), you can counterfeit a twenty-dollar bill too, but that doesn't mean a twenty-dollar bill isn't real.

By mid-afternoon, as I moved the cursor down my computer screen in the CSETI story to where I wanted to insert the first quote from Colin Andrews, I was thinking the Brit would be my last interview. Then, BAM! I am so out of here. Adieu, little green men and your psychic game playing.

The story was all but finished aside from this last insight from Mister Andrews. As the cursor came to rest pre-insert, I heard a loud noise that seemed to come from both inside and outside the room. It was startling and chilling. It pierced through the quiet of my attic office and I literally jumped to my feet.

My only frame of reference for identifying this sound leaped to mind within a millisecond of hearing it. The Bible describes in the Book of Revelations the sound of a trumpet blown by an angel heralding the end of time. That is how this sound announced itself to me before I fervently rationalized what it really was—either the lid of a garbage can blowing up the street or the sound of metal being scraped or clanged by guys remodeling a house down the street.

Yet I knew what those sounds were. And what I had heard that almost launched me into the roof was neither of them.

By the time I got the genial and well-spoken Andrews on the phone, I prefaced our discussion with a description of the strange things that had been transpiring in my house—the weird noises and lights; the little red balls; and the calamity caused by placing the cursor where Andrew's quote would go.

He laughed heartily. And then in a serious, more simpatico tone, he described how once his work on the circles began by performing tests inside them and making detailed observations, he started hearing strange sounds as well, usually when he wasn't even within twenty miles of crop-circle country.

He recalled how he and his wife would be driving in the city and suddenly, from the backseat or trunk, or someplace inside both, strange beeps would begin sounding in odd sequences along with other inexplicable noises. And not always in the car. Eventually, he said, the high strangeness became too much for his wife and they parted ways.

By now, the writer in me wanted to know as badly as the guy known to my longtime friends and acquaintances—what was it all about? Why was it happening, and how? What did it *mean*? I was hoping Andrews could explain precisely what it was, or at least present another piece of the puzzle.

Again, I heard gentle laughter and he explained that there is so much that's unknown—with all of this stuff. Then he laughed again, almost a giggle this time, and I could hear camaraderie in it. But there was also the sound of futility and expectation as the interview wound down, his words flying on an invisible wave of electrical current to a man half a continent away.

He composed one last thought and we were done. "You're in the slot, mate," he said, laughing softly and ambiguously. "You're in the slot!"

CHAPTER FOUR:
DRAGGING THE COSMOS IN SEARCH OF INTELLIGENT LIFE

"Time past and time future
Allow but a little consciousness.
To be conscious is not to be in time
But only in time can the moment in the rose-garden,
The moment in the arbour where the rain beat,
The moment in the draughty church at smokefall
Be remembered; involved with past and future.
Only through time is time conquered."
– *The Four Quartets*, "Burnt Norton" by T.S. Eliot

I submitted my finished profile of Dr. Steven Greer and CSETI to a few publications such as *Vanity Fair*, then I pulled back off the trail. Or tried to. I simultaneously laid off all matters CSETI and started reading three books on related topics: *Encounters,* Edith Fiore's book on so-called abductions; Jacque Valle's *Passport to Magonia*; and parts of Raymond Fowler's *The Watchers*. Infrequently, I started guarding my bedroom window at night, the one that faced the street and the long, vegetated slope down to Minnehaha Creek. My threadbare logic was that if I could properly tend the blinds that covered the view outside, things would be good, things would not go sideways like they had been. Things would reset.

The implications of the Cannon material and the five cherry bombs in the bedroom were as jarring as the quiet consciousness awakening in Boston. As the bright fall colors began fading in Minneapolis, both weighed on me in equal measure.

My expectations for publishing the Greer piece were low. I sensed that no matter how well written, it was not a mainstream print story. And it was long! The internet, where any number of sites could publish the story now, was still in its infancy.

Despite a noticeable amount of programming about these topics on TV and radio, much of the mainstream media coverage amounted to brief news reports of UFO sightings and the emergence of a soon-to-be blockbuster show called *The X-Files*, which launched in the fall of 1993 and has become a convenient trope for journalists when covering the UFO/ET topic.

After finishing the piece, I wanted a cooling-off period to reflect. I didn't want to focus on recent nocturnal events, which I felt I had no control over, but maybe on finding the threads in my past that would tie to my present-day predicament. I resigned myself to the feeling that an unanticipated expansion of consciousness had occurred, and with it the recognition that the universe really was what British biologist Haldane proclaimed, "not only queerer than we suppose, but queerer than we *can* suppose."

As intrigued as I was about the connections CSETI had made between consciousness and extraterrestrial contact, I was equally intrigued by the implications of consciousness itself, especially its non-locality and all the questions that arose from this gnarly neuropath like: Did consciousness lay solely in the fleshy cauliflower folds of the brain, stationed there like a train in a roundhouse, or did it also lay outside of it, moving on the many possible tracks of reality that are unseen until one is personally localized on an individual track and it becomes visibly "real?" Or could it lay both inside and outside the mind simultaneously? Quantum Entanglement would make it so.

Dr. Robert Lanza is a leading stem-cell researcher, medical doctor, and scientist, and the author of *Biocentrism: How Life and Con-*

sciousness are the Keys to Understanding the True Nature of the Universe and *Beyond Biocentrism: Rethinking Time, Space, Consciousness, and the Illusion of Death.* Lanza views life and consciousness as being essential to the existence of our universe. Numerous experiments show that everything we see, every single particle, depends on the presence of an observer, Lanza told the Art Bell show *Coast to Coast*, a national radio show for all things out and off the ledge. Without conscious observers (in the form of biological life) there would be no universe at all, Lanza claimed. Space and time are not external objects and do not exist independent of an observer's mind.

But here's where my main man got the music writer in me jazzed. Lanza likened time to a record on a turntable. All the songs exist simultaneously even though you experience them one at a time (give this man a humble Space Pen Club membership to go with the other accolades he's received such as *Time* magazine naming him one of the world's 100 great thinkers in 2014.)

During my "cooling-off period," I also wondered if I could start reliably remote reviewing everything (not) in sight? And if so, how could I leverage this to the greatest benefit possible, not just for me, but maybe for others? Would I also start "seeing stuff" I didn't want to see—bad or painful things before they happened, like Christopher Walken did in the movie version of Stephen King's *Dead Zone?* Walken's character, a teacher, has fleeting precognitive or psychic impressions of people after coming out of a coma following a car accident. If I started meditating again to sharpen my mind, like I did in college as a Space Pen adherent, would I have similar pre-cognitive views like the Boston one I perceived in sleep?

I had many questions about consciousness, so I asked an old friend and occasional PR client, Jane Barash, for a good definition of it. Jane has run the Continuum Center in Minneapolis almost forever and is one of the most intelligent people I have ever met. Her understanding was this: "Consciousness is a creative, self-organizing intelligence that interconnects the universe (and everything/one in it) across time and space and comes from beyond space-time (creating matter in a gravitational collapse of quantum waves of possibility.)"

As for the brain's role, Dr. Larry Dossey, MD and author, noted during a 2016 Continuum Center lecture, "Consciousness works through the brain, but is not produced by the brain and cannot be explained by it. The brain is a *transmissive*, not a *productive* organ." This summarized the interrelated views of William James, Henri Bergson, F.C.S. Schiller, Aldous Huxley, Rupert Sheldrake and others. But for every Jane-, Rupert- and Larry-like view, there were more strident "mainstream" scientists and thinkers on the opposed side of consciousness who completely negated its role in the affairs of humans and the universe and the implications of consciousness like non-locality.

"[The brain's] workings—what we sometimes call mind—are a consequence of its anatomy and physiology, and nothing more," believed Carl Sagan, the dashing young astronomer who influenced an entire generation with his exploration of how the universe *might* work on the 1980 PBS show *Cosmos*. Yet, Marvin Minsky, of the Artificial Intelligence Lab at MIT, threw an even wetter sheet over the "C" word with this bone-crushing view: "The brain is just a computer made of meat."

During that fall, I discussed the strange events I'd been through more freely with select friends and acquaintances. I felt like was living in two worlds, one rich with daily activity, the other rich in nightly activity. But their cumulative meaning still was not clear. I went to lunch with one of my former editors at *The Twin Cites Reader*, Deb Hopp, and others who had an interest in the topic.

Over lunch, Deb listened politely as I explained CSETI and its thinking around the ET issue. She made some skeptical looks when I got into some of the dreams and the night-time strangeness in my house. I thought, "Oh boy, now I've gone too far. I'll be walking out of here with a fringy Scarlett Letter on me." Instead, she calmly offered this assessment, recounted here as a paraphrase: *I would imagine if another planetary group—thousands of years evolved beyond ours, or maybe even on some different evolutionary track than ours—were to try to announce itself to us for whatever reason, they would start doing so in as many ways as they could without being so alarming. And one of those ways would be through sleep, or the subconscious.*

"That is a great statement!" I told her excitedly, suddenly considering her prime Space Pen material; the club was always short of females, the same way the UFO ghetto was totally lacking in diversity, especially in the US. "I think you belong in CSETI," I joked.

She vigorously shook her head, countering that she had enough to do in her very Earth-bound life.

Word had leaked out among some of my music-biz friends and acquaintances that I was seriously interested in the UFO issue and writing about it. One such friend was Owen Husney, the man who discovered and first managed Prince, the superstar from Minneapolis who blew up on my beat in 1984 with *Purple Rain*, the movie and the album. I'd interviewed the rigorously shy and guarded 17-year-old Prince in the apartment kitchen of his drummer Bobby Z (nee Rivkin) just before his first record came out.

Thereafter, I covered his rapid rise in the Twin Cities, his surprise gigs at First Avenue, going on the film set, attending birthday parties and after-parties, and catching him and his band at many other locales, including the Hollywood premier of *Purple Rain*. Many years later, when he was internationally famous and all too willing to talk to the press about his split from Warner Bros. Records, I interviewed him at Paisley Park, his recording complex, for a *Minnesota Monthly* magazine cover story. In my weekly "Martian's Chronicles" music column at the alt paper *City Pages*, I dubbed him "His Royal Badness." It stuck!

That handle has survived three decades in popular culture, and the column earned me my Martian nickname for just as long among friends, many of whom also remembered the popular '60s sitcom *My Favorite Martian*. Its main character was a Martian anthropologist who crashes on Earth and is found and befriended by a newspaper reporter who chooses to cover up the alien character's real identity—a highly implausible premise, even for a sitcom.

The man who discovered and signed Prince experienced a dramatic sighting in Minnesota farm country, then some bona fide high strangeness in his home much later (Photo: James Steinfeldt)

(Photo: Greg Helgeson)

Husney, who long ago had turned Prince's purple reins over to an LA management company, agreed to have lunch with me at a Chinese buffet in St. Louis Park, a Minneapolis suburb. He sweetened the "UFO date" by offering to play me some old unreleased Prince tapes in his car. Deal!

At lunch, I let him go first. He and his soon-to-be-fiancè Connie Olson, with Norwegian ancestry, decided it would be fun to have a few beers and play pool at a small bar near Hutchinson, Minnesota, about an hour west of the Cities. It was dusk in late autumn. I knew the area, especially the curious little farm town of Cosmos another twenty miles or so up the road, which was founded by a bearded Norwegian settler named Daniel Hoyt, described in the booklet *The History of Cosmos* as "a cultured and highly educated man from New Hampshire who arrived in 1868." This "visionary and eccentric character" gets credit for changing the township of Nelson to Cosmos Township.

Hoyt apparently also lives up to his visionary characterization. He "prophesied that a railroad would pass through the section of land he homesteaded that was fulfilled when the tracks of the Luce Line were finally extended to Cosmos in 1922." Named after the Arizona businessman and his son who bankrolled it, the train originated in Minneapolis and allegedly followed a trail the Native American Dakota had used before the colonialists came. It was supposed to go all the way to Brookings, South Dakota, but only made it as far as Lake Lillian, just west of Cosmos.

"Luce" is also Italian for "light." How would you like to ride the Luce Line—the train of consciousness—through the Cosmos? During that period, I was beginning to feel as if I were on that line, chooglin' fast to somewhere unknown with many surprising stops ahead. I didn't know the Side Hustle Bus stopped in such small, peculiar places.

Road sign photos: Chuck Statler

In Cosmos, all the streets are named after places in the known cosmos, and for a long time, the town featured an old-fashioned water tower in the shape of a rocket. Its main drag, for instance, was called Astro Boulevard, my kind of place! At the corner of Milky Way and Gemini is the former exotic dance club the Juice Bar, now falling apart, its building parts peeling off like articles of clothing from the young strippers who once worked there. In the shadow of a very large grain silo in the middle of town that rivals the big rocket water tower for size, the Juice Bar in its day caused quite a stir after the locals lobbied to close it down. Ironically, the strip club butted up to a former mayor's house and business, like they were getting a lap dance.

Cosmos was also on the way to my in-laws, to the southwest in the Granite Falls area. A little further west of Cosmos, where the Great Plains start unraveling into prairie grasslands, Ufology meets the great expanses in Canby, home of the creator of the "UFO bible," Jerome Clark, who ironically—like many "in the field"—has never seen a UFO. But for years he has judiciously recorded the history, events, sightings, shakers and movers, and minutiae of the UFO phenomenon in his most famous book, the multivolume *UFO Encyclopedia* (1990-1998), and others including *The Unidentified* (1976) and his most recent, *Hidden Realms, Lost Continents, and Beings from Other Worlds* (2010).

Cosmos water tower (Photo: Chuck Statler)

Every July, Cosmos features a weekend Space Festival, with kiddie activities, live music, food, arts and crafts. There was nothing very space-age about it. But after all, these folks woke up every morning on streets named Jupiter and Comet, as if they were living inside some real-time planetarium. You couldn't get more space-age than that! During one visit to the event, I talked to a couple of event organizers, two women in their 60s, about the history of the festival. After a good discussion of how it got started and some of the little bands that had played there, I said, "Given that your town is called Cosmos and you have all these space-age streets around here and this annual space fest, it begs the question, have there been any UFO sightings here?"

The two glanced at each other and then down at the ground. They looked like I had just asked them if they had any incarcerated relatives or something.

Finally, after an uncomfortable silence, one said softly, "No, nothing like that." And the subject was dropped like a bad piece of meat. It's true, for all its cosmic city planning, there have not been any sightings identifiable or unidentifiable in that location, according to Clark.

The town's yearly Space Festival always reminded me of Space Pen Club events. Annual "Spring Rites" and "Peak with the Leaves" usually were held at a de-sanctified chapel that sat on a beautiful lake point away from the main campus at St. John's University about an hour northwest of the Twin Cities. It had been founded and run by Benedictine monks "behind the pine curtain."

Husney's sighting had been just a few years after I had left music journalism for a long-running role in public relations with large corporations, small businesses, non-profits and artists of all stripes, while still accepting music-related assignments on the side. Before Husney saw anything while driving in the country that day, his CD player, spinning classical music, started to skip around like static was frying it. And his radar detector kept going off and on, irritating him.

He prefaced his next remarks by saying he had had absolutely no interest in the ET/UFO subject—zero, NADA. "I didn't give a shit about it." Until he saw the object.

"At first, I thought some cop was screwing around with me, with my radar," he recalled. "The scratching sound the CD was making was getting to me so I pulled it out to check it and slowed the car down to a crawl. There was nothing there, no cop. 'Why is this cop fucking with me?' I thought. 'Just bust me and give me a ticket but stop playing with me!'"

He slammed on the brakes and turned on the brights to find the cop. And then he saw it, "a chunk of metal about the size of two cars, oblong and flying low to the ground. I can't say it was a 'flying saucer'—although Connie took one look at it said that's exactly what it was! That's just so Norwegian of her, so Connie! It just looked like a chunk of metal in the sky, flying silently right over us, across us in the car and not more than thirty feet above us. It gave me a freaky feeling, as if it were watching me. Once the thing got near or over our car, the engine hesitated."

The object continued moving beyond their vision. Connie, who had so matter-of-factly pronounced it a saucer, now wanted to follow it. When they finally got back to Minneapolis, Husney called the Hutchinson Police Department to ask if any weather balloons had been in the area. He described what he had seen and the person advised him that no weather balloons had been launched in that area since the '60s because radar was used to chart and predict weather.

Later that evening, WCCO, the AM radio market leader in the upper Midwest, reported that two police officers had seen the same thing in that area. So Husney's Close Encounter of the Second Kind had been corroborated. Husney said that the event changed the way he thought about everything.

In many ways, that is how I still feel about the run-up to meeting Greer—and later working with CSETI.

Husney's story, told over lunch back in the '90s, was updated twenty years after I contacted him to get his approval to use it in this book. He admitted he had not told me everything the first time, perhaps through simple forgetfulness. But two decades later, he told me that about ten months after the Hutchinson sighting, while asleep in his Edina, Minnesota house at four in the morning, he felt as if "10,000 volts went through my body and I woke up suddenly."

He thought he was having a heart attack. "It was a weird sensation through my entire body, like an electrical charge," he said. "But once my eyes were opened wide, from the bedroom I could see that all the lights were on in the house. I wondered if there was a burglary going on. I closed my eyes for a second to get my bearings while still feeling the sensation in my body, which scared the hell out of me. When I opened my eyes again, it was completely dark!"

Lights on in the house… that sounded familiar. Was this the pro-verbial card left under the mat by the boys upstairs, just like the lights had been consistently left on in my house?

Husney says two things went through his mind. One, that there really was a burglar in the house! The other: "I felt like somebody came back to check on me, or to test me, or maybe to remind me, be-cause I completely flashed back immediately to what I saw that day in Hutchinson."

After we first explored his sighting over the Chinese buffet, we started talking freely about what it all might mean. He expressed interest in CSETI's contact methods and over-arching philosophies after I shared my early experiences with Greer and a little of the weirdness in my home. He mused about how people interested in the topic most often were artists or had artistic sensibilities. "Their minds were more open to the idea and other levels of reality than others," he said, pointing out that Budd Hopkins had been an ab-stract expressionist painter before he started hypnotizing alleged abductees in New York City, and that Whitley Strieber was a short story writer and novelist before his strange "Visitor" experiences in an upstate cabin in New York, which he rolled into his book *Com-munion.*

Husney speculated that a lot of the events in world religions might indeed be more about extraterrestrials and less about God. He is Jewish and wondered if the "burning bush thing" in the Torah (or the Old Testament for Christians) and that whole pillar of cloud leading Moses and the Jews in their exodus from Egyptian captivity through Sinai, might ultimately be about this topic. Later, I would run across similar theories in UFO books and at UFO events. But that day, Husney and

I agreed, everything was up for reinterpretation after what had transpired for both of us. Cue Prince's "1999."

The other music contact I met had a personal story based on two UFO sightings as a teenager that continued to inform his artistic work in elaborate, sophisticated comic-book collages he created. These stunning artworks have been exhibited in the Twin Cities and are full of flying saucers, superheroes, bad guys, men in black, reptilian monsters, government agents, besieged men, women and children on the street, iconic religious and pop-culture figures, all exported from the comic book medium into a highly stylized world inside framed pieces. Every loaded picture tells a story.

Curtiss A (nee Almsted), who was named after the now-demolished Curtiss Hotel in Minneapolis, is for many fans and critics across the US one of the most powerful contemporary rock singers alive. A potent songwriter as well, he's also among the least known. Whether belting out tunes from his considerable output, covering Howlin' Wolf or crooning Hank Williams, Curt can raise the hair on the back of your head, bring a broad smile of appreciation for his dark-witted, between-song observations *du jour*, and make a sentimental tear drop from your eye.

Known as the "Dean of Scream," he is also well known for his annual John Lennon Tribute every December eighth at First Avenue nightclub, amassing twenty-plus players to joyously explore the Lennon Songbook from early '60s hits with the Fab Four to familiar and obscure solo work and all stops in between, including the Beatles' psychedelic period of "I Am The Walrus," "A Day in the Life," "Tomorrow Never Knows" and other songs the legendary band never played live. For many, the tribute—which has been going on since the night Lennon was gunned down in 1980—jumpstarts the holiday season.

The rocker confessed that he took "a vow of poverty" and has never wanted to tour, become famous or play the game it takes to build a massive fan base and respectable commerce. He gets the occasional fanzine feature story or mainstream reporting about his gigs, releases, and rants (often about "aliens,") and a local filmmaker is working on a documentary about him. But Instead of being on the cover of *Rolling Stone* or featured in a Pitchfork post or thriving as a king of iTunes downloads, Curt has remained a best-kept secret except among those scenesters near and far who love what he does. He infallibly rocks!

He has spent his free time offstage and away from his part-time job at the Comic Book College store building, an unbelievable basement-level, fan-driven, pop-culture diorama that features different sections, including a Beatles and rock 'n' roll section plus areas for Batman, Superman, ET and saucer swag, and other themes. It's a sprawling, shrine-like companion to his framed artwork filled with figurines, posters, toys, memorabilia—you name it, it's there! I've never seen anything like this rich, spectacular repository of cultural artifacts that belongs in a museum like the Smithsonian. It's like stepping into another world.

Coincidentally, the young Curt was also a victim of the zinc-and-cadmium-sulfide spraying of grade-school children by Army personnel (referred to in the previous chapter) at Clinton School in south Minneapolis as part of a "test." The potentially toxic dosing was dispersed as "simulated biological warfare agents," according to the *Chicago Tribune*, June 15, 1994. "One hundred biological warfare simulation tests were conducted by the Army in urban and rural areas between 1952 and 1969." Duck and cover, here's a different kind of hard rain.

Curt's first UFO sighting was at the end of a long night on the outskirts of his then-home in Neillsville, Wisconsin, as he was returning from a gig in the upper peninsula of Michigan. It was the last day of Woodstock back east, he remembers. He and his bandmates in the group Cold Turkey—Randy Berdahl on drums, James Solberg on guitar and bass player Rick Clark—were together in a car pulling into town just before sunup on a cloudy morning. Though tired, they were all sober.

According to Curt, in a profile of him in the late '90s Twin Cities rock 'zine *Cake*, the sighting was dramatic: "As we approached the north end of town we stopped at a stop sign. From the west I saw a glint out of the corner of my eye. Randy must've noticed, too, because he was pointing his finger across my face...

"At first 'they' looked like inflated dimes. As they crept through the sky, closer, the impression was of deflated footballs. Rick and Jimmy were still asleep in the backseat, while Randy and I sat with our mouths agape at the sight of five flying (floating) saucer shaped vehicles in a 'V' formation approaching as we sat like deer in the headlights. Was I unable to move or speak? I don't know because this is the point where I experienced 'missing time.' My next conscious memory was of all four of us standing outside the car as all five craft hovered about us.

"The most eerie part was seeing them above the white church steeple (since burned down). I would estimate each disc to be approximately fifty-feet in diameter. They couldn't have been more than a hundred yards above, while the house of worship was two to three blocks from our hilltop position."

The craft eventually disappeared into the clouds but then "a giant burst of red illuminated the sky. But no thunderclap was perceived." Weary and bewildered, the four musicians reached an old schoolhouse that Curt and Rick were renting. Randy and Jim split in their own cars while Rick and Curt went straight to bed.

"I think we slept a long time. We talked about what happened [when we woke up] and slept some more."

After interviewing Curt in early January 2012, his story was virtually unchanged from his account in *Cake*, although he added that "as soon as I realized that they were flying saucers, they became like a

119

still picture in my mind. I stopped having control of my own vision! I tried to scream but I felt like I was in a 2D movie. I think I blacked out. And I have no memory of what happened to the other guys. But it was frightening—horrific, really."

The incident didn't really end, however, until two days after the Sunday experience/sighting. Curt was outside his house relieving himself in a ditch at about seven-thirty in the evening because the outhouse for the rental he shared was "infested with wasps." As the *Cake* story continues, Curt explains what seems to be a revisit of a craft: "As I drained, I noticed a dizzy feeling accompanied by what I can only describe as a 'hum' inside my head. I began to lose balance and stumbled backward... Across the field, behind a line of trees there was a red glow. It looked like a beautiful sunset, except that the sun was still yellow and plainly visible several inches above the northwest horizon (to the right, as I faced west.) As I watched, I saw what was obviously one of the same crafts I'd seen Sunday morning, levitating above the tree tops pulsing red. With each pulse the humming seemed to increase in intensity. Suddenly... the floating disc turned a white light brighter than a welder's torch and shot straight up, until it turned into a speck amongst the azure."

If you ask him now about that long-passed incident, he might be willing to show a scoop mark on his leg—a common indicator among abductees who believe their DNA had been sampled by the visitors. Was his?

I don't know if I will ever have that answer for myself, since I can't even answer to my own experiences by truly *knowing* them. Curt believes it. And he believes my story. What does it get us? Derision occasionally, and tinfoil rolls to wrap everything together. And a sense of isolation, knowing not everyone has had these experiences or even cares to consider the possibilities. Curt's bandmates from that event eventually went their own ways, one becoming a born-again Christian because of the incident.

Rocker Curtiss A reading the original version of "Fake News"—Tabloid UFO
propaganda (Photo: Bonnie Butler Brown)

After telling him about CSETI, Curt says he can't believe the phenomenon is benign if these events are occurring the same way his did.
But for Curt, his experience is a reality that he lives with, and it's one
that has inspired at least one solid song in his repertoire, "The Unidentifiable." It embraces all the black-helicopter terrain that plagues and
populates the UFO ghetto, where paranoia is a poor person's membership perk. But more urgently, it underscores the bigger issues of
how we perceive what all the data—the anecdotal stories and scientific
evidence—really means. And what do we do about it once we think we
think we understand it? For me, at that time CSETI seemed to have a
correct view—make contact, then create sustainable relationships between the visitors and this planet to enhance life on earth and possibly
out into the galaxy.

While I had known Curt professionally for years, I didn't become friendly with him until a mutual acquaintance, Tom Tulien, introduced us to swap stories and experiences. Tom was a videographer and filmmaker, and an avid researcher/hunter-and-gatherer who hosted a respectable community cable TV show in the early '90s called *Dialogue with the Universe*. Like many working in the creative world of production, he had a good side hustle and skillfully supplemented his income with hard work, carpentry and home-maintenance and remodeling jobs. Eventually, after I took on the PR duties for CSETI, he had Greer on his show to talk about the CE-5 Initiative.

But perhaps Tulien's biggest contribution to the UFO puzzle was his exhaustive research done years after an incident a hundred miles from where I grew up and had my first sighting in Dickinson, North Dakota. That incident clearly underscored the security threats that some unidentified craft—or other phenomenon—posed to the country's nuclear defense arsenal. His work on this case, *24 October 1968-Minot AFB, North Dakota*, is readily available online at http://minotb52ufo.com/index.php, and parts of it appeared in a Peter Jennings ABC Special in February 5, 2005, "UFOs: Seeing Is Believing." Some of the critical excerpts from Tulien's excellent research include the following details taken largely from official case documents but boiled down a bit here:

- The two air wings headquartered at Minot AFB included the 5th Bombardment Wing, with 15 B-52H Stratofortress strategic bombers capable of delivering nuclear and conventional ordinance worldwide, and the 91st Strategic Missile Wing, responsible for 150 Minuteman Intercontinental Ballistic Missiles (ICBMs) housed in underground Launch Facilities scattered across an area of more than 8,500 square miles. Today, both wings continue operations under the major command of the Air Force Global Strike Command.

- The 24 October 1968 Minot UFO case is remarkable because reporting was continuous over three hours and involved more than 20 military personnel at locations across the missile complex surrounding Minot AFB. Two distinct communication networks facilitated reporting from remote locations. During this time, a B-52 returned to Minot and the B-52 navigator observed and filmed on radar a large UFO pacing the aircraft. During the encounter, the B-52 radios lost their ability to transmit. Later, radar ground controllers vectored the B-52 to the location of a stationary object on or near the ground, where they flew over a large UFO at close range.

- In the early morning hours of 24 October 1968, United States Air Force maintenance and security personnel at the Minuteman ICBM missile complex surrounding Minot AFB observed one and, at times, two UFOs. The Base Operations Dispatcher established radio communications with the ground personnel reporting in the field; Minot AFB, Radar Approach Control (RAPCON); and the crew of a returning B-52H Stratofortress aircraft.

- RAPCON alerted the B-52 pilots to the location of the UFO high in the northwest quadrant, which was observed on the B-52 radarscope maintaining a three-mile distance throughout a standard 180° turnaround. As the B-52 initiated the descent back to Minot AFB, the UFO closed distance to one mile at a high rate of speed, while pacing the aircraft for up to 20 miles before disappearing off the radarscope. During the close radar encounter, the B-52 UHF radios would not transmit. Radarscope film was recorded.

One UFO hovered close to the ground above the Air Police security vehicle. Two men inside "were scared to death," recalled navigator Captain Patrick McCaslin, who was in the air flying in the B-52H Stratofortress with the rest of the plane's crew. More telling—and a worst-case nightmare scenario for U.S. Command and Control—was that one of the missile silos had been compromised to the point that the twenty-ton concrete "lid" over the Minuteman ICBM silo had been opened and the interior alarms set off.

According to Captain Bradford Runyon, who was with McCaslin in the B-52H Stratofortress at the time of the incident, "There had been outer and inner alarms activated and Air Police [Security Alert Team] had been sent to investigate. The first Air Police had not reported in. Other Air Police were sent to check and found the first Air Police either unconscious or regaining consciousness, and the paint was burned off the top of the vehicle. The last they remembered is that something was starting to sit down on them—and they started running. The Air Police did go onto the missile site and the 20-ton concrete blast door—he might have called it blast door—anyway, the 20-ton concrete lid had been moved from the top of one of our Minuteman missiles, and the inner alarm had been activated. He also mentioned that Air Police had seen us fly over, and had seen the object take off and join up with us." It was an astounding story that was well researched by Tulien and corroborated by witnesses.

I also shared my UFO interest and the rank strangeness in my pad with Laurie Brown, a client who later became a friend. Laurie had opened the second "green" retail outlet in the country, Restore the Earth Store, and the first in Minnesota, using my PR-consulting services to drive a highly successful launch in print, radio and television. Open-minded and interested in the topic and other related phenomena, including psychic ability, Laurie had limited background but suspected there was more to the story than what she could discern from traditional media coverage, the net effect of which was almost zero. She found my tale intriguing and profound. And without missing a beat, she sagely pronounced, "You are going to do PR for the ETs!"

PR for the ETs. I was certain no one was in that niche yet.

* * *

Sometimes the search for present answers lies buried in the past. But the gaping chasm between my first UFO sighting in the winter of 1969 and the rich weirdness of 1992—twenty-two years of mostly *not* thinking or caring about flying saucers, let alone having close encounters with them—seems staggering. When did it all begin? Maybe this always has been a part of my life and those of my peers. As space-age babies, we had been media-fed images of sci-fi saucers winging through black-and-white TV sets, during Technicolor flicks at the Saturday cinema, and in the richly inked pages of superhero-supervillain comic books. Or were we the mind-expanding byproduct of a very real space age, with primitive but aerodynamically state-of-the-art capsules roaring into the star-spiked darkness bearing dogs, monkeys and eventually humans in a quest for a new frontier?

In the days after sending off the CSETI article, I began looking back at my life and first sighting, still wondering if my interests in the ET hypothesis and UFO analysis were completely separate from my experiences in the house, often described as "paranormal." Certainly none of my closest friends or professional colleagues were experiencing these fragmentary, but generally not frightening, nighttime episodes. And if they were, they clammed up.

Was I undergoing some kind of psychic or spiritual attack that just happened to be occurring at the same time I was reporting on Dr. Greer's CE-5 work? Or had my greater consciousness opened wider like a super-sophisticated camera lens to a greater reality, a once un-seen spectrum? Had my crown chakra really opened, as Howard suggested? And as a result, was I somehow attracting broader frequencies into my consciousness, like a radio picking up more stations? Was I expanding my bandwidth like my grandfather's tube-based radio expanded its range with magnetic tuning for foreign stations? Had I just simply turned the dial too far left?

In reading the abduction/CE-4 literature, I noticed that with some abductees the experience was occasionally generational; a mother or father could have had similar encounters that would repeat with their offspring. But as far as I knew, this didn't run in my family—although it may now.

We were mostly middle class, second generation, and shared the same belief systems as most families in that isolated farm town stuck out on the Great Plains during the nation's post-war boom and the dawn of television. Heavily Catholic, we hit church often like hard believers. My two brothers and I served mass frequently and went to Catholic schools.

Aside from that training, we had the parental wisdom of Mom and Dad in our heads—use your common sense, think for yourself, and don't run with the wrong crowd. We played baseball, fished with Gramps, hit the movies, played with friends and wondered what the rest of civilization might look beyond the wheat fields that bordered our little dot on the map—and how far the sprawling night sky might really go.

One really terrible movie we saw during a classic Saturday afternoon matinee in 1964 was *Santa Claus Conquers the Martians.* Calling it a B-movie is too kind. The film was so bad that is has made many "Worst of" film lists and has been mercilessly spoofed by those masters of movie riffing, Mystery Science Theater 3000 (MST3K) and Cinematic Titanic, both created by Joel Hodgson.

During the '80s, I covered Joel's early comedy career in the Twin Cities before he created MST3K. And when he put Cinematic Titanic together, I did publicity for the troupe at the Parkway Theater in south Minneapolis in 2011. Had the Titanic crew known I'd had any *unusual* personal history with this cosmic clunker of a film, however, they would have razzed me big time, or filed me in their own Tin Foil archive!

As laughably horrible as the movie was, it terrified me—again in dreams. Complete with a red devil character with a schlocky red pitchfork, the dorky flick scared me for no apparent reason—and not just for one night but for about two months. It got so bad, my old man threatened to take me to a shrink. My brothers couldn't believe it. How could a film like that scare anyone?

We also watched as much television as we were allowed. I remember watching the Amazing Kreskin on *The Tonight Show* as he tried a telepathic trick with Johnny Carson where the mentalist would concentrate on a card he held and Carson would try to guess what was on it. We tried doing it many times ourselves and actually got fairly good at guessing the correct card around 50–60 percent of the time. Kreskin also had a game used to develop your psychic skills. That was about the extent of our exposure to psi knowledge.

We got our spiritual knowledge and morals in school. Our nun-run grade school was a block from the main public school, and at noon recess a few of those kids often would walk through the alley leading to their school. They would vehemently flip us the bird, which was alien to us. At home, full color pages of saffron-robed monks in Vietnam bursting into flames stared at us from magazines. These sedate and terrifying human sacrificial candles were as unknowable and alien to us as the venomous wrath of the fire hoses and attack police dogs loosed at black people in the south on TV.

We lived through the harrowing Cuban Missile Crisis, knowing the fertile farm fields around Minot and across the state were filled with the bitter, exotically foreign fruit of destruction. We shuddered at the thought of cowering in the basement like we did occasionally for tornadoes, waiting like fools for the final fireworks should the Kennedy brothers, Nikita Khrushchev and Fidel Castro not avert the unthinkable catastrophes that could be unleashed on the people and their planet. By comparison, space—or what we could find there, or what might find us there—didn't seem so foreboding or lethal, even though it was a dangerous vacuum, seemingly void of life (because that's all science knew at that point.)

My earliest conscious memory of space exploration is of my mother in her long housecoat sprawled on the couch with me on the floor at four-thirty in the morning watching Mercury astronaut Alan Shepherd blast off from Cape Canaveral in Florida. Despite the impossible hour—and the fact that we had only one TV station out on the western plains of North Dakota—it was a school day for this star-giddy eight-year-old. While my dad and baby sister slept soundly upstairs and my two younger brothers were lost to their dreams in another bedroom nearby, mom and I were caught up in the excitement of the American space program after the Russians had gotten the edge. It somehow seemed important, at least to me. And my loving mother indulged my interest by getting me up to watch the flight.

Invariably, through most of the Mercury launches, the liftoffs were put on hold, sometimes for hours at a time. I would miss some of them because I had to get to school. The voice of NASA's Flight Controller Christopher Kraft became so prominent announcing delays on TV that my friends and I would do poor imitations of him. "Ah, this is Mission Control, at T-minus eight-thirty p.m. we are putting the math homework assignment on hold. Repeat. The math homework is on hold." And so it would go, over the phone or walking to school, trash talking about the dawn of the space age and the beginning of our young lives.

That same interest in space became as pronounced as my lifelong interest in music. Of course, like any boomer, it began with The Beatles on Ed Sullivan. What I like to think was really a global-consciousness event and/or cultural-epiphany served up through television, the earliest form of mass media and awareness-making. In the Keller household, a regular soundtrack played. The Ray Charles, Hank Williams, Billy Vaughn, Al Martino and Pat Boone records my parents liked would later be supplanted by the sounds booming from hip teenager radio stations as far away as KOMA in Oklahoma and WLS in Chicago that we turned in while dragging main street in our parents' cars back and forth...

Today, reducing these memories to their simplest meanings, I would connect those trillion teenage trips up and down the four-mile Dickinson strip to the silent survey of large radio telescopes that the Signalers set in motion, fanning back and forth across their designated coordinates in space... back and forth, looking for signals, sweeping the gateways to the stars... Back and forth, seeking data, trolling for knowledge, anticipating cues from the blackness of space and hoping for communication.

Back and forth on Main Street we repeated our search, dragging our *American Graffiti* cosmos, looking for signals from friends, girls and strangers, seeking knowledge, cues for parties, expanded friendships and communication, always with the radio on. That's how it went. Turn around, repeat. Is that all there is in this one-TV-channel town?

* * *

Every time I pass through Cosmos these days—dragging its brief main street, Astro Boulevard—I'm reminded of this adolescent rite, and of Greer's basic pacifist-like beliefs compared to other Ufologists. I was sympathetic not only to the implications of consciousness he had spawned in the literature, but to his ET politics, just as I had become sympathetic to the moral consciousness-raising of the Berrigan Brothers, Phil and Dan, two Catholic priests who practiced civil disobedience to try and stop the Vietnam War by raiding draft offices or trespassing on nuclear sites to do a a symbolic dismantling of warheads.

Was this the intention of the boys upstairs who illegally trespassed at Minot AFB and moved twenty-ton concrete silo lids and set off ICBM interior alarms, as well as in similar jarring incidents at Malmstrom Air Force Base and other national missile sites? Were those acts cosmic civil disobedience? Or were the boys upstairs probing our systems, as some have suggested, looking at how soft our defenses may be.

Toward the west edge of Cosmos as you drag Astro Blvd., a non-descript house sits on Comet Street South set back from the road and easy to miss as you accelerate to hit the open road. The Lennon house I call it. The Peace place that seems incongruent in a town where the rest of the signs all seem to say, "dying farm town, fading light."

Part of the chorus to "Imagine" is painted on the garage door—a voice in the wilderness of space and the little town of Cosmos: "Some may say I'm a dreamer. But I'm not the only one." Eleven simple words with implications that reach across the universe. They're comforting, somehow, those words painted metaphorically in the deeper, broader cosmos. And it makes all the difference. Every time I see them, increasingly weathered against the wood, they put a calm on things swirling inside my head or in the general flux of news events. They call to mind similar sentiments of a decorated old warrior, World War II American General of the Army Omar Bradley, who said, "The world has achieved brilliance without conscience. Ours is a world of nuclear giants and ethical infants. We know more about war than we know about peace, more about killing than we know about living."

Though described as an experimental endeavor, Greer's ET contact mission had peacemaking at its core. After having been "radicalized" by the devastating Southeast Asian war, assassination events and space-age triumphs of the American '60s, I was drawn to CSETI's vision and simultaneously intrigued and skeptical of its contact methods. I didn't see anyone else in the phalanx of UFO researchers or activists who had this platform or the call to action inside Working Groups to make contact by remote viewing, using their coherent thought-sequencing projections, sending out repeated imagery about location and intention. These redundant tracer thoughts would result in a hoped-for CE-5, dragging the cosmos with the groups' minds, cruising the invisible borders of inner mind and outer space, while doing their best to shut out the rest of the mind's endless and mundane chatter.

He "traveled the spaceways": Legendary jazz composer, keyboardist and band leader Sun Ra, who believed he was from Saturn—and that humanity needed to wake up!

No, it wasn't hard for me to make that big leap from our adolescent car rituals back and forth on Main Street to understanding and participating in the primitive remote viewing exercises taught to CSETI Working Groups. I had space jazz in my blood—similar to but nowhere nearly as dense as the legendary Sun Ra, leader of his colossally rich jazz Arkestra, who claimed he was really from Saturn and had been transported here in the '30s. "He read the ancient texts of Egyptians and African and Greeks, the works of Madam B. Helena P. Blavatsky, Rudolph Steiner, P.D. Ouspensky, James Joyce, C.F. Volney, Booker T. Washington," reads his redoubtable bio on his official website. "He read about the lost history of the American Negro and studied the origins of language. Sun Ra knew Biblical scripture better than any preacher, read Kabbalah concepts and Rosicrucian manifestos. Through these texts Sun Ra learned it was possible for the chaos of human knowledge to be ordered."

How bad did I have it?

While plenty of '60s kids spent time and money on buying 45s and albums and joining fan clubs, or playing sports like there was no tomorrow, I wrote to NASA for information and photos of the astronauts and the space programs. And I heard back via pre-autographed photos of the space voyagers and background documents about each program. A letter I'd written to Senator/astronaut John Glenn after his three orbits around the Earth even got a personal response signed by a NASA employee for the astronaut and an autographed photo! And when it came time to do a science-fair project in seventh grade, my creation of a space flight complete with all my NASA dope and some glue-heavy space capsule models I'd constructed courtesy of Woolworth's and a homemade flight plan—earned me a trip to the state science fair (from which I came home with squat).

Yeah, I was a total space geek. Many years after middle school geekdom, former Nevada Senator Harry Reid wrote in a *New York Times* Op Ed section in 2021 that Senator Glenn was interested in looking harder into the UFO topic after Reid attended a scientifically focused presentation by mostly academics in 1996: "'Over the following years, as I became increasingly interested in U.F.O.s—in part through my conversations with former astronaut John Glenn, a fellow senator with a similar curiosity—my staff warned me not to be seen to engage on the topic.' Stay the hell away from this,' they said. I politely ignored them. I was inquisitive and, like Senator Glenn, I thought it was an issue that demanded attention, and I was in a position to act. And act I did.'" Another Space Pen ally, if not a Hall of Famer member recognized, Senator Glenn.

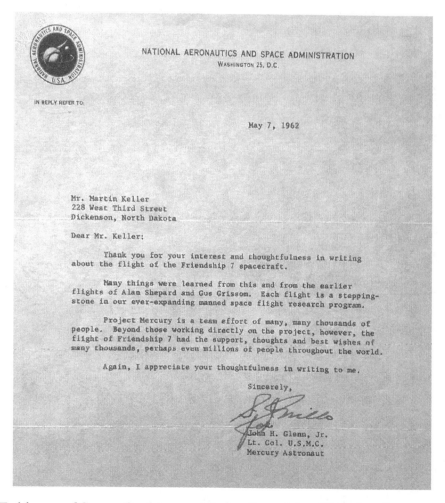

NATIONAL AERONAUTICS AND SPACE ADMINISTRATION
Washington 25, D.C.

IN REPLY REFER TO:

May 7, 1962

Mr. Martin Keller
228 West Third Street
Dickenson, North Dakota

Dear Mr. Keller:

Thank you for your interest and thoughtfulness in writing about the flight of the Friendship 7 spacecraft.

Many things were learned from this and from the earlier flights of Alan Shepard and Gus Grissom. Each flight is a stepping-stone in our ever-expanding manned space flight research program.

Project Mercury is a team effort of many, many thousands of people. Beyond those working directly on the project, however, the flight of Friendship 7 had the support, thoughts and best wishes of many thousands, perhaps even millions of people throughout the world.

Again, I appreciate your thoughtfulness in writing to me.

Sincerely,

John H. Glenn, Jr.
Lt. Col. U.S.M.C.
Mercury Astronaut

Evidence of Space Geekiness: A letter from John Glenn's office and a signed photo

Best Regards

Lieutenant Colonel
U. S. Marine Corps

I still can't pinpoint exactly when I became aware of UFOs, but it likely coincided with the rise of the great Cold War space race with Russia since the early exploration programs of both countries were littered with UFO incidents. With my best friend Jim Reichert (JR), whose house butted up to Rocky Butte Park (although I'm sure the native inhabitants of the land have another name for it), I often discussed the possibility of life "in outer space" capable of visiting this planet.

JR and I became a pretty tight team, later joining as debate and speech partners, elected student-council leaders, and one-time hosts for the talent show as Reichert and Martin, after the popular Rowan and Martin comedy show on TV. Without his personal encouragement to join high school debate and speech teams, where critical thinking was learned along with confidence in public speaking, I would have never gotten elected to the American Legion-sponsored Boy's State my junior year, and then voted by many peers from across the state to attend Boy's Nation in Washington, D.C., as one of two representatives from North Dakota. It was one of the awards that my parents and I shared as a genuinely proud accomplishment despite our growing mistrust of the institutions behind the achievement.

Reichert (aka JR, Zod) & Martin—playing off the popular '60s TV show *Rowan & Martin's Laugh-In*—host their high school Variety Show the same year as they had two UFO sightings

Behind that abutted park, near JR's house, the city had built a metal five-pointed star the size of a billboard facing I-94. It had all-white lights in the star outline and could be seen from far off. We sat at its base in almost any season pondering our little lives, our music faves, our teachers and classmates, the subjects we liked and hated, the news of the day and our own adolescent inventions.

We each had a brother one year younger, plus other family, but somewhere around the time of our sighting, his brother John, my brother Ted and several of their friends started reading *The Urantia Book* and creating their own language. *The Urantia Book* (in the book, "Urantia" is introduced as the word for Earth) was allegedly channeled from "celestial beings" by a group of Seventh Day Adventists in Chicago during the '20s through the '50s and written down on volumes of papers, or "The Papers," according to the Urantia Foundation website, which first published the book in 1955.

The writings in *The Urantia Book* "instruct us on the genesis, history, and destiny of humanity and on our relationship with God the Father. They present a unique and compelling portrayal of the life and teachings of Jesus. They open new vistas of time and eternity to the human spirit, and offer new details of our ascending adventure in a friendly and carefully administered universe. *The Urantia Book* offers a clear and concise integration of science, philosophy, and religion." As with most organizations formed around such high and higher-minded ideals, there was always a gray area where outsiders might see the Foundation as being cultish and out of step with other more accepted "isms" that constitute life as most of us know it.

Even though Urantia sounded intriguing to JR and me, we ignored it. We spent our time reading "Classics Illustrated" comics, recording fake radio programs and making a bad little film or two of rock songs we liked—early music video, Dakota style. The Urantia turf was a playground for our bros and their buds—not us. And they owned it.

A passerby had left a flyer about the book on the car of one of the guys in my brother's circle. The result of that classic marketing tactic was that all of them were reading the massive tome, in which the cosmos is defined like this: "The Papers make use of the word 'universe' in several different ways: They speak of *local* universes and *super*universes, of the *central* universe, and the *grand* universe, and the *master* universe."

The Urantia Wikipedia entry presents a definition of the book that is as good as any: "It has been described as 'a rich and complex moral

narrative, equal parts Tolkien and St. Paul.'" And the Wiki overview
suggests that, yes, the universe(s) are teeming with life, material and
spiritual: "Part II [of *The Urantia*], 'The Local Universe,' describes the
origin, administration and personalities of the local universe of 'Nebadon,' the part of the cosmos where Earth resides. It presents narratives
on the inhabitants of local universes and their work as it is coordinated
with a scheme of spiritual ascension and progression of different orders of beings, including humans, angels, and *others* [my italics]." The
entry also cites claims for a cosmos jammed with life: "Urantia is said
to be located in a remote local universe named 'Nebadon,' which itself
is part of superuniverse number seven, 'Orvonton.' The physical size of
a local universe is not directly stated, but each is said to have up to 10
million inhabited worlds." That sounded faintly, perhaps, like an example of string theory.

Like Greer's Bahá'í Faith, and the cosmology expressed in *The
Book of Mormon* (not the smash Broadway musical by the religious-
ly irreverent creators of *South Park*), the Urantia religious group also
believes that life on other planets is a *de facto* no brainer. But the Wiki
money quote for me is this one: "Urantia is said to be a markedly confused and disordered planet that is 'greatly retarded in all phases of intellectual progress and spiritual attainment' compared to more typical
inhabited worlds, due to an unusually severe history of rebellion and
default by its spiritual supervisors."

Great, this planet is the way it is—"confused and disordered"—
because some of the Star Forces upstairs have not towed the line hard
enough! They don't have their shit straight and can't dance to the real
celestial music everyone else can supposedly hear playing. That adage,
"As above, so below" never made more sense in light of this damning
judgment. Thank humans there was art and rock 'n' roll to help us get
through it all outside the walls of a church, mosque, synagogue, ashram or name-your-favorite-spiritual-center-here. As Urantia called it,
Earth was clearly not playing with a full set of cards. We'd been cheated
from the get-go, born into the one universe among universes like true

losers, the most dangerously alienated and magnificent outliers in the known universe. "Like a rolling stone."

As a former music journalist, I'd be remiss if I didn't note that several prominent musicians found much substance inside the profuse, esoteric pages of *The Urantia Book*. Reported avid readers of the book included artists like Jimi Hendrix, Jerry Garcia (one of the Space Pen Club's saints), Stevie Ray Vaughn and others, including former Twin Cities jazz bassist Jaco Pastorius (who wrote "Havana" for Weather Report's *Heavy Weather* album), and iconic modern composer Karlheinz Stockhausen, who scored a complete, seven-cycle opera based on the strange book's daunting cosmology. Curtiss A keeps his copy by his bedside.

Still, if the bleak takeaway from *Urantia* was that our blue planet had been poorly mismanaged by, ah, upper management, was it any wonder the alleged visitors were treading carefully when interacting with us here in one of the far-flung armpits of the cosmos. The bros and their friends read most of the book, from all reports. But they only got up to around fifty words in the development of their own teenage lingo before they threw in the towel. Nevertheless, their handle for my BFF Jim stuck, "Zod."

The UFO sighting that Zod and I experienced took place on the other side of the park from his house, about a mile west on Empire Road, not far from our Catholic high school, which we could easily see from the hillside where the big star was planted. Empire Road constituted the edge of town then and was the street of a childhood sweetheart, Peggy. The dirt road was home to a handful of other families and a large section of land owned by the North Dakota State University (NDSU) Agricultural Extension office. It was commonly called "the experiment station," although I never knew what they were experimenting with—grain or livestock, most likely. It was in that direction we saw the UFO parked in the air roughly forty feet above the ground on that bitterly cold night in February.

The incident happened during the middle of an intense varsity basketball game and a week in which numerous UFO sightings were reported across that end of the state.

One of our friends burst into the game at halftime from outside, where he'd gone to smoke a cigarette. "There's a big honkin' UFO out by the experiment station!" he shouted.

JR, another friend and I didn't need any encouragement. We dashed outside, leaving our winter coats in the bleachers, and raced toward the far end of the parking lot where you could see the craft silently hanging there, defying gravity and belief.

My admittedly faded memory is that it had structure and was silent and bathed in a yellowish-white light. Zod, decades removed from it as well, remembered, "It was a small-to-midsized white-light object that moved in the sky from the northwest toward the extension station." Zod said it didn't seem to have structure, per se. It was "only a round light." It was "noiseless" and "moved back and forth slightly." The only sounds you could hear "were other people off in the parking lot by their cars."

We stood hunched up to stay warm, watching it and making comments. "I can't say there was any 'excitement' among us about seeing it," Zod recalled, "It was just viewed and discussed very matter-of-fact, maybe because all of us were a little awestruck." Then one of our friends made a daring suggestion: "Let's get in my car and go see it!"

I'm not sure, but I think it was me who poo-pooed that idea. I'd reverse that, if given the chance, and would have raced closer to see what it was doing.

"Nah, it's too cold and we saw it now," I offered. "Besides, I want to see the end of the game and we left our coats in there." That seemed to be okay among the rest of us, too. Dumb!

That sighting might have been beginning of it all, although in our own way, Jim and I had been tracking every report we could find about UFO incidences in the local paper, and we often read the UFO monthly magazines at the newsstand in White Drug, just down the hill from his house, until an angry pharmacist would chase out of the store for not buying anything. I also shared this fascination with my next-door neighbor, Rodney, who was a couple years older than me.

Rodney suffered from a kind of growth deficiency and compared to his siblings looked completely out of place. But he knew the subject matter much better than Jim and I ever did at that time. He ordered books about it and took it very seriously. He also scoured the heavens at night with expensive binoculars from atop the two-foot concrete wall that ran along our driveway and his parent's property. My younger brother Tom always said of him, "He wasn't just interested in aliens, he was one!"

It wasn't long before I got my own "bnocs" to search with him. Occasionally, Bob Lenhardt from across the street would join us (a lifelong UFO seeker, he still sends me stuff today). Besides looking for anomalous objects and talking up the UFO stories we'd heard, we just liked being under the stars, finding major and minor constellations, spotting the few satellites that crawled across the black night like insects moving slowly over an inky, distant pond. I thought of Rodney during other nights with CSETI teams in different locations. Those nights never disappointed, even if there was no UFO action, simply because the night sky has rare gifts that quietly feed the psyche and the imagination.

Rodney and I also poured over the two October 1966 issues of *Look Magazine* when they came out, especially the one with the ravishing Elizabeth Taylor and her plunging neckline on the cover, in a pictorial story about the filming of *Taming of the Shrew* with Richard Burton. That issue featured a major story on Betty and Barney Hill, who had one of the most publicized Close Encounters of Fourth Kind ever. An interracial couple allegedly taken aboard a craft by classic gray-looking entities while traversing Route 3 in New Hampshire around Indian Head, the pair was given a battery of tests and experienced two hours of missing time. They later began having dreams and nightmares about the incident. Barney developed anxiety and an ulcer. Eventually, they both underwent hypnosis to uncover and understand what they had experienced.

Look Magazine, October 4, 1966: One of the first mainstream American magazines to carry the Close Encounter of the 4th Kind (CE-4) account of Betty and Barney Hill in New Hampshire

Cannon's monogram about it, based on telling details of the encounter that were tape-recorded during a series of hypnotic regressions, argues persuasively that they could have been victims of a covert psychotronic operation. He makes such a good case that it created doubt in my mind about it, even though a few years ago, while in New York with a client, I attended a presentation by Betty Hill's niece, Kathleen Marden. Marden had coauthored a book with Stanton Friedman called *Captured! The Betty and Barney Hill UFO Experience: The True Story of the World's First Documented Alien Abduction.* The event was sponsored by the Intruder's Foundation, Budd Hopkins' organization, which was based in the Big Apple.

"Yes, I really know how to live it up on a Saturday night in New York!" I muttered to myself, as I walked to the event from the Waldorf Astoria, passing throngs of theater-goers on Broadway and pausing briefly to munch a slice of pizza. Hopkins, who died shortly thereafter from cancer, looked like he was in full battle with the disease. Also there was journalist Leslie Kean, whom I had met before, and a film-maker who was doing a documentary on a well-publicized African CE-4 case in which a craft landed and several beings interacted with a host of children in a small village. This event was studiously reported in the five-star 2021 documentary *The Phenomenon*, which included interviews with the children who are now adults! But in a story I had read long ago about the same incident, an ET reportedly told one child who asked if he could go back with them to their home planet, "No, your thoughts alone would pollute our planet," or words to that effect.

Kean and I chatted briefly before and after the talk. Her book, *UFOs: Generals, Pilots and Government Officials Go on the Record*, was coming out soon and she was excited. We touched on Greer, whom she disliked as a journalistic source, but she wouldn't say what had transpired between them to produce this reaction. Perhaps it was simply the non-strategic way she thought he handled the second Disclosure event—now 20 years ago—at the National Press Club in Washington. The May 2021 New Yorker story "How the Pentagon Started Taking U.F.O.'s Seriously" may shed some light on it: "Leslie Kean, an independent investigative journalist and a novice U.F.O. researcher who had worked with Greer, watched the proceedings with unease. She had recently published an article in the Boston *Globe* about a new omnibus of compelling evidence concerning U.F.O.s, and she couldn't understand why a speaker would make an unsupported assertion about alien cadavers when he could be talking about hard data. To Kean, the corpus of genuinely baffling reports deserved scientific scrutiny, regardless of how you felt about aliens. 'There were some good people at that conference, but some of them were making outrageous, grandiose claims,' Kean told me. 'I knew then that I had to walk away.'"

By then, I had not seen Greer or talked with him for several years, but after working in CSETI, I knew the powerful effect he could have on people, both positive and negative.

That night in New York, I sat with about thirty others in a small, second-story space that doubled as a metaphysical bookstore and listened to some of the chilling tape recordings Marden played of Betty Hill's hypnotic reliving of the event that had become *the* UFO story of the era. The unsettling tape-recorded sections at key points in her CE-4 were persuasive, disturbing and unforgettable. Having read the story several times after it happened and discussed it repeatedly with Zod and Rodney, I knew many of the details. But hearing Betty's voice on tape made the incident even more powerful.

As I combed through the details of my adolescence that fall as a thirty-something, I could find through-lines to my adult world that had become more layered with complexities while I was unraveling the night-time events in my house and processing what I had learned in CSETI. As winter made its approach, I rapidly raced through Edith Fiore's book and started seeing parallels between some of her clients alleged abduction experiences and mine, especially the person obsessed with blotting out the night sky by drawing the shade tightly.

But one early morning, when the blind in my bedroom had not been turned down entirely, I awoke and automatically turned my eyes to the window. Suddenly it hit me, a white light—not intensely bright but with a glow like the nearby streetlight but without any incandescence. The light hit me not from the sky—or from any saucer-shaped beam—but from the hillside. I glimpsed it briefly flashing in my direction, then shot straight up in bed so that I was in a sitting position at a severe 90-dgree angle. I was conscious enough at that point to feel that I was not in control of my body. I had one vivid thought—that this was probably not a good thing. Then I went unconscious and back to sleep. Susan again slept soundly beside me.

In many ways, the episode disturbed me more than the night of the five red orbs in the bedroom (created by a psy-ops team if you go with the Cannon explanation) and their after-effects. Things seemed to have moved too far. Some force or manipulation had become physical rather than just perceptual. A line had been crossed. Or had it been crossed previously?

Fall gave way to winter. Rejection letters came in on the CSETI story. I talked to Greer about rewriting the piece or finding new outlets for it. I also put another option on the table—to become the PR person for his organization. I'd been thinking about the possibility and knew it was a priority role for this nascent group that was starting to get its act together. I also knew that the focus on consciousness would serve as a massive learning experience. I was ready to take the rest of the course.

"I can probably do more good for you and CSETI and the objectives you have by providing these services than just placing one story," I offered.

He thought that might work but cautioned there was no budget for such a role, only enough to cover expenses like travel to Asheville for meetings, long-distance phone calls, etc. Knowing that as with any nonprofit organization, there were always fundraising needs, and having met some of his early benefactors in Los Angeles, I suggested making a PR job one of his funding goals. "I'm always looking for another full-time job in public relations or back in journalism," I told him (although those jobs were starting to dry up because of the internet). "But it has to be the right situation. And CSETI might be just that."

He acknowledged that, saying he would welcome help on the PR front. Could I come to a meeting soon? I knew that Howard from Canada was involved at the organizational level, and I had met other key people like Shari in Denver. By now, Dr. Joe had signed on in in advisory role too, and Dick Haines. So without much fanfare, I stopped trying to place the story and moved to the other side of the desk.

The first meeting at his home was largely uneventful. But the good doctor did hand out red carnations to us, like the Maharishi did to his disciples, including the Beatles. The agenda included planning for a spring training session in Arizona and a discussion about a membership filter of sorts that Howard was working on to weed out CSETI candidates who might prove unstable or detrimental to the organization's values, the regional Working Groups, the visitors and even themselves.

In my attempt to figure it all out, I continued reading from the UFO literature. In the 1969 book by Vallee, (or Partridge, using his Aviary name) *Passport to Magonia: On UFOs, Folklore, And Parallel Worlds*, the author suggests that many strange figures in folk tales from the Celts and other cultures—magical creatures from parallel and unseen "fairytale" worlds—often shared a common ground with figures in modern UFO stories, not just in the current era but throughout the centuries. Knowing the limits of human knowledge on this planet then and now, I'd say *Passport* is really a book about how human interpretation of reality works, or attempts to work, when trying to put all indecipherable phenomena (including the world's fabulist literature and folklore that has survived as long or longer than written language) into some context, to codify inexplicable weirdness, without having all the tools or ultimate understanding to do so.

A fascinating read (especially for an English major), *Passport* made a deep impression, not only for its high level of arcane historical research, but because of one simple passage that whiplashed me back to my dream in which a small figure offered me a tablet—or something to ingest—in order to create force fields with my hands after he had made a pile of silver dollars appear out of the air with his own hands. Partridge recounts both the warnings of Celtic folk tales and the instructive account of a UFO case from Eagle River, Wisconsin, in 1961, in which a chicken farmer was offered three wheat cakes or "cookies about three inches in diameter and perforated with small holes" by three five-foot beings wearing black "outfits with turtleneck tops and knit helmets" from inside a twelve-foot by thirty-foot "silvery saucer-shaped object" in exchange for water.

Although there are many more details to this odd encounter, Partridge goes on about the parallels between this police-documented encounter and select folkloric tales that guard against taking anything like food in these "fairy" realms, less one become a captive of the realm. Was it possible these realms, though innocently named, were metaphorical mind zones that we don't physically inhabit but intersect with metaphysically? Are they really intricate yet subtle levels of consciousness? Was the "pill" I had ingested from the small boyish "visitor" really an ethereal communion wafer, a spectral tablet of consciousness, a mind seed to prepare me for the future events following that night, which was when I surmised it all had begun?

And was this really an initiation like the one Dr. Stringfield described in the previous chapter? A bridge into the waking world of events that had unfolded inside my house and then into the consciousness-driven platforms of CSETI? I cannot know, but I continued then—and to some degree do so now—to bump about my unknowingness by searching for clues and answers looking for, as Thomas Wolfe's words describe in the epigram that frames this book— "A stone, a leaf, a door. And of all the forgotten faces—" clues that might bring closure and not more passports to levels further down the rabbit hole.

Years later, while researching this book, I stumbled on an interview with the brilliant French Partridge/Valee at Ufoevidence.org called *Scientific Study of the UFO Phenomenon and the Search for Extraterrestrial Life*. "In his recent autobiographical book, *Forbidden Science*," the posting states, "Vallee summed up his views about the provenance of UFOs, a viewpoint that he's developed through decades of research: 'The UFO Phenomenon exists. It has been with us throughout history. It is physical in nature and it remains unexplained in terms of contemporary science. It represents a level of consciousness that we have not yet recognized, and which is able to manipulate dimensions beyond time and space as we understand them.' So much for anti-gravity-powered starships ferrying Big Brothers from outer space. Vallee thinks UFOs are likely 'windows' to other dimensions manipulated by intelligent, often mischievous, always enigmatic beings we have yet to understand."

Of course, I hear Greer dissing this idea, as he often did with any that didn't fit his cosmology, by saying that "humans are by nature inter-dimensional," and that ET should not be confused or confabulated with other beings that may be astral, folkloric, spiritual or something else. I tend to agree with him, despite all the ideas I entertained to solve my inexplicable experiences.

* * *

As Christmas approached that year, Susan and a friend of ours, Angela, who had been in the seminal Twin Cities "folk punk" band Tetes Noires, went to see Handel's *Messiah* performed at the Cathedral of St. Paul, a massive, beautiful European-style church on a hill overlooking downtown St. Paul and the Mississippi River. While the choir exquisitely performed the exalting music, especially the piece's signature "Hallelujah Chorus," my eyes darted to the beautiful stained glass windows depicting various scenes with Jesus and his apostles, all with halos— glowing, numinous light circles around their crown chakras denoting a Christ consciousness. Momentarily I flashed on one of Willie Nelson's many one-liner statements about how the Christ consciousness and the Krishna consciousness appear to be one and the same.

Even though I had given up on the orthodoxy of Catholicism and the dictates of Rome before college, I still occasionally enjoyed the art and music they inspired and the steadfast rituals of the Catholic mass. Looking into and through these stain-glassed images, staring as hard at them as I stared at my own inner life, I felt a comfort zone of nostalgic innocence wash over me. With the choir, organ and instruments blazing, this was a perfect wrinkle in time that revisited my young years serving at the altar and in the congregation, hoping and praying the world was the way they said it was in church, at home and in school. Praying that it was all real and black-and-white simple. Praying that it would stay that way as time wore on, but knowing deep inside that just wasn't going to happen.

Glancing at the stained window frames of the cathedral with those halos, I thought of Howard's "third-chakra installation diagnosis." Of Husney on UFOs and religion. Of cosmically compromised nuclear payloads buried deep in the Minot, North Dakota snow. I thought of it all. But I didn't go there. Curtiss A could go there with his dense visual art and his guitar. The Partridge could too with his intellectual theories and brainy extrapolations. PR for the ETs? Hmmmm… Even Greer and his teams could go there by remote viewing seen and unseen skies, back and forth, back and forth and overhead at the zenith.

I put it all out of my thoughts. Not this time, not now, as I tried to focus solely on this traditional spectacle before me in the big cathedral. This was a true, beatific Christmas epiphany like something from my past, experienced in a fleeting, present moment, finally unspoiled, uplifting and inspired. Santa Claus, and the Martians, would have to wait.

CHAPTER FIVE:
THE SPACE PEN CLUB—THE FELLOWSHIP OF THE PEN

"BYOMZ (Bring Your Own Mind Zoomers)"

—Space Pen Club invitation to Peak with the
Leaves

Six months into my side hustle at CSETI—and longer since things inside our house careened outside the lines—my thinking demanded rearrangement. Beginning with my early interest in space exploration, I now reasoned that maybe my early outer space fascination was really a placeholder for a later exploration of inner space, mind, consciousness. And the club—how did it fit into the puzzle? Or could I fit it into the puzzle without diminishing its members, or the elegant engineering of the long line of Fisher Space Pens, which reached the fifty-year mark in 2016? There did exist among the many members of the UFO ghetto and the core and ad hoc members of the club distinctive ties that bind. But at the heart of both, an almost obsessive and yet free-form fellowship existed that "non-members" probably found foreign, curiously silly and or without merit.

As the riveting "Handel's Messiah" performance in St. Paul Cathedral faded, the holidays passed, and the cold, short days and long frigid nights set in again. After a few weeks and several unreturned phone calls to editors who had been sent the Dr. Greer/CSETI profile, it seemed as if I had launched a dud—twenty-some pages, double-spaced and maybe just too far out or too spaced out for most sensibilities. My dad, a former staff sergeant in the US Air Force with a national security clearance, liked the story. He thought it was very convincing—"and this guy just might be right about the whole thing." Too bad he wasn't on an editorial team I had pitched.

So, I embraced the publicist side of the desk to try and raise the visibility of CSETI and its Close Encounters of the Fifth Kind Initiative to the general public, hoping that "the boys upstairs" would show up and make it worth the effort. Greer and Howard, who was on CETI's executive team with five or six others, including Shari and Dr. Joe from LA, were happy I closed ranks. Dr. Haines played an advisory role. My job entailed getting the necessary tools in order—writing a PR plan, creating a media kit and a targeted media list, developing pitch letters, outlining topics for Op Ed or Commentary pieces that might run in mainstream media publications, and doing media relations (i.e., calling reporters and producers to discuss covering the story). One of Greer's goals with media was to see this subject move from the tabloids to the front pages of *The London Times* and *The New York Times*.

On one of my earliest weekend meetings with his team, I met Bob Dean, a lanky, gray-headed fellow with a Beatles haircut that was sometimes pulled back into a flimsy ponytail. He was a special guest, along with his wife, Cecelia, at Greer's seven-bedroom home in Ashville. We set out to do planning for media engagement and the creation of outreach activities to set up Working Groups and seminars around the US and in England.

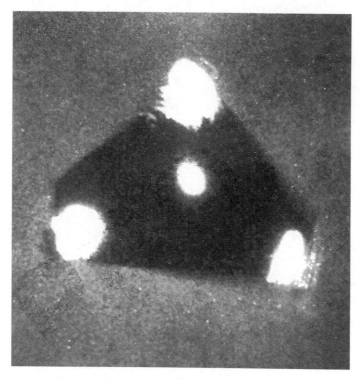

Another part of the early CSETI Media Kit: A photo of a triangular craft with energy signatures at each apex, allegedly taken during the "UFO wave" over Belgium from November 1989 to April 1990.

Cecelia Dean was a pleasant, soft-spoken Hispanic woman in her 50s who helped Bob book gigs on the UFO circuit and with various media outlets. Bob had his story, like so many in this world did— a run-in with the phenomenon, or they were self-proclaimed keepers of the secret knowledge. But Bob's story was more robust than most—if it were true. And it may well be, although his credentials and other details of his service have been questioned by a historian at the Supreme Headquarters Allied Powers Europe (SHAPE), where Bob claims he read a life-changing document. In retrospect, it seems as if anyone who makes big claims in the field is going to get their entrails read and their garbage studied to discredit them (as with Bob Dylan, whose trash was rifled through in the Village during the '60s by A.J. Weberman who was futilely trying to prove the singer was a junkie).

Dean was an affable, grandfatherly type who had many adoring fans at UFO confabs around the country. A friend eventually nicknamed him the "Pope of Ufology" because of the veneration his flock proffered to him. In reality, he was also a retired US Army Sergeant Major.

His story? He claims he read an eight-inch thick report, "The Assessment: An Evaluation of a Possible Military Threat to NATO Forces in Europe," allegedly commissioned in the early-to-mid-1960s at SHAPE, a full-blown analysis of the UFO/ET issues and whether they were a threat to NATO forces. They weren't, the document concluded, according to Dean. However, the more I read other officially published assessments over the years stating the same thing, the more I began disbelieving that conclusion.

Why all the secrecy? Nick Pope added perspective many years later. Pope was a former British Ministry of Defence insider who was tasked with investigating UFOs in the '90s and offered this insight in an interview with the British *Sun* tabloid in 2018: "We told Parliament, the media and the public that UFOs were of 'no defence significance,' but this was a meaningless soundbite designed simply to get people off our backs."

"Pope" Bob claimed that he had obtained access to this "cosmic top secret" document, which, when on duty, he could retrieve from inside a locked, caged room located on the floor on which he was stationed. He says he read it many times late at night—just him and the cosmic top-secret secrets—to recall its contents. Copying it would have tripped all kinds of legal military and security wires, The age of the noble whistleblower a la Daniel Ellsberg and the Pentagon Papers was still a few years away.

Only fifteen copies allegedly existed of "The Assessment." As Bob discussed at UFO conventions and in many interviews, the analysis estimated that hundreds of advanced civilizations existed and many had been visiting earth. Other highlights included the revelation that four races of ETs supposedly looked very much like us, spooking the military officials who had been briefed about the report since these illegal aliens could blend right in.

It wasn't that far afield of the Rand Study entitled "UFOs: What To Do?" written by George Kocher in November 1968 and released in 1997. According to Jeff Cook, Rand's Director of Public Information, that report "was not a Rand Study as such," and not an official Rand document even though it was written by a Rand researcher. It was never peer-reviewed, Cook says, and never became part of the official Rand process. The corporation decided to release the report on its website because it had had so many requests for it over the years, especially from "the UFO community."

The unofficial Rand doc looked at historical sightings as far back as the 1500s, including "the large number" of UFOs around atomic and military installations like White Sands, New Mexico, and the Hanford, Washington atomic plant. And it contained some telling information about how sightings should be handled, speculating about the possible numbers of intergalactic civilizations that may be far advanced beyond our own.

Kocher's study said there were so many UFO reports in the '50s that "the CIA was concerned that an actual attack on the country might not be immediately recognized... In order to unplug the military intelligence channels, however, the CIA recommended that since the UFOs apparently posed no threat, the Air Force should debunk UFO reports and try generally to discourage public interest in them, in the hope that they would go away. It was the CIA's recommendation, apparently, that was made policy, for their investigative procedures used since 1955 have been vestigial and the handling of the subject by authorities tended to make witnesses look ridiculous."

Of the chances that life exists elsewhere, the Rand study says there are probably 30 billion stars with one or more planets, but if we select those similar to the sun, only one in 30 might be able to sustain life comparable to Earth. "Therefore, we would expect about 1000 million suitable solar type stars exist. Of these, it is estimated by various astronomers that 200-600 million have planets at about the right distance and have been around long enough that life forms as developed as our own could exist."

U.S. Army Sgt. Major Bob Dean, "The Pope of Ufology" whose life was changed by "The Assessment"

Given the fact, the report continues, that Earth science and technical development are roughly only five hundred years old, "among the populated planets those younger than the sun would be peopled by beings very much behind us technologically, while those on older planets would be extraordinarily advanced (remember our progress of 500 years and note that some planets could be as much as a few billion years older)... We are left with the possibility of 100,000,000 planets in the galaxy having life forms very much advanced from us."

The report goes on to state that it is very likely that some civilizations may have found ways "to circumvent the speed of light restriction [sounding a lot like Steve Greer] ... Thus, we may conclude that it is very likely that at least one, and probably many of the 100 million advanced planetary populations is capable of interstellar travel... The next question is, of course, have any of them been here?" The hunt for earth-like planets in other solar systems with modern space telescope surveys have certainly begun to affirm those Rand assumptions early in the 21st century.

So *maybe* Bob's "assessment" story passed all the smell tests. On the 50th anniversary of the alleged 1947 Roswell, New Mexico UFO crash where four ET bodies were allegedly recovered from the wreckage and a coverup ensued after international headlines, Dean told a Roswell crowd, "We are apparently dealing with advanced intelligence that seems to be multidimensional in their source... Some of the more advanced species, more advanced races were apparently multidimensional." This passage comes from Dean's talk as excerpted by master debunker Philip J. Klass in his Skeptics UFO Newsletter, as reprinted by *Parascope.* Of course, I hardly knew anything about UFO debunkers at this point in my jagged little journey through the rabbit warrens.

At Greer's house that first night, Bob and Cecelia shared an impressive collection of UFO images from around the world. Included were photos of a bevy of historical art pieces that told strange UFO stories in paint. Bob commanded the room with his slide projector and provided a colorful narrative. It was like watching scenes from a family summer trip to the forbidden galleries. I liked this kind of pictorial data as much as I did the alleged government documents and the anecdotal things I would hear for the next few years while traipsing around the ghetto.

Later, Bob claimed he had an audio recording from one of the Minot AFB incursion incidents on which a couple soldiers freaked out and futilely fired on a craft. He referred to it as the night the electronic military perimeter around the north edge of the country went down. I heard snippets of it over the phone once and asked for a copy, but never got one.

So now, by Major Sergeant Dean's reckoning and that of Rand Corporation, there were lots of boys upstairs—and girls—to contend with. Hundreds of 'em, perhaps, who could move undetected like stealth actors on and off the world stage as I started doing PR for the ETs, er CSETI. I was now in the ranks, not of "believers"—since that connotes a religious aspect that misleads and misinforms even by implication. But of those who knew "The Big Enigma" was credible, if not also incredible (the "enigma" phrase used frequently by the engaging *Herald-Tribune* writer and De Void blogger from Florida, Billy Cox.) In knowing of that credibility, I'd become a pledged member in a fraternity, a cosmic club whose aspirations reached into the planets and stars and all the space debris in between. I figured I'd already had my high-strangeness hazing in my house in advance of attaining the quirks of membership.

* * *

Back in Minneapolis, after I'd agreed to help set up a CSETI Working Group, and arrange and promote a spring lecture here by Dr. UFO, I went about my day jobs, filing freelance stories and trying to grow my PR practice. Somehow, for a ridiculously low price, I was able to rent the World Theater in downtown St. Paul. The World later was restored and named the Fitzgerald Theater after the city's most famous literary son, F. Scott Fitzgerald, who had grown up nearby. The Fitz was where Garrison Keillor later would frequently air his legendary live radio show, *A Prairie Home Companion*.

Keillor had helped raise the dough to restore the theater, and I deeply respected him for that, but more so for his incomparable writing and broadcast abilities. I had interviewed the self-described Old Scout a couple times and written about the show often as a pop-culture reporter. But I knew of him even back in college at St. John's where he first went on the air at Minnesota Public Radio's original station, KS-JN-FM. You could see this tall Paul Bunyan-like bearded figure who spoke in soothing tones and jazzy cadences traipse across the quadrangle to the tower housing the station… or some nights leaning over the urinals after a few cheap beers at the La Playette in nearby St. Joseph, Minnesota.

The official Space Pen flag, commissioned by Boston, and mounted at the "de-sanctified" chapel across the lake.

Some of Keillor's friends became formidable Space Pen Club members, like the Little General, who was highly respected for organizing anti-war protests on campus and being a genuinely likeable guy and gifted English major. But among club members, the General became best known for donning diving gear during one of the club's "spring rites" at the old chapel out on Lake Sagatagan. He later surfaced with his Space Pen ('73 model) in hand and a plastic baggie containing a note he had written on paper underwater while Albert Hofmann's chemicals coursed through his head. He held the silver beauty in the air like a trophy fish as he came up from the depths and exclaimed, "It really does write underwater!" And, "The Fisher Space Pen saves another life."

Of course the pen could write underwater! It could also write "over grease, at any angle, upside down, three-times longer than the average pen, in extreme temperatures ranging from -30°F to +250°F), and in zero gravity," according to the Nevada company that produced it, Fisher Space Pen. Fellow members and astonished onlookers—many in costumes—wildly cheered the Little General's announcement. But they applauded even more his spectacular arrival from the lake's nether world as a modern, modified creature from the black lagoon bearing a primitive tool of space-age communication.

For Greer's all-day Saturday lecture at the World following his speech Friday night, I lucked out getting a smaller venue pretty much gratis. The struggling Cedar Cultural Centre was a poorly rehabbed movie theater turned performance space on the west bank of the Mississippi near the University of Minnesota. I was on the board of the Cedar for a couple of critical years, helping to save the place from closing. The artistic director who had run the joint was losing the reins and sliding headfirst toward the cliff. A defender of hers vowed it was because she was "a triple Taurus." A bull times three or not, she was overthrown and replaced by a board and membership vote. The new director was a college friend of mine, Bill Kubezcko, who had managed a great little night club outside Chicago called Harry Hopes.

Kubezcko was also an ad hoc member of the Space Pen Club, another hairy member who was defined by and helped define the counter-culture zeitgeist of the early-to-mid '70s. The beloved line of pens represented a real and a symbolic community—a semi-secret student society of the pen. And the club became my catch-all for ideas, individuals and notions that pushed status-quo thinking out of the way to look at life's deeper issues and possible meanings. It was not to be confused with tinfoil.

Graciously, Bill and the Cedar board offered the venue to us for a few bucks to pay for lights. The lecture had received a decent amount of publicity in the mostly alternative press and during key radio interviews. Nearly two hundred people turned out. I introduced the good doctor, who began a lecture that I knew so well I could almost give it myself. Greer was brilliant as always, deftly articulating his assessment of the phenomenon with a historical timeline; how our responses to the visitors were always wrong—the fight and flight one and the "blast them out of the skies" strategy, for examples; and how CSETI's contact protocols for the Close Encounter of the Fifth Kind Initiative were developed based on previous Close Encounters cases and the fundamentals of universal consciousness. His condensed view of the role that consciousness played in trying to make contact mesmerized many. A longer version dominated the Saturday presentation along with field work under the stars that night. But I could see some converts being made even before the intermission Friday night.

I could also see some skeptics clinging to their skepticals, especially Alex Heard, a writer (and later the Editorial Director) from *Outside* magazine, who had heard about CSETI's adventures and wanted to write about them. Greer and Shari Adamiak, his right-hand person, were leery of Heard from the get-go, but begrudgingly comped him and his gal pal into both events. I argued that if CSETI wanted a wider audience, this was one way to expose the message, even if it meant risking a negative story that was written cynically or missed critical points and lacked deeper thinking.

It turns out, Heard's take was all those things—in spades.

Stylistically, parts of Heard's occasionally entertaining harangue reminded me of my old pop-culture work. It deployed clever word play and seasoned story-telling tropes: "UFO skywatch clubs are nothing new—they've been around since flying saucers whooshed into the American consciousness with the first big wave of alleged sightings in 1947, kicked off by pilot Kenneth Arnold's famous report of metallic, disk-shaped objects flying near Mount Rainier, Washington. The CSETI difference is Greer's impatience with the traditional notion that we have to wait passively for them to show up. He believes we can prime the pump. Armed with a hardware cornucopia (high-power halogen lights, radar detectors, walkie-talkies, still and video cameras), Greer and his followers do exactly that, gathering at darkness-swaddled mountains, fields, and woods, where they beam photons and positive energy into the inky infinite. Greer claims an astonishing success rate at calling in UFOs; he says he's scored more than a dozen sightings in countries all over the Western Hemisphere."

But Heard's piece consistently and carelessly threw around many mainstream presumptions and mostly failed to challenge media prejudices about the UFO issue that an uninformed reader would never think twice about. And he offensively relied on zoomorphism—the use of animal attributes to create an offensive caricature of the doc: "Greer is a well-built 37-year-old whose sturdy neck supports a simian head decorated with red-blond hair, a beard, and glasses. The overall impression is of a bookwormy, partially sheared Sasquatch." And of me: "…friendly, basset-faced Martin Keller—CSETI's media-relations specialist." My two brothers never let me forget that one.

That bespectacled, weasel-faced scribe's story—what Doctor Joe described as a "hit piece"—was eventually folded into a 1999 book of Heard's (of course!) *Apocalypse Pretty Soon: Travels in End-Time America.* As the year 2000 approached, Alexander the Not So Great had the audacity to call and email me to see what CSETI was doing for the big millennium (long after I had parted ways with the org.)

He wanted to know if there were any special plans to reach out to the ETs (what, they're on the same Gregorian calendar as Earth?) I never returned his calls, not because I resented his story so much as I mistrusted the millennium-associated math and year-counting that we all accept chiefly because we can't really trace our history back far enough to know when the count began, or what time it really is. In the Jewish faith, the millennium year 2000 was year 5761. Cue that old Chicago tune.

But for every Heard in attendance the night of Greer's Twin Cities debut, there were others who had seen UFOs or were more open-minded, like Terry Townsend, a burly guy who had driven forty-three miles from Elk River and shared his UFO sighting story with me in the hallway at the World Theater. He described coming upon a thirty-foot craft hovering in a rain-soaked field on September 16 at midnight as he came over a hill during a good thunderstorm. Townsend wrote a letter to the editor of the *Elk River Star News* recalling "this very powerful ordeal" in defense of an area woman whose UFO sighting had been reported in the news section the previous week. A wave of sightings near Elk River had taken place in 1992, and his seemed to be right there in prime time.

"It's like they wanted me to see them," the shaken man said. "I was scared mostly because it was such a surprise, coming over that hill and all of a sudden, here's this silvery object hovering right there in front of me with strange lights around it. But I never felt threatened by it."

Saturday morning, Alex Heard was among the fifteen people who lined up at the start of the day, nowhere near the participant numbers I'd seen in LA. Some of the others had been at the lecture, and a few knew of Greer by word of mouth or from things they'd seen in *Omni* magazine or elsewhere. And there were a few "just curious" attendees anxious to see what the show was about.

Looking around the circle as Dr. UFO began the proceedings, I could tell who the best prospects for my Working Group might be based on the questions they raised, the looks on their faces or the things they said in passing. Heard never said anything. Not a good sign. A good reporter at least asks some questions. Maybe he was saving them for later in a one-on-one with Greer.

There was a thirty-something hippie couple, Lisa and Elias, who were all pumped up for both day and night events (they didn't come back for a second excursion a few weeks later.) Young "blue eyes," a handsome twenty-something male who worked in a food coop and had intense irises, was a go. Debbie, a quiet U of M student who I'd seen at a UFO conference someplace was already an ardent CSETI supporter. Jesse, a friendly retired gentleman and former English teacher whose wife had recently passed, was definitely CSETI material given the amount of lonely free time he had and the smart questions he asked (he eventually became a co-organizer of the Twin Cities group.) Then combover Bob. No brainer. He was a fiftyish 3M engineer with thinning hair who knew all the players in the UFO universe and went to as many UFO conventions as his life and wife would allow.

Bob later admitted one night under the stars that even though he'd read and heard so many conflicting theories about the UFO issue and alleged ETs, he had "made room for them all in my mind." I think I may have cynically joked to him that going to UFO conventions to find out the truth about UFOs was like standing in a rainstorm to see if the sun might be shining. And yet, there we were, both wet behind the ears but with minds lit with the prospect of "what if?"

As evening approached that Saturday night, our group headed northwest of the Twin Cities for star time away from city and suburban light pollution and Saturday night revelers. Our destination was Sand Dunes State Forest, a state park near Princeton, not far from Elk River. We set up and divided into small groups with designated CSETI tasks as light signalers/sky watchers and those who do the CTS process for a time. Later we reversed roles.

Early on, a noise in the forest sounded a lot like the strange tones CSETI had allegedly recorded from a downed craft. Even Heard, in his story, says the sound was strange, "spooky: metallic, ringing, metronomic."

Greer and I decided to investigate the sound, leaving the group to its paces. Heard volunteered to join us. Great! A publicist's concern in any setting, whether during a business story interview or a live demo of how to meet the boys upstairs, is allowing too much access too soon to all aspects of the story, if only to ensure the reporter is understanding what is being said and the client is communicating clearly.

"But what the hell?" I thought to myself as we snapped branches and headed toward the sound's origin. "I'd do the same thing in Heard's shoes." Besides, it was a lovely night to be under the stars as we lit the dark forest ground with our flashlights. *I don't care if anything transpires out here of an ET origin*, I kept thinking, *I like the night sky.* That has always been my attitude doing what Greer calls an "experiment." And that's a part of the CSETI mission that Heard blithely chose to ignore in his published tale, including the way this part of the adventure transpired—tracking the mystery sound at Sand Dunes

As told in Heard's shade-throwing prose: "At the edge of the woods, before we duck in to meet our destiny, Greer tells Keller in an excited whisper that he wouldn't be surprised to see a UFO hovering in a clearing. Crunch, snap. After a few minutes of pinpointing, the tone is directly overhead. Keller shines a light. It's an easily identifiable flying object: a perched owl. And not just any owl, but one with an especially grumpy glare that seems to say, "What in the *hell* are you doing?" I turn to Greer to see how he handles this particular CE-zero.

"Interesting," he says thoughtfully. "The tone was similar to a crop-circle sound, but it was aurally distinct enough to not *quite* match it." He turns to the expressionless Keller and says, "Well, that's what field work is all about."

"CE-zero." Good one, Alex the Not So Great.

* * *

Besides PR duties, I also began looking for ways to help fundraise for the cause. That meant finding individuals with means who were open-minded and willing to do a CSETI mini-training that would include a night under the stars using the contact protocols to initiate a Close Encounter of the Fifth Kind.

I had a few friends with big dough from the music biz, and someone from one of the wealthier families in the state. But they didn't seem right for this mission. I racked my brain's Rolodex and landed on Horst Rechelbacher, the man who would revolutionize the beauty world with his trend-setting company Aveda and later with Intelligent Nutrients.

I'd met Horst many times over the years, from the late '70s when he was just starting out as a newly arrived immigrant and hot hair stylist to the early '90s when he was honored with an award by the *Minneapolis-St. Paul Business Journal*. I also happened to have a client, Kim Carlson, who was getting the same award at a noontime luncheon for her environmental work in the real estate industry with her company Cities Management.

There was the usual mix-and-mingle social hour before the ceremony, so I made a beeline for Horst. I re-introduced myself and soon was rambling on about CE-5s, Dr. Greer, UFOs and consciousness. He stayed with me, smiling occasionally, which he hadn't done that often in my experience. I'd touched some neurons.

He invited me to sit with him through lunch. Kim, who also knew of my interest in the high strangeness realms, encouraged me to go break bread with him. Throughout lunch, while I talked and he asked questions and offered comments, Horst often tapped into his little tool-kit of tinctures and added dribs of this and drabs of that to his food and water, sometimes explaining what each one was while someone was talking about business leadership and innovation from a nearby podium. By the end of the luncheon, he had made me an offer to continue the discussion at his compound in Osceola, Wisconsin, an hour's drive away, and yes, he was very interested in meeting Dr. Greer and trying the contact protocols.

A couple weeks later, I sat in Horst's big "museum" room that held hundreds of empty perfume bottles and sundry other beauty-industry ephemera he had amassed through the years. The minutes I spent waiting for him added up. Soon he came to where I sat and apologized, saying it would just be a little longer. Visiting relatives from Austria had arrived and he was hosting them as only a relative could, showing them around his woodsy estate. Eventually returning to the room of many bottles and much who-ha, he said again that he would be right back. Meaning two-plus hours later.

He apologized profusely upon returning to the room that I had circled several times, trying to absorb what such a collection could mean to me and to him. But in short order he offered possible dates for Dr. Greer to visit, and the names of friends who might be interested in this unusual experience.

"Add some of your own people," he said in his delectable Austrian accent, smiling and waving to his rellies to indicate he would be right back with them.

A few weeks later, sitting in a large circle in a farm field near Horst's home as twilight slid to darkness, I watched his people and a couple of mine settle in as Greer was preparing to begin the event. Earlier in the day, he had presented his shorter lecture on the non-locality of consciousness and how it could "in all probability" be harnessed to remote view ETs in their flying machines in our galaxy or beyond. Good old quantum entanglement, or Einstein's spooky action at a distance, at work.

Dr. Dean Radin, Ph.D., writes in his book *Entangled Minds,* "Individual minds may combine into networks of entangled minds, giving rise to more complex mind circuits, forms of awareness, and collective psi effects beyond our conception... Minds are entangled with the universe, so in principle minds can nonlocally influence anything, including a collection of other minds or physical systems." Whether by physical systems Radin meant saucer, or cigar-shaped, or triangular-looking crafts like the many that were reported in UFO literature, one can only speculate.

Radin goes on to explain how this across-the-universe quantum channel then could be used, for example, to communicate an intention to interact with the Horst group in a kind of interstellar meet-up set right there in the Wisconsin field.

Some of the people gathered on their blankets appeared nervous, others were silent in anticipation, and still others seemed giddy and not dialed in, like this was a dark picnic of sorts under the stars. In a way, it did have the feeling of a midsummer's night festiveness, driven by an earlier social hour and light dinner after the lecture. Attendees also had the chance to peruse CSETI brochures and reports, as well as the cool T-shirts that space artist and CSETI Denver Working Group member Ron Russell had created using images of various crop circles from around the world. These were given gratis to participants for their time and curiosity.

One of the guests I had invited, an heir to the Phillips liquor family, looked comfortably ready to begin. Further around the circle, sitting next to Horst, was Kevin Foley, who ran a special-events business. Foley's company had done work on the first Bill Clinton presidential campaign, for the unveiling of the Women's Vietnam Memorial, for a large alternative health-care event in Washington, D.C., that Horst had helped underwrite and for other occasions, including John Denver's Futures Symposium in Aspen, for which he had hired me and a marketing friend, Lisa Proctor, as publicists. On a break during a planning meeting at Denver's mansion on a mountain outside of town, he and I had talked briefly about Greer. Denver was highly interested in the subject. But he looked at me and rubbed his fingers together and asked, "Got any pictures?" as if he were going to buy an antique guitar from me.

With Foley in Wisconsin were two very tall, bald and handsome shamans from Estonia, friends that he and Horst had met on one of their many world travels together with Horst's partner, the lovely Kiara. Those three clearly were in "play mode." One of the shamans immediately got very friendly with an attractive young female singer from Minneapolis who sat next to him. Later in the evening, I saw them sneak out of the circle into the night. It wouldn't be the first time there was CSETI heavy petting, or starlight sex, despite guidelines about no drugs, alcohol or hanky panky onsite. Even though his organization was only a few years old, Greer had seen it all by now, humans being what they are.

As was custom at the outset of a CE-5 exercise or experiment, and I regarded each CE-5 excursion as the latter, a tape recorder was passed around to record names in case an "off-planet" opportunity presented itself. The recorder would be left behind to notify next of kin that, yes, they'd taken the express bus to the stars. Foley shouted his draft number into the recorder before offering his name, address and the name of his wife, drawing laughs before Greer began the verbal meditation designed to put people in a clear frame of mind to undertake the coherent thought-sequencing process. Soon a small group got out the high-powered lights and moved to the perimeter, and the etheric sounds of the alleged downed ET craft started playing on a loop.

The event went on for several hours, and while there was no activity to report, before leaving, one of the shamans said that he had received a message that something would come the following night. Greer and I retired to the guest rooms Horst had provided, and in the morning had a healthy breakfast in his large dining hall. One of his assistants said that Horst wanted to talk to Greer before his departure back to North Carolina.

While we waited, Greer noticed a weight room nearby and wondered if he had time to lift, his firm biceps being one of his more noticeable physical qualities, especially under tight-fitting polo shirts with the CSETI logo that he liked to wear. But before Greer could begin pressing iron, Horst appeared and motioned to follow him to his office.

"I wanted to thank you for making this trip. I am filled with so many ideas about your theories about ETs and making contact," Horst said, smiling through his accent. "And last night! Last night, I felt like I was worshipping under a starry cathedral. It was magnificent. I felt so charged by it!" Greer and I thanked him, but before we could finish, Horst wrote a check for $13,000 and handed it over to the doctor. "Do something good with it."

A couple of days after the event, Horst called and said someone had reported strange, small colored lights in the field where the group had been the night before. Would I let the doctor know? Perhaps the shaman had been right after all. But were small colored lights or orbs, UFOs, and by extension ETs, some kind of intelligence waiting to manifest somehow? Or something else?

A critical practice I learned in high school debate—to define the terms or subject matter you were debating so that everyone was clear about meanings—was often lost in the entire UFO/ET discussion. Were orbs UFO's? Were they ET's? Were they spiritual entities, natural or supernatural phenomenon, or truly unknowable and therefore undefinable? What constituted an ET being, anyway? It was an answer that I hoped would present itself as I continued to learn from CSETI, the ghetto and the books I ploughed through while riding the side-hustle bus. I would continue to browse any internet posts on topic that seemed credible, as the UFO discussion eventually flooded the web with the force of a firehose.

* * *

Herr Rechelbacher, the assorted people in my Minneapolis Working Group, strangers I'd met at different UFO events and even some of the Birds in the Aviary shared a common interest that reminded me of my college friends who'd formed the Space Pen Club. Most were interested in challenging preconceptions about reality and unlocking Huxley's doors of perception by as many ways at their disposal as possible.

Most of my Space Pen chums lived in the dorms on campus, but some lived off campus and a few a little too much in the hippocampus. Pot, beer, booze, 'shrooms, acid, hash, all could bring on altered states of consciousness (and, of course, pure inebriated stone-iness). And while many used each or all as recreational accoutrements, there was a prevailing Tim Leary/Richard Alpert subtext to those times for anyone "tuned in" to "turn on" to what these experiences might lead to, aside from mere euphoria.

For me and others, it was an invitation to explore the transcendent pathways leading to a greater awakening of mind, a deeper dive into alternate consciousness that might lead one "Further." That one word was the ultimate destination plastered on the front of a psychedelic bus piloted by Ken Kesey, Neal Cassady and others less than a decade before we all headed off to college to commune behind the pine curtain in central Minnesota. "Further" was an unintended result of our schooling, part of the long strange trip the Grateful Dead sang about, and was not to be taken lightly.

The Space Pen Club's origins are prosaic and inspired. Clean-cut Keis—who started out as all-American as you could get—discovered that his roommate, Dennis, had come across a Space Pen in the college bookstore where he worked part time in 1972. He eventually shared the shiny item over cheap beers and handmade bongs. The bongs were created by Dr. K, a pre-med student who stood six-four and whose thundering laugh seemed to accompany even the most serious statements he might make. It could be heard a floor down—and he laughed a lot! His THC delivery systems were the best, intricately designed to deliver maximum smokeage before retail head shops and record stores regularly stocked similar commercial versions.

At first, the pen and all its far-out features were treated as a kind of an inside joke. But then the curious utensil soon became a "thing" among a small circle of friends, only to become bigger when the space-age writing tool became the iconic instrument of celebration each fall and spring for the next three years.

Not long after the founder discovered it, the aspirational quality of the sleek but sophisticated item soon revealed itself, according to Handsome Harley who roomed with Dennis their first year. Inside their small collegiate barracks, they had a terrarium with two chameleons, named after the then-current Secretary of Defense, Melvin Laird, the other after Nixon's despised Attorney General, John Mitchell, both men architects, in part, and drivers of the Vietnam War. Mitchell aggressively denounced anti-war protestors and pursued "draft dodgers." For our founder, that was personal: He was a conscientious objector. And a Classics major. "A Classics major! There weren't a lot of those in our community."

"For Dennis," Harley added, "it was all about the *possibilities* that the Space Pen represented." One included a ritualistic nighttime debrief among college friends. Core members would regularly gather around 10 p.m.in someone's dorm room after the books were put aside. And, usually over a bowl and or a beer, they would ceremoniously open their Space Pen salon by reading *Alice in Wonderland*. "When that was done, we'd all share what we had learned that day, whether it was philosophy, theology biology, art, whatever new knowledge we had acquired."

With a new pen minted every year, the Fisher Pen company seemed to be making them just for club members. Never mind that astronauts were their elite, first-tier customers.

The Fallen Angel (center) and her two acolytes raise up a funky facsimile of the cosmic writing tool. (Photo: Mike Schroetke)

Soon, younger classmen and women, and a few outsiders from the city of St. Cloud and St. Cloud State University, became involved. But at the heart of the Club, the main characters "built the brand," as they say in Marketing 101, and created club assets that exist to this day. Handmade invitations to "Peak with the Leaves" or the "Rites of Spring"—one reminding Space Pen members to BYOZ, i.e., "Bring Your Own Mind Zoomers"—were hand-delivered, slipped under dorm-room doors or handed out in bars. "Boston," a long-haired brunette from Beantown who always had a wry smile on his face, had a red-white-and-black Space Pen Club flag sewn, which he and others paraded during events or ceremoniously draped from a fir tree or on the side of the old stone chapel across the lake from campus where the psychedelic bacchanals were usually held. And they were usually held with everyone in costume – "an idea gleaned from an art class lecture about the Dadaists, taught by Bela Patheo, the artist and St. John's instructor," Harley recalled. "But there were some political overtones to the club, too. With the draft, there was always a fatal feeling that you were going to be dragged off to war."

Another member, HairDog, already had a reputation as one of the smartest guys and the most likely to be most loaded on weekends in the class and club. :He earned even more stripes just for being one of the original Space Pen clubbers. The Fallen Angel, Morris, claimed he taught her about feminism. A pre-med student, National Merit Scholar, native of Rochester, Minnesota, and son of a Mayo Clinic surgeon and nurse, HairDog sported long, curly, golden tresses that made him look like a classical Renaissance figure reincarnated as an enlightened, beatific hippie who let it all hang out after a hard week of hitting the books on his way up the steep summit to medical school.

One autumn, taking a page from Yossarian in *Catch 22*, HairDog once climbed stark stupid naked into a magnificent, flaming Maple tree near Tommy Hall in the center of campus during Parents' Weekend, taunting and greeting others' loved ones amidst the bright red, yellow, gold and green foliage. How the monks never found him out that day, no one knows.

HairDog was an admirable, furious feast of a young man, who also christened me with the nickname "Hawk" during an intramural basketball league game dominated by "freaks." We shared bench space more than playing time. But when I finally got it in, I took a forty-foot jump shot before there was a three-point line. Swished it!

"Martin Keller, the 'Hawk,' hits one, ladies and gentlemen, from way out there!" he shrieked in his mock sportscasting voice from the bench. The rest of the team erupted in cheers. The name has stuck among many of the old club members, especially my college roommate for the first two years and again for a few months after we graduated. The roomie—tagged with the "GhoulDog" name by his peers—sported a big, bushy, dishwater blonde Afro, even though he was a skinny white dude from Park Rapids in northern Minnesota who loved the Stones, Taj Mahal, John Prine and Joni Mitchell. Most everyone in the club or at its outdoor functions had a deep interest in music. You could tell who was home by what tunes were blasting behind their dorm doors— the Allman Brothers, the Dead, Todd Rundgren, REO Speedwagon (a favorite of Dr. K) the Beatles, Fairport Convention, David Bromberg, Loggins and Messina, Carole King and many others.

GhoulDog claimed to be a theater and psychology major. But I regularly had to get him out of bed so he wouldn't miss class, any class!. He often was out past midnight at Brickey's or the Mantle in St. Cloud with MurrDog, that other fourth-floor Johnny dog directly across from our room, who played a pretty good acoustic guitar and sang well with my occasional roommate, who was also fond of quoting Max Erhmann's calming prose poem *"Desiderata"* (written in 1927 but re-popularized in the '70s). It was mistakenly said to have been found in an old church and was anonymously written, thus giving it a kind of folkish, spiritual mystique that the flower power generation dug.

Queen of Hearts, Mary E: Half the straight males at college were probably smitten by her, even if she scared them shitless (and she saw "one" while living on a kibbutz)

If HairDog had a female club counterpart at the "girl's college," the College of St. Benedict three miles away in the half-horse town of St. Joseph, it was probably Morris, who had a wicked wit and tongue and enjoyed the group's "community" aspects. She dressed for one fine Spring outing as a pregnant angel in an all-white, seemingly vintage wedding dress. Mary E. was another female Hair-Dog and a local St. Cloud native. Mary E. was a no-nunsense (sic), take-charge personality with lovely chestnut hair and the whitest teeth I've ever seen. She often had run-ins with the Catholic sisters and their strict rules. Alpha and Amazonian in stature, E. could rival HairDog or any of his peers with acute brain capacity, a cutting sense of humor, and her fierce presence. Half the straight males at St. John's were probably smitten by her, even if she scared them shitless.

Word of the club somehow got to the maker of the Space Pen line and its founder, Paul Fisher, in Boulder City, Nevada. During an engineering symposium someplace 15 years after college, CV encountered Mr. Fisher at the event and introduced himself while also telling him he was member of the Space Pen Club. Fisher grew excited and told him, "You guys are legendary at the company!"

Entrepreneurial to the core, Fisher was a self-made visionary. His pens defied gravity and made it possible to communicate in the harsh vacuum of space using an earthbound tool. The best part of his story (much more interesting than this abbreviated version) was that his idea for the space pen came from a dream.

"'Some of his more profitable ideas—and he has had a few—have come to him in dreams,' he said. For instance, that's how he successfully invented the space pen, first used by the Russian cosmonauts and then by U.S. astronauts to write in outer space," according to a *Washington Post* profile of Fisher in 1980.

"'In the early 1960s when the Russians started to fly in outer space, it occurred to me they had no pen to write with,' Fisher said in an interview yesterday. But Fisher couldn't perfect a way for the ink to flow under pressure without dripping in globs.

"'One night I had a dream,' Fisher continued. 'Somebody came to me in the dream and said, 'Paul, if you use a minute quantity of rosin it would reduce the drip.' The dream messenger was his deceased father, who gave him the solution to challenges he was facing with ink flow and anti-gravity.

"Later Fisher learned from his chemist that his dream messenger meant to tell him 'resin', not 'rosin.' The resin worked."

Greer's experimental contact protocol was his tool to communicate into the time-space continuum using concepts of universal mind or consciousness as the invisible ink that would convey CSETI's messages of interaction and intentionality. Even in the early '90s, as I became more engaged in the organization and enthusiastic about the advanced thinking that lay at the core of its CE-5 Initiative, I realized I might have started to sound like that character, Miller, one of the many lovable misfits in *Repo Man*, one of the best "B" movies ever made. In the film, a young punk played by Emilio Estevez goes in search of a stolen car with "other-worldly" contents. But first he has to learn the code of the Repo Man.

At one point, his friend Miller makes a speech in an effort to bring some perspective to their seemingly mundane lives: "A lot of people don't realize what's really going on. They view life as a bunch of unconnected incidences and things. They don't realize that there's this, like, lattice of coincidence that layers on top of everything. Give you an example, I'll show you what I mean. Suppose you thinking about a plate of shrimp. Suddenly somebody will say, like, plate or shrimp or plate of shrimp out of the blue, no explanation. No point for looking for one either. It's all part of a cosmic unconsciousness."

Still, for my money, Paul Fisher was the Exalted one of the club—a group, at least in my way of thinking, that included anyone who explored the realms of dreams and tapped the vast, infinity of consciousness that lay inside one's head. But when one of his regional sales reps showed up at the school to inquire about the club, he opened the trunk of his car to reveal a bunch of old political merch with Paul Fisher's name on it! Fisher had made a run for the Democratic presidential nomination against JFK in 1960, and again in '68 against a crowded field of more likely contenders. It's a good thing the rep didn't venture out to one of the gatherings though. There he would have witnessed a deep woods costume drama at the old chapel along the lake shoreline. Among the many gathered, stood two English majors including a young woman reciting Shakespeare from memory to a young man, who listened intently while taking his first Albert Hoffmann-esque trip, about fifteen yards away from spontaneous group dancing to the Dead banging on Buddy Holly's "Not Fade Away."

Weekend Wizard, Dr. K, cutter of flying carpets, maker of bongs. (Photo: Mike Schroetke)

Hawk striking a missionary pose. (Photo: Mike Schroetke)

Mike, the roaming WWI soldier-reveler. (Photo: Mike Schroetke)

Joints and wine sheaths passed through the gathering like plates at the Sunday collection while Dr. K boogied to the Allman Brothers' "One Way Out" in a long robe with a tall wizard hat emblazoned with a lightning bolt. He looked like the fucking Sorcerer's Apprentice, cutting a flying carpet with some local hippie chicks in loud, tie-dyed T-shirts. Boston was dressed up like Raggedy Ann, or was it Andy? Another Johnny named Mike wandered around dressed like a shell-shocked World War I soldier with a camera.

That he never met Keis is probably a good thing, or the company might have filed an injunction to cease and desist this extended college caper. I wish I could think of someone from the UFO ghetto or maybe one of the birds in the Aviary who was Keis' equivalent. But there simply are not enough Keis characters in the world, then or now. And most likely fellow club members haven't met anyone like him since they scattered to do their life's work. Even though he started out all-American, even taking ROTC classes and once considering joining the Green Berets, Keis took a hard-left turn and, before long, became a hardcore hippie.

Before his "transfiguration:" Der Keis (center) on the Rugby field at St. John's University, Collegeville. (Photo: Dan Johnson)

He was an avid club attendee, the farthest out of the far out—plus a vanquishing, muscular rugby player, a talented drawer, and a practiced hash eater who rivaled the appetites of Fitz Hugh Ludlow, a lost 19th century American "drug writer." But Keis was also semi-trained as a survivalist who had maxed-out the Eagle Scouts' Nature Badge before he went to college and truly got his wings, an Eco Warrior before there were Eco Warriors. He was all that. Rumors of him eating a live frog during a first-year rugby practice were not put to rest when he broke the record for swallowing the most live goldfish during the freshmen talent show the first or second week of school. Actually, they were live minnows, since a good supply of goldfish could not be found on short notice. But Kies downed more than Guinness had on the record books for goldfish so he had that going for him too, all minnow-sized fish, gold or otherwise, being equal.

Perhaps his crowning achievement, however, came during a Spring Rites event during the club's last year on campus. For some reason, this particular sybarite celebration took place not at the chapel across the water but inland within one of the college's natural bowls behind the football field where the school later built a baseball field.

As the sun began to creep toward what was the horizon in that dug-out landscape, someone spotted a figure on a hill in the distance with shoulder-length hair and beard dressed in a white robe (or was it a bed sheet?) and carrying long sheaths of tasseled grass in each hand. And as the sun set in that precise spot, the figure in white extended his arms horizontally, his body forming a cross. The sun's rays brilliantly illuminated him as if it were a holy transfiguration, totally biblical. Down below the hill, the vision of the guy on the hill gave the rabble of Space Pen partiers pause.

Then someone in the crowd shouted, "It's Kies! It's Kies!"

Gasps and shrieks came from the horde as everyone turned toward the illuminated man. Then applause. And more applause and wild cheers for his exalted trippiness.

"I think everyone thought I was going to give the Sermon on the Mount after that," Keis admitted years later with a gleam in his eyes and a wide smile. He also confessed that it wasn't planned, he was just there when he noticed the sun going down behind him and seized—then suspended—the moment.

Years later, as I explored the UFO canon of both credible and crackpot writers, some key "supernatural" moments recorded in the Catholic faith and in other faith traditions were often reinterpreted as UFO events. The alleged appearance of the Virgin Mary at Lourdes, France, in 1858, is just one such event given to UFO revisionism. But many decades later—as rumors of the Vatican's interest in ETs (along with its fabled Advanced Technology Telescope atop Mount Graham in Arizona) reached a fevered pitch—one of our fellow Space Pen members would put a finer point on that aspect of the church and the outer limits (but you'll have to keep reading to discover which one). And the beat went on.

The club represented a piece of the countercultural zeitgeist, a time and a place, a cast, and a platform for active consciousness-raising, and idle hellraising too. But it also framed my own clumsy, juvenile odyssey into mind to test the inner limits.

Not merely content to derive pleasure or high strangeness from the mind-expanding contraband of that age, in my junior year I decided to take an interim Hatha Yoga class one very cold January, a time when most students vacated the campus for warmer destinations or self-made studies off-campus approved by their professors.

In an earlier chapter I related how Greer's remote-viewing mind projections to contact visitors reminded me of the time I tried to do the same in the Canadian Rockies to escape a deep heartbreak. As I said then, there was one other instance where his meditative technique held some resonance with me. This incident took place one night after having taken three-and-a-half weeks of notes full of historical and practical information about yoga and attempted to practice meditation in the lotus position on a daily basis, with direction from our teacher. Of course, this was decades before two-hundred dollar Lole Van Malli yoga pants were available and the practice became as trendy and mainstream as braised brussels sprouts with olive oil, garlic and bacon bits.

I vacated my room in 4th Bonnie Hall, then the outer-most dorm on campus, for the study lounge down the hall. It was empty, dark and quiet. My breathing technique had come along pretty well, and as I sat in the lounge, I was getting into a good meditative state. About twenty minutes into mediation, I felt like I was in deep, even allowing for the sounds of a closing door, the occasional burst of music, a TV and distant voices down the hallway. The sounds mingled with my mind's errant thoughts but did not distract. Then I felt my head emptying, detaching from it all.

Despite the fact that I hadn't given one hoot about UFOs or read any materials about them since I'd left for college, an image of a flying saucer aiming a beam of light at me suddenly flew into my mind's eye. I sensed that I was about to receive some kind of downloaded transmission via the beam, an inter-dimensional data dump from the Unknown, the Great Unconscious, the Galactic Federation, the mental memes made in my head. My eyes sprang open as my lotus position collapsed in fear and confusion. End result, I gave up meditation for the next twenty years until I relearned it in my work with CSETI to try and vector in the boys upstairs.

Even today, the episode makes no sense. Maybe none of this does, rationally. Only a crazy person would think an invisible saucer could transmit anything to the black awareness of the mind, to somebody just test-driving hatha yoga, right? Who did I think I was, some rube trying to stumble forward in the footsteps of Ram Das, aka Richard Alpert? The former Harvard professor and colleague of Tim Leary's gave up the lysergic chemistry of the West for the timeless mysticism of the East. But there it was, and here it still is, embedded in my memory along with all the other memory pictures from the period, flickering like glowing, magical embers before they burn out. Some things one never forgets, though. This is one of mine.

Sometimes, as I have related strange bits and often inexplicable pieces of my CSETI experiences to my old, now reformed college roomie GhoulDog (meaning he gets up on his own accord every morning to take on his substantial business interests and responsibilities out in South Dakota), he listens like a good friend should. He listens without prejudicial judgment or friendly derision. And often he still quotes his favorite part of *Desiderata*, perhaps to remind me that there are not answers or explanations to everything that we encounter.

"Hawk," he says with a cackle that is equal measure an utterance from an occasional trusted mentor and a somewhat skeptical brother, "Hawk, remember... 'Nurture strength of spirit to shield you in sudden misfortune. But do not distress yourself with dark imaginings. Many

fears are born of fatigue and loneliness. Beyond a wholesome disci-
pline, be gentle with yourself. You are a child of the universe no less
than the trees and the stars; you have a right to be here."'

CHAPTER SIX:
HYPNOTIZED IN THE LAND OF THE KACHINAS

The Hopi believe their ancestors came from the Pleiades, the place, or people they call Chuhu-kon, or those who cling together, a reference it seems to that tightly grouped starry cluster, as it appears to the naked eye.

—"Legends of the Star People," by David S. Lewis, *The Montana Pioneer*

I felt like I was at the crossroads of Kafka and Castaneda.

Actually, I was lying on the beige carpet in a hallway of my sister's house in Phoenix unable to move. Completely immobilized. Damn near paralyzed, it seemed. Helpless and in pain, I laid there slowly eating toast and an egg on a plate, breakfast fit for a rug rat. I ate for twenty minutes and then laid there another twenty minutes wishing I'd never made the trip, thinking that maybe I'd come a bridge too far—or at least an airplane ride too long—what with all the CSETI activities that had entered my life. Was this whole business patently absurd with a strangeness bordering on fable and or foolishness? Where indeed had this side hustle taken me as I searched my weird experiences, futilely looking for a rational explanation. And if that was not available, then for an irrational one I could live with?

As to what could be construed as the mystic-like trappings of everything to that point, was I on a path to investigate the UFO phenomenon *and* on the threshold of some shamanistic journey into multi-dimensional consciousness like Carlos Castaneda's? Or was I just caught up in a Kafkaesque crisis phase of my life? Castaneda was a doctor of anthropology at UCLA whose mysterious primary teacher was a Toltec descendant and Yaqui Indian named Don Juan Matus. He'd been described as a sorcerer from northern Mexico. However, I didn't have a ton of Castaneda coursing through my system, having only read one of his books, *The Fire Within*, although I read plenty about him in magazine stories and related literature at the height of the so-called counter-culture era.

I winced as I tried to crawl back toward bed. I waved off my youngest sibling, Marybeth, who stood in the kitchen forty-five-feet away washing the morning dishes and glancing over every few minutes to make sure she shouldn't try to help.

"I'll be okay, if I just lie here until the spasm stops and I can regain some strength," I told her "That's what I did at home when I collapsed. This is some kind of hospitality you have here in Phoenix, I tell ya!"

She laughed and I laughed. But laughing hurt, so I shut up. My back had gone out four days earlier in Minneapolis after a run around the lake without the dogs. Apparently, I hadn't stretched and now I was paying the consequence. Not good timing, as CSETI was about to launch the first "Ambassadors to the Stars" program near an old mining outpost that had been turned into an isolated getaway called Wickenburg about ninety miles away in the Arizona desert.

Howard (my Canada bro), Shari, Ron Russell from Denver, Steven Greer and another Steve, and Mary from Ashville—the whole inner core of CSETI—had prepared for the three-day training that included lectures during the day and CE-5 exercises under the stars each night. Dick Haines and Dr. Joe also joined in, along with forty-some people who had paid their fees and trekked across the country, plus a thirty-something couple from Germany, Hans and Greta, whom I'd met previously in Denver. I remembered Hans clearly because he had lobbied to slow down the pace of CSETI functions because between the daytime instruction and the nighttime work, which often lasted until two or three in the morning, he was just plain too tired.

When I tried to get out of my bed in Minneapolis, I fell to the floor twice, so I called Howard and Greer to tell them my chances of showing were dim. Howard encouraged me to rest and drink a lot of fluids. Steven said he'd send good thoughts my way. The night before my plane was to leave, I felt pretty good, so I packed my backpack and gathered my binoculars, the big light for signaling, a tape recorder, notepads and some Arizona clothes.

I hobbled off the plane, got to my sis' place and went to bed early, anticipating that I'd get a car in the morning and head out to the site. Instead, the only thing I got the next morning was breakfast for one on the floor and a heap of frustration. I called Howard and told him what had happened. He said maybe I'd rally, and "Oh, the sky is fantastic!"

I laid in bed and tried to read the UFO lit I'd brought along, probably Vallee again, who had written many books on the topic, each with a different thesis as to what the real UFO/ET deal might be—fairies, demonic presences, covert programs, real space visitors, or all of the above. But my reading just raised unsettled issues: What was the true nature of the phenomenon? Why had I experienced the non-linear events in the house, the pre-cognitive dream set in Boston, and the deep meditative yoga state "ambush" of consciousness back at the inception of the Space Pen Club?

The ancient Sanskrit Vedas talk of flying vimanas, sky-bound chariots of various eternal deities. Perhaps one had found me in my college dorm circa 1974 while I was in a righteous Hatha Yoga meditation. Yeah, that must have been it....

* * *

The next morning, I had enough lower-back strength to eat at a table with my kin. I'd decided to return home if I could change my ticket. Things felt too precarious to venture into the desert for a rigorous couple of days with my fellow saucer-seeking Earthlings.

I had selected a couple late-day departure times for my return and was just about to call the airline when Howard called from Wickenburg.

"How are you feeling?"

He didn't wait long enough for me tell him I was returning home.

"We're coming to get you!" Then Howard excitedly described the two women who would be assisting me, one a chiropractor and the other a "healer," and both part of the Ambassadors' event. They would be arriving in Don's big RV so there would be plenty of room to stretch out and be comfortable. I protested but to no avail. They'd be there within the hour.

Sure enough, Don's RV was big. I got comfortable on a long couch until we hit a bump and moved to a pile of blankets the ladies arranged on the floor. Much better.

The chiro (I can't recall her name) worked on me and I felt better as she finished. After chatting about how things were going, the healer casually went to work. She placed healing crystals on my backside as I lay flush against the floor. I was wary of these treatments. When I was heartsick prior to hiking in Montana, a similar "healer" had put a collection of "therapeutic rocks" along my spine to heal my energy and chakras, especially the heart. Rocks!

By the time we got to the mine site, I felt well enough to move on my own power. I thanked Don for the smooth ride and went into the main building. Howard greeted me and shared that both Greer and Steve, his helper, claimed they had seen a couple of swift-moving daylight discs yesterday streaking through some hills nearby. I was dubious. I had to be.

"What about last night?" I asked.

"Nothing really," Howard noted, "although our group, the one you'll be in tonight with me, kept seeing a light in the distance toward ground level. No one could be sure what it was."

"Probably just a car headlight on the road."

"I don't think so. There's nothing moving around here at night. I mean *nothing*!" Canada Bro explained how three groups in different locations all had been connected by walkie talkies around a large perimeter. There were enough people to allow each group to do its CSETI thing without disturbing the others. Shari was leading a group, Joe another, while Greer was in charge of ours.

Howard led me into a large room inside one of the buildings where people had gathered for the afternoon lecture. He introduced me to the assembled and the place burst into applause, while a few people shouted, "Welcome Marty!" Apparently, my name and rep as the PR guy had been put in play well before I was able to get out of bed on my own. Slightly embarrassed, I thanked everyone for the warm greeting and took my seat.

After the lecture, night fell fast. The desert quickly gives up daylight, as if it is of no value. Greer's walkie talkie was cranked up loud enough so that most in our group could hear him as we walked toward our patch of dirt.

Joe radioed that his group was getting a slow start. "Ah, one of our guys fell into a cactus, so we are checking him out."

"Roger," Greer replied. "Is he okay? Make sure he's okay and you get all the needles out. Who was it?"

I won't say who it was, but this same individual had been exhibiting high anxiety all day according to Dr. UFO, which Howard confirmed. He was fairly well known too, with connections to former President Jimmy Carter, who'd had his own well-publicized UFO sighting, which Greer later leveraged in Project Starlight. Suffice it to say, Cactus Man went on to write his own book about remote viewing and set up a team of remote viewers to forecast future events for clients. But for now, his status was prickly and perplexing.

Then Shari clicked in from an area away from Joe's group and twice as far from us.

"I thought I should let you know, there're some other people out here near us, wearing something like fruit and odd things on their heads, like feathers or ornaments, I can't see them that well." She gave a few other details, but my first thought was that she was describing Kachinas, Hopi spirits that played an important ritualistic role in the lives of the Hopi, Zuni and other tribes in the desert Southwest.

Or perhaps Shari and her star seekers had seen some local First Nation people out to perform a ritual or practice something at night dressed in ceremonial costume. But why hadn't anyone heard car doors closing or footsteps approaching as our groups fanned out across the desert floor? Later, when searching for more information about kachinas, I browsed reliable sources but one line in a Wikipedia entry jumped out at me: "*There are a number of kachinas that represent space and time in the Zuni religion.*" Maybe the visitors CSETI sought in the heavens already had been among us on the ground. Or maybe I was grabbing at the long straws and trying to connect dots that didn't exist. Regardless of who or what they were, no more information ever came in about them as the night at Wickenburg played out over the next five hours.

A desert chill set it in as our group started its Coherent Thought Sequencing (CTS) process with light signalers a short distance away armed like sentries with powerful search lights and CSETI tones playing on a tape recorder. After about forty minutes of sky watching, Dick Haines and I were chatting informally when we were interrupted by the sound of Joe on the walkie talkie saying that they were tracking a faint light high above their group at an eleven o'clock position. Everyone in our group whipped their binoculars toward the sky. Shari chimed in that they could faintly make it out.

Greer cautioned everyone to remain alert and aware. Dick and I agreed that the light was too distant and faint to discern what it might be, but it wasn't an aircraft and didn't seem like a satellite given the direction it moved. Yet maybe it was, and no one had noticed this trajectory the night before. The light slowly crawled across the inky expanse.

"We're still tracking it," Joe radioed in. "It could be for real."

Greer followed it with his binoculars, then radioed with the authority of a military commander, "It's a UFO. Repeat. I declare this is a UFO. Do you copy?" Standing far enough away from our leader that he couldn't hear us, Dick and I burst into laughter. We both thought the object was too far away to declare it to be anything. It certainly was not the classic "UFO craft" we were looking for. Was it?

"In another life, I think Steven must have been an officer in the military," I joked. Dick nodded in agreement, his brushy moustache bouncing as he laughed. But as that pinprick of light faded from view and the radios fell silent again, we both spotted a buttery yellow light—

much more prominent and likely just two or three miles away and lower to the ground. The light started to move slowly from the south. Soon, most of our group were watching it. Light signalers flashed in sequence try to get a response. Nothing.

They flashed again, with Steve leading the way. Nothing again.

"What do you think that is?" I asked Dick. "I can't make out any structure."

"I really don't know what it is," he replied, observing it with his binoculars. He was taking this one seriously. But then it simply faded to black.

Howard walked over to us from the tip of our staked-out territory and addressed Haines. "Well, doctor?"

"I don't know, Howard—I don't know."

Howard asked how I was doing, and I said I was OK but needed to stretch my back out.

He led me to a tent, a kind of safe house away from the group activity and opened its flap. "Just yell if you need anything," he said as he moved away. I stumbled inside and saw there was another occupant. I dimmed my flashlight so it wouldn't disturb whoever was in there.

"Oh Mar-tcc," a voice said with a slight German accent. "Come in, come in. Just taking a break."

"Hello Hans," I smiled. Poor Hans, all tuckered out before midnight.

After stretching out for twenty minutes and massaging my lower back with the end of my flashlight, I told Hans to sleep tight and we would wake him if anything crazy started. He laughed and waved me out.

* * *

Back out in the dark desert landscape, Ron Russell strolled over to where a few of us including Greer, Canada Bro, and Haines were watching the sky and making idle conversation.

"The light's back again," said Ron. Howard nudged me as if to say, "This is what we observed last night."

We walked out beyond the signalers to remove any interference from their hand-held light sabers. Over a hundred yards ahead, a silver light glistened. It looked like part of an illuminated stadium girder. At first it appeared pixelated, then momentarily lost its brightness only to regain it, as if something might be materializing. There is such a thing as a night mirage, but usually it is associated with an external light source to illuminate it. Was it a classic Fata Magana?

"I'm going to it," Ron said after we watched it for about five minutes. After some strategic planning and a handoff of his walkie talkie, the space artist from Denver set off for the glowing girder that seemed to rise up from the sandy desert floor. We watched until he and then his flashlight halo disappeared. The luminous girder faded in and out and then went dark. We looked at each other quietly.

"Can anyone see anything in their binocs?" Howard asked.

No, too dark.

Then we began to see the small oval of light from Ron's flashlight moving through the darkness. In a couple minutes, he was back.

"There's nothing there," he said. "Not a trace. No light. I must have walked two hundred yards and I never got within reach of it, and then it went dark. I couldn't even really locate where it was, let alone what it was. But there's a helluva lot of cactus out there! Man!"

We laughed and someone joked about the mishap Cactus Man had had earlier in the evening. We walked back to the bigger group and shared the non-news. A few people seemed crestfallen. Others were growing tired and starting to pack it in. It was already one in the morning and Greer had pleasantly released from duty anyone who wanted to retire if they hadn't already.

Haines was about to set off for his room, which was also Howard's and my room. We helped each other pack up our things. As we did, I started to tell him that I had done a little research into hypnogogic experiences and how it didn't seem to fit what I had seen in my room—those five solid red orbs, those cherry bomb gooba-gooba mind zoomers that threw my being off its gyroscope. I wondered if it might involve something else.

"Like what?" Haines replied.

"Well, I dunno," I said, "but I want, you know, a second opinion."

Howard laughed at that suggestion as he grabbed my backpack of CSETI stuff to carry.

Dick started walking up the trail. He turned and asked, "Should I hypnotize you and explore it that way?"

"Uh, sure. I mean, I think so." I was suddenly alarmed and excited by the prospect, knowing the good doctor had worked with many alleged abductees using hypnosis. Maybe this would put an end to the mysteries. "When?"

"Right now. I'll meet you in the room. You shouldn't be that hard to hypnotize," he declared.

Was he saying I was a "suggestive," a light touch, a pushover? Okay, maybe I was. Before I could protest, he walked away at a brisk pace toward the buildings in the distance. We could see others down the way filing in from their groups as well, or at least we could see their flashlights.

Out in the first group location, just Greer, Howard and I remained in desert, the pitch-black night owning us. We started walking silently when all three of us noticed odd, ground-lit, plantlike things to our left, sporadically lighting up about twenty yards away. What the hell?

"Should we investigate?" Howard asked, flashing his light at one. It reminded me of a scene in an early *Star Wars* movie where the plants suddenly illuminate.

"No," Greer said sternly. I couldn't tell if he was too tired to bother any more or if he had already figured out what the strange things were. Uncharacteristically, we walked away from more high strangeness in low places. But the night in the land of the kachinas wasn't over quite yet.

* * *

Howard flopped onto his bed and Haines positioned himself about twenty feet from mine. We flipped on our respective tape recorders.

"I should have asked if you mind if I sit in," Howard said, suppressing a yawn.

Although apprehensive about what I might say or do if hypnotized, I approved his presence. The induction part seemed to be fairly textbook: Relax, take deep breaths evenly in and out, and focus on the sound of Haines' voice. Barely two minutes into the ordeal, a startling image appeared in my mind's eye. I ignored it and tried to clear my head, listening intently to Haines' voice.

The doctor continued, telling me to imagine going into a deep place of comfort and relaxation. He added that nothing that transpired would cause harm but would take place at a safe distance.

"Are you doing okay?" he asked gently. Then the image appeared again—three tubular-looking life forms staring at me, their small heads and narrow eyes fixated on my consciousness. The one in the middle kinda looked pissed.

"I'm doing fine," I replied. "But I've got to tell you that I've been seeing strange images of these three things—beings or something—in my mind's eye, ever since we started the hypnosis." Dick calmly asked me to describe them, and I did.

"What do you think they want?" he asked me.

"I get the feeling they don't want me to talk about it."

The doc assured me they were harmless and would not interrupt again. We continued and these slender looking forms, which reminded me of Ren and Stimpy cartoon characters, seemed to fade away. He asked me to imagine that my right arm could float and would slowly rise up to prove it.

Seconds later, my right arm slowly climbed into the air. The room was only lit by a small deskside lamp near Haines' bed. And it was very silent, until… Suddenly, I heard Howard snoring. I thought this was funny, but the occurrence didn't break what seemed to be a moderate state of hypnosis. I had always imagined that hypnosis would block out the "real world" or real-time activities like my compadre falling into slumberland. But it didn't.

Dr. Richard Haines, Research Scientist at NASA AMES; Chief Scientist at NARCAP (National Aviation Reporting Center on Anomalous Phenomena); CSETI advisor; my Arizona Hypnotist

He had my zenith: **Canada Bro, Howard** Schachter twenty-eight years later.
(Photo: Rachael Schachter)

For the next half-hour or so, Haines took me through a series of questions. The early ones focused on my youth when I may have met "people or strangers who were different." Nothing really clicked. He moved on, probing more recent times, including what was going on in my bedroom the past few months with the lights and strange sounds.

This triggered heavier breathing on my part and a good deal of avoidance. I couldn't or didn't want to articulate what had happened. Maybe I didn't know the answers. Or maybe I didn't want to know the answers. Haines sensed the conflict and moved on.

"Let's talk about those small red objects in your room." He asked me to describe them again and wondered if I knew what they were.

"I dunno, some kind of measuring thing or tool."

"Oh. Why do you say that?!"

"I don't know, just guessing maybe." My breathing got labored again and the hypnotist said we would return to those "things" later. He took me back to that sighting with my friends in high school outside the gymnasium where we all saw a white object "down by the agricultural office out on the country road nearby." I talked about it in rather prosaic terms and heard Howard rustling in his bed, awake now and listening.

"What do your buddies think it is?"

"We all think it's some kind of UFO, like the ones we'd heard about on the news all week. My best friend Jim—all of us think that."

"Well, what does Jim say about it?"

Without missing a beat, a long-lost memory surfaced, and I said, "It's not like the one we saw in the park."

Bingo!

Haines asked what I meant, but I seriously didn't know. It's as if a fragment of the past had mysteriously risen from my unconscious but without any context. We tried to return to the more recent events in my home, but we were both tired and the hour was late. He wrapped up the session saying I would recall it all. He also shared a personal password so that if he hypnotized me again, I would go under more quickly.

Slowly, I felt as if I was coming up from underwater after a dive into a pool. In my mind's eye, I saw a large white orb and then a purple one, both shaped like moons and each softly abutting the other. And I felt extremely at peace.

As we prepared for bed, Howard said he would share his thoughts with me in the morning on the ride back to Phoenix. Dick said he thought it had gone well, even if we never reached any understanding about the five cherry pits in the bedroom, then added, "I seriously suggest that you call your friend Jim when you get home and talk about 'the one in the park.'"

I assured him I would.

A brief closing ceremony was held the next morning. A young woman played a lovely violin piece. A few people wept. Dr. Greer encouraged people to return to their communities and set up Working Groups to continue the CE-5 work. With that, the first Ambassadors to the Stars program came to a kumbaya close.

I rode back to Dodge with Howard and another participant. I had the whole backseat to myself and sprawled out to get comfortable and safeguard my lower back. Canada Bro said he thought the night session had gone well and laughed when I asked how would he know? "You slept through most of it!" I said.

"Some," he said, "some. And listen, I know you didn't like *Communion*, the movie. But I really think you need to read the book. Read Whitley's book, because it will illuminate some of the things you said in hypnosis and some of the things you are wrestling with." He mentioned Whitley Strieber, the book's author, like he was a close friend.

"Oh, and don't forget to call your old best friend Jim about the park. Then call me." Good old Canada Guy, another brother from the mother planet. He had my zenith.

CHAPTER SEVEN:
UNDER THE VOLCANO WITH CBS'S *48 HOURS*,
GIVE OR TAKE A DAY OR TWO

> For five years [early in the 20th century], the editors of *Scientific American* refused to acknowledge the aviation achievements of the Wright brothers because the magazine had been told by trusted authorities that manned, heavier-than-air flight was a scientific impossibility. To *Scientific American*, the claim of powered flight was simply a ridiculous hoax. As proof, the magazine's editors cited the lack of press coverage of the Wright Brothers activities. It was a classic case of the blind leading the blind.

> –Terry Hansen, *The Missing Times: News Media Complicity in the UFO Cover-up"* (Xlibris Corporation, copyright 2000, www.Xlibris.com)

When Susan asked at the airport how the trip was, I cut to the heart of it. "I got hypnotized." I quickly explained why and touched on the weird stuff we'd seen in the night desert, adding, "I've got to call Jim!" Through the years since this unexpected journey had begun, Susan had tolerated the adventure, the kookiness of it all and the information I shared from books that might put a simple framework around it. Truthfully, though, it was a complex riddle and neither of us was fully prepared to deal with it. She had expressed concern that maybe I was moving too fast downstream with CSETI, giving too much time without any monetary benefit, although my freelance work was steady, and the org was paying my travel and office expenses incurred on its behalf.

"A long time ago, I worried I'd get involved with someone and they'd suddenly turn into a Jesus freak or something," she said. "I hope this isn't the case here. I hope this isn't a cult or something." I tried to assure her that my part-time cynicism made me cult-proof and that, while Greer did attract some individuals whose devotion to him and the organization were borderline zealous, this was not the case for me. (Nonetheless, a few years later, CSETI would be listed as "a UFO cult" by one of the alphabet-soup intel agencies, most likely to discredit it.) As the millennium approached, ABC News erroneously—and inexcusably—included CSETI in its list of millennialist cults posted on its website, including everything from a secretive Japanese neo-Nazi group called Sukyo Mahikari and Elohim City (with ties to alleged Oklahoma City bomber Timothy McVeigh) to several other Christian-based groups: Among them The House of Yahweh and "Concerned Christians," and something else called the Order of the Solar Temple, an apparent suicide cult with rumored gunrunning and money laundering activities ! Gaaaak!

I served Greer and company out of a deep sense that this "visionary" and experimental mission, built on the emerging science of consciousness—a field that was just beginning to come into its own—seemed viable. And I had a firm sense that the UFO issue was a well-kept national security secret, and that most of what the government and media said about it was dubious, if not an outright sham. I'd seen such obfuscations with the Vietnam War and the Pentagon Papers, the civil rights movement, the testing of the atomic bomb on soldiers and radiation tests on American citizens. So, I got a pass from her. For the moment.

My old friend Jim was intrigued when I rang him up that day. I said, "I need you to rack your memory cells about something that happened—or may have happened—in the park behind your house." I explained how Haines had taken me under to explore the strange incidents—CSETI or otherwise.

Ever since getting involved, I had been conveying little updates on our minor teenage obsession to Zod at lunch visits or during extended phone calls. I told him that the hypnotist was aware of our sighting outside our high school long ago and of the more recent paranormal events in my Minneapolis house. When I mentioned what he said under hypnosis—"It's not like the one we saw in the park."—I heard him get excited. "Oh yeah, I know exactly what you're talking about!"

For the next five minutes he continued in very precise detail about how, during the same week we had seen the white object to the west of the school, he and I had also encountered a small reddish object at eye level near his house in Rocky Butte Park while making our way one night for a student council meeting at school.

As he talked, I slowly began to remember the scene—the red, ping-pong-ball-sized orb seemed to fly down toward us from the top of the butte and then hang in the air about ten feet away. It made no sound—it just seemed fixated on us.

"What do you think it was?" I asked.

"I don't know," he replied, breaking into a half-hearted chuckle, "but the first thing you said was, 'It's the devil,' 'cuz it was glowing red, and we're good Catholic boys, and we both kinda laughed." The minute he said, "It's the devil," I regained near-total recall of the event and told him so. The intruding object had come very rapidly toward us with intention, as if confronting us.

Then my memory stalled. "Well, what did we do?" I asked.

"Ah, here's where my memory peters out too," Zod confessed. "We either went back to my parents' place [about a block-and-a-half via the snow-covered, unpaved park road] or we went ahead to school. I mean, we were student council officers. We had to be there. Can you remember it?"

I was still blank. I assume we went to school and the thing disappeared. If we did go back to his house, I think his parents might have asked us why we were back so early and we would have had a conversation about the experience in the park.

196

Or was there a third scenario with the red dot that neither of us remembers for whatever reason?

In the ensuing years, I have often wondered if "the red one in the park" was somehow related to "the five red ones in the bedroom." They were the same size and color and had movement—at least two of the five did in my bedroom before I blacked out and woke up the next day with a soul-scarred mind and body malaise. So now I had one more jigsaw puzzle piece and it did not complete the picture.

As the second year of my CSETI participation rolled around in 1992, I continued to do whatever was required to garner coverage for the group and plan for other Ambassadors events. I also kept up with my local CSETI team—ol' Jessie, Combover Bob, Young Blue Eyes and occasionally a few others—although I made a point of not riding to our sites with Jessie. His old-man driving—hitting the gas hard, then the brakes, then the gas harder again—made me car sick.

I kept in touch with many Space Pen Club friends, attending our 15th college reunion and beginning to communicate with a few on something called email over a noisy dial-up connection. I look back at the evolution of communication tools in my lifetime and wonder, from simple pen and pencil to typing on an old, thirty-five-pound Royal that I christened the Orbit Express (pasted on top with a decal found in box of Cracker Jacks), to Space Pens, to floppy discs, to the experimental psi attempts at remote viewing and remote communicating. Could tools to enhance telepathic communication be next?

A few Space Pen buddies at the reunion had heard about my UFO interests and engaged on the topic. One, Handsome Harley, asked me in a loud, pot smoke-filled St. Cloud hotel room if there was anything to it and what should he read? Over a boombox blasting out Dead tunes, I tried to explain about the Roswell case. We shouted at each other trying to be heard.

Another, John P., whom I had worked with on the college grounds crew, later asked if I was still writing anything. Now a medical doctor, he was aware of my coverage of pop culture in the Twin Cities. Before

I could even answer, he opined, "I hope you aren't writing about any of that flying saucer shit!"

The next day on campus before an afternoon picnic, I sat in a car with the Club's High Priestess, Big Mary E, waiting for some fellow classmates. She was beautiful as ever—hardly a thing about her had changed except that she was married now, like many. Even her brown hair was the same, hanging just off her strong, broad shoulders an inch or two. The curious, mischievous look in her light-filled eyes was still there, along with that hearty, dusky laugh that came from deep in her chest. She too had heard a little about my UFO interests, and she was eager to share the sighting she'd had in Israel while living in a kibbutz.

She described how a distant white object seemed to leap across the sky from point A to point B and then to another place in the sky with little effort. This display went on for at least a half hour, she said. *Of course, she would have had a sighting!* I thought quietly as she continued her brief account. She had everything.

"I'm sure it was one of *them*," she said, laughing.

"Sure sounds like it," I replied.

"The world's full of some crazy strange shit, huh?" Then she looked around for our compadres so we could head to a bar. "Where are those effin' guys anyway?!"

* * *

While the world kept spinning, I flew down for a CSETI planning meeting in Asheville with the key leadership team. A videotape surfaced at the end of a long day, *Messengers of Destiny*, produced by a ufologist and filmmaker named Lee Elders. While the tape suffered from a cheesy new-agey soundtrack like a lot of the work produced in the ghetto and tried to tie the mass of sightings in Mexico during the total eclipse in 1991 to ancient Mayan prophecy, the footage was astounding, especially of numerous daylight discs, which was much rarer than night objects and often more clearly identifiable as true, anomalous aerial phenomena.

"Wait until you see this!" said Barbie Taylor from California, another early CSETI member in the field of psychology, as she slipped the tape into the VCR. An Amazon review I found many years later of *Messengers* did a tidy job of summarizing it right down to the historical backdrop of the total eclipse:

> "In 1991 a number of (unrelated) people obtained chance footage of an unidentified aerial object hovering over Mexico City, while they were filming a solar eclipse. Much of the footage came to light when the Mexican version of 60 MINUTES canvassed their viewers to check their tapes and forward anything remarkable to the show. Subsequently, some 2,000 tapes were submitted during the time when these videos were produced (and reportedly some 5,000 to date).

> "Most of the shots are of extremely clear daylight discs, some of which are seen to be metallic and rotating on their axis. A set of "A-B" comparison videos [four as I recall], are showcased next to one another, then compared by an analyst. A propulsion expert reviewed some of the footage [in Messengers], exclaiming that these were the best UFO films that he had seen. There were some other shots from around the world, which appeared to show the same structured object. Fascinating! Some memorable UFO clips presented are: 1) an object that seems to be performing a "hyper-jump" 2) near misses with commercial jet aircraft 3) a chase by Mexican fighter aircraft as shot by a local TV news team 4) a night shot of the so-called stair-step maneuver 5) a "swarm" of objects in the sky 6) a cylindrical object a mile or so long dispatching objects... [the list goes on].

"Some of the oddest footage shows objects darting in and out among the clouds which reacted as though they knew they were being filmed and made attempts to both hide and 'tease.' Very weird and quite alarming, especially when one thinks of the ramifications. This footage was quite creepy to see, as was the clip of the large cylindrical object. Of interest is that the footage was shot while computers were in their infancy, thus practically eliminating a clever hoax."

What the reviewer didn't say was that Jamie Masson, the host of the Mexican version of *60 Minutes* called *60 Minutos* was so taken with the collection of tapes and the fact that a major "UFO wave" was taking place over Mexico City that he eventually left his position to begin reporting almost exclusively on what the Mexican media called "Los Ovnis," the Unknowns. I thought it sounded like a good name for a band. Masson eventually went totally ghetto, appearing at UFO events and conferences and becoming one of the more trusted authorities in the field.

Halfway through watching the tape, Greer paused it and said CSETI had to activate its Rapid Mobile Investigative Team (RMIT) as soon as possible. Barb said that as far she knew, the "wave" was still going on, especially in the volcano zone about eighty miles southwest of Mexico City near Puebla. This really sent the juice through us.

Consisting of four to five seasoned members, an RMIT would deploy to UFO hot spots like those in Mexico, or to crop circle country in England and other places. I knew that as a relative newcomer I would not be making that run south of the border. So as Dr. Joe and Sheri checked their calendars and Barbie began looking for Mexican contacts in her notes, I went off to bed.

About ten days later the team took off for the *zono volcano,* where twin volcanos Mt. Popocatepetl and Iztaccíhuatl lay waiting for them like giants—one sleeping, one awake—in the great Valley of Mexico, a land mass lying atop an ancient lake bed. Popo, the active, smoldering mountain and highest peak in the country, and Izty, the dormant one, are part of at least two mythological stories in Aztec culture not dissimilar from the Western world's stories of gods or those in First Nation stories from the gone, gone, gone past.

Mt. Popo: A highly active volcano and UFO hotspot 43 miles from Mexico City.

I was eager to hear about the Mexico RMIT results but went back to my business in Minnesota and started reading Strieber's *Communion* book as Howard had recommended. I thought a more fitting title would have been *Confession*, but it was indeed better than the film. I also decided to investigate more of the items Dr. Joe had sent in his care package, from whence Martin Cannon's alternative theory of alien abductions came. There was an obscure feature-length film I decided to watch later and a couple of *Sightings* tapes from a TV show in the early '90s on paranormal activity that featured numerous UFO stories. *Sightings* first aired on Fox, then moved to the SyFy Channel for a five-year run until 1997, about the time I slowly started to uncouple from CSETI.

Joe had left a note on one of the VCR tapes about Professor John Salter, Jr., and his son, John III. The pair had gotten "lost" or turned around somehow on a back road in Wisconsin on a car trip south from Grand Forks, North Dakota, where the elder Salter—who had been very active in the civil rights movement, like Betty and Barney Hill—was a professor of Sociology at the University of North Dakota (UND). UND was a place I knew well from attending several high school debate and speech tournaments in the dead of winter near the Canadian border where the land was table-top flat, where B-52 bombers from a nearby Air Force base would fly right over your car in the middle of the day and rattle everything around it for miles, and where the bloody northwest wind blew all the time.

Joe's note read. "You've got to watch this one, a positive encounter NOT recalled under hypnosis!" I asked Susan if she wanted to watch it with me in our bedroom. She suddenly started kneading her hands and grew anxious.

"Um, I, I, I don't think so, I'll just watch something else downstairs." More handwringing. "Maybe later." She exited abruptly as I started the show. Salter's account was mesmerizing and indicated he'd had several CE-4 encounters in his lifetime that altered his body chemistry and boosted his immune system. Years later I read his comments posted on what appeared to be his website (hunterbear.com) to see if his story or reaction to it had changed. It had not. If anything, the time between the incident in March 1988, the full written account of it in 1989, and his retrospective web post in 2011 had crystallized the encounter details and acutely sharpened his analysis of what had transpired with "the boys upstairs."

The incident began inside Salter's Ford pickup with both father and son suddenly experiencing amnesia while driving at twilight, "not unconsciousness…. When I think about what came immediately after that, I sometimes get waves of strange, 'electrical-like' sensations—vibrant chills—throughout my body." John III talks of "spooky feelings.'" And this was the point of interception and close encounter—"very close!"

Over time, they both gradually recalled what happened to them through conscious recall and in dreams as if their wired consciousness were protecting them from the dramatic episode. The next morning, they again saw the craft they had been allegedly taken to as it shot into the sky on another secluded section of road as if the visitors were saying, "Don't forget what happened."

Other highlights from the report about the on-board incident and the father's later thoughts on the topic include:

- "It is almost dark. Completely at ease, I can see two or three small humanoid figures climbing up on the back bumper, looking at our gear in the back of the truck. Up closer, they are four to four and one-half feet tall, thin bodies and thin limbs—but comparatively large heads and conspicuously large, quasi-slanted eyes. There are several of these small people—perhaps six or seven—and a taller humanoid figure, almost as tall as I (six feet) and not as proportionately thin as the others. His features are more, as we would use the term, "human"—and he may well be a mixed-blood. Whatever clothing type they're wearing, it's tightly fitting and, to us at this point in recall, non-descript. Our communication with them is more than thought-impressionistic; it's telepathically specific."

- "John III sits down. Three of the small humanoids gather around, viewing him with as much fascination as he does them. Everyone is very pleasant. The tall humanoid is attached to us in a special fashion and is obviously our key liaison. Now we are walking through the darkening woods, up a ravine and over a small ridge, to the UFO which is in a rather secluded clearing, some distance from the pickup. I stumble and fall backward but am immediately cushioned by a (telekinetic?) force. Very, very gently, several of the humanoids reach for me and pull me to my feet."

- "Throughout this entire, still continuing recall process of mine is the clear, persistent definite sense of a brightly lighted room—a kind of white light—and a deep-blue glowing panel. An implant is placed very carefully up into my right nostril and well beyond. There is a strong sense that the last time this happened to me was a long time ago, when I was John III's age, in 1957. There is now an injection into my neck, at the thyroid area; and then an injection into my upper, central chest (thymus gland). John III's face is scanned very thoroughly with a 'flashlight' type instrument whose head is so soft that it melds into the contours of his face; special attention is given to his chin and jaw area. Then we are out in the open again."

- "The feeling is downright powerful that the meeting has gone very well indeed from everyone's standpoint. Our tall humanoid friend walks with me back through the woods to the pickup. He is carrying some sort of light, obviously for our benefit. John III is slightly ahead of us. I believe the smaller humanoids have remained with the UFO. John III goes into the passenger side of the pickup, closing the door. I feel an extremely strong, poignant sense of farewell toward the tall figure, sensing equally strong reciprocity. (His emotional and intellectual reactions are like ours: sharp intelligence, good-natured, smiled a great deal, eager, very interested in things and sad—very sad—at parting. Basically, I think all of this holds true for the smaller people.) The tall figure and I tell each other (and John III is included) that *we will see one another again in another place, in another time.* Now, John III and I are by ourselves in the pickup. We wait. Very shortly from his window, John III watches the UFO rise and, brightly lighted, move diagonally up into the dark clouds and beyond."

- "I believe these encounters are specifically selective (anything except random) and, as such, necessitate among other things a good deal of careful planning and maneuvering by the humanoids. I do believe that, across the Creation, there are certain universals: e.g., principles of logic, scientific methodology, and the concerns of bureaucrats about cost and time factors. It probably took several days and a good many humanoid-hours to set up and implement the 1 1/2-hour meeting with John III and myself on March 20, 1988. I believe these are extraterrestrial persons similar to ourselves and perhaps even related in some intriguing fashion or at least the results of a parallel evolutionary course. They are solid and physical and "all-around" tangible entities, sharply intelligent (as one would assume trained astronauts and scientists and perhaps even professors to be), and their range of emotions is comparable to ours. I categorically do not see them as angels/devils/psychic manifestations."

- "Their actions (motivations and effects and related factors) are quite positive. While I think it's possible that there may be some 'experimentation' involved, I think this is ethically and honorably done—and to good ends. However, I believe the basic thrusts focus on helping some of us (directly) 'keep on keeping on' in the business of edging humanity closer and closer to the Sun—figuratively speaking and sensitizing humanity with respect to the relatively nearby presence of other forms of intelligent life."

- "New as I consciously am to the UFO situation, it may seem more than a little presumptuous for me to (paraphrasing, I believe, Koestler's Ivanov in *Darkness at Noon*) point out that there are some strange terrestrial birds in the trees of 'ufology.' Without getting shrill about it and recognizing that there can be 'reasonable differences of opinion between reasonable people' (as I was reminded occasionally a long time ago and still am from time to time), I do believe that the 'gloom and doom' people in UFO research are often either downright paranoid, motivated by commercial con-

205

siderations, or ideologically endeavoring to resurrect a new version of the Red Scare (but I don't think they'll be able to do *that*)."

The positive narrative sounded like one Greer could have written or incorporated into CSETI's instruction manual, it had so many of the shared affirmative beliefs about ET—at least the ones that Salter had encountered. In 1993, though, Greer was busy with the RMIT outside Puebla, in a little oasis forty minutes away called Metepec, closer to Popo and Itzy. I had gotten bits and pieces from Emily Greer, who had talked to her husband while he was down there—silver discs seen during daylight, dramatic stories told by the locals, beautiful terrain under the volcano. I was skeptical; I had to be. But I watched *Messengers of Destiny* again with a more critical eye and gave the crew the benefit of the doubt.

When the RMIT members got back to the states I heard confirmation of all the above and then some. Joe was the most excited. They had seen a low-flying, silent, large, triangular-shaped craft at night during one of their CTS exercises. Joe said it was massive, floating over the valley with the volcanos in background.

Could it have been a stealth military craft of some kind?

"I don't know. But it's the first thing I think of in the morning when I get up now, and the last thing I think of before I go to bed at night," Joe rhapsodized. Clearly, they had gotten an eyeful of something.

Sheri relayed how two families who could speak fairly good English had related how their young children were playing on the lowest slopes of Popo one day when they'd met two humanoids about their same height. The children thought they were other kids at first until they realized the strangers on the slope had very big eyes, no real mouth and were communicating telepathically.

One humanoid told them that the Earth's environment was in danger and there was going to be a war in New York City, although the child's mother admitted her kid didn't know what New York City was or how you could talk with your mind like they did! When I shared the account with Susan later, she laughed and said, "You don't need ETs to know the environment's in trouble." But when 9/11 hit eight years later, I wondered if that event was what the alleged small strangers in the ancient valley had conveyed to the children in this hardscrabble rural place.

Greer's fascinating account of that trip, the lucid dreams he'd had before traveling and what might be transpiring with the sightings and the volcano are well detailed in an RMIT report on CSETI's website. It is worth reading in its entirety. But some of its more salient and insightful moments are worth including here. Greer writes:

> "There is speculation that the intense presence of ETS in the area is related to this recent upsurge in Mt. Popo's activity. Some believe the Extraterrestrial people are monitoring the situation and may even be involved in a project to somehow reduce the force of any future eruption. I must admit that both our retrospective survey of past sightings and our own real-time observations lead me to conclude that the Extraterrestrials are there for reasons related to the volcano's recent increase in activity. To precisely what end remains to be discovered. Even during our brief stay in the area, we observed an increase in the steam and smoke coming from Popo, and given our very close proximity to it, I wondered more than once if my 'last will and testament' was in good order! Certainly, we discussed an evacuation plan of our own but luckily never had to use it. The spacecraft which have been seen and videotaped from a distance are of two types:

> "(1) A large, triangular craft with a light at each apex and a red light in the center, very similar to those seen in Russia and Belgium: These are 300-

800 feet in diameter, and appear at night, usually fairly late, in the areas adjacent to the volcanoes.

"(2) The second type is a silver disc, probably 20-30 feet in diameter, seen at night and during the day time. Multiple daylight videotapes of these exist.

"Then, at 11:45 pm, a CE-5 of profound significance occurred. The entire group was performing CTS, and I was in a state aware only of 'one mind.' Suddenly, I sensed—knew—to sit up and look to my right, and there it was: a large amber craft moving obliquely away from us in the northwest sky. My immediate sense was that it was looking for us, that it was over the area of the pyramid-shaped mountain and the field of the eagle cloud. I immediately notified the team saying: '*This is it - this is the real thing!*' With both CTS and powerful lights, we signaled for the spacecraft to come over to our location. IMMEDI-ATELY, it turned off its present course, and moved directly towards us. Initially, the spacecraft was 2-5 miles away, but as it silently glided towards us it came within 1500-3000 feet, and only 200-500 feet in the air! We immediately realized the historic significance of this event: A team of humans had consciously and intentionally vectored a spacecraft into a research area. It was clearly responding by changing course and coming directly to us, now in an apparent landing approach, or at least landing approach simulation.

"By now the exact shape of the ETS could be seen—it was a huge 300-900-foot diameter trian-gular-shaped structured craft, with a light on the underside at each apex and a reddish glowing light in the very center on the underside. This was no vague distant light in the sky, but a large craft with technological lights. We noted that even though the wind was coming from its direction, no sound was heard whatsoever!

"The excitement, if not astonishment, of the team was obvious, and yet all performed beautifully in the coming moments. Jeff moved the video camera to the adjacent field and set out our portable landing strobe lights - indicating to the E.T.s that we welcomed a landing, should this be safe and feasible for them. The rest of the team prepared for boarding and I sent signals with the high-powered light. The spacecraft made a sweeping arc, approximately 180 degrees, and then came straight towards us in an apparent landing approach. As I signaled to it, it returned by illuminating large and powerful lights on the now 'front' antero-grade of the triangular craft.

"It descended to 200-300 feet, coming straight towards us, and as it did so, it greatly increased the luminosity of the front lights, as if signaling to land. We could also see a small 'scout ship,' red-orange in color, floating alongside and behind the large triangle."

Ultimately, the craft did not land, and all the team's video and photographic equipment failed during the encounter, even Sheri's Instamatic camera. Of course, skeptics, debunkers and Greer haters can pile on here with their rants about the convenient failure of the equipment and why should we believe Greer's written account. Nonetheless, the rest of the events that night bear repeating:

"About the time Jeff tried to film the spacecraft, it aborted its landing approach, turned to our left (east-northeast), and began moving away from the site. However, in a beautiful gesture of continued communication, the receding spacecraft illuminated its retrograde lights and clearly, unequivocally signaled with us as we flashed our lights to it. It was a lovely and poignant 'good-bye.' In one to three minutes, it dipped below a nearby ridge, and was not seen again at close range that night."

Later, Greer asks in his report:

"Why did the cameras fail just at that moment, when they worked fine before AND after the event? Was this an inadvertent side-effect of their energy and propulsion systems on our electronics at very close range or was it evidence of deliberate "jamming" of the equipment, with the message, 'NO, not now, not at this close range with a high magnification camera. We do not want to be documented for the world at close range yet, and if we were, it may endanger our mission, and your (CSETI) mission as well...?'

"Were we 'breaching diplomatic protocol' by unilaterally attempting to film the event at close range? Our policy is to document fully SO LONG AS THE PROCESS OF DOCUMENTING DOES NOT INTERFERE WITH THE CONTACT-EVENT ITSELF. Had we crossed the line and shortened the event by trying to document it? These and many other questions occupied our thoughts and continue to be a source of policy discussion within CSETI to this day."

CSETI's insistence on not just doing proactive research in the field but also trying to forge a relationship with the visitors is what still separates the organization from many researchers in the field, from the high-tech SETI radio telescope hunt to MUFON's reactive investigative fact-gathering. The handful of journalists and researchers with any integrity (versus anyone else in media who's reported on the topic) like the late Terry Hansen and the grand dame of the Washington press corps Helen Thomas, Leslie Kean and Richard Dolan, Tom Tulien and a just a few others did the most concisely focused and clear research and reporting. And yet, it was hard to discern if only the people in the choir were buying it. These few were able to see beyond the generally shoddy and shallow media treatment of the subject—the ever-present noise from the UFO ghetto and its own preconceptions—that "the biggest story of all time!" as many ghettoites claimed it to be, was in fact viable and worth telling. Just maybe not in such grandiose terms. Unfortunately, the telling often resembles 500 blind folks and naysayers simultaneously trying to affirmatively describe or negatively debunk the weird elephant in the room.

The "rest of CSETI's mission," so to speak, was as inspirational and in some ways just as far-fetched or visionary as its CE-5 contact trilogy. My job as the PR person communicating its far-out methods and objectives was challenging and exasperating. But I knew it would be difficult, simply because there were more cynically tuned Alex Heards from *Outside* magazine running around in mainstream journalism crying "conspiracy theory" or "conspiracy theorist" than there were level-headed thinkers and writers like the Whitely Strieber's of the realm.

Moreover, most journalists and the public at large were not aware of how well the subject had been manipulated and/or managed in secrecy and broad daylight since the early 1950s. ET knowledge was driven to the margins of modern thought through a well-conceived strategy of official denial and public ridicule of UFO reports and those doing the reporting. It's as if the Flat Earth Society had begun telling the media and the masses that flying saucer sightings were for suckers and psychological weaklings.

The reality is that this obfuscation has worked for almost seventy years, thanks not to Flat Earthers but to our own government. The Robertson Panel was established at the CIA under the Truman administration in part because a fleet of radar-tracked unknowns had buzzed the capitol in July 1952 over two separate weekends. There was also the fact—alluded to in the Rand report —that the big brass had become increasingly concerned that the volume of UFO reports, both the good and mistaken ones, could clog the channels of the military and intelligence agencies, posing more of a national security threat than the actual objects that had been vetted. Even the CIA's own website today lays out the Robertson strategy in stark detail:

> "The panel recommended that the National Security Council debunk UFO reports and institute a policy of public education to reassure the public of the lack of evidence behind UFOs. It suggested using the mass media, advertising, business clubs, schools, and even the Disney corporation to get the message across. Reporting at the height of McCarthyism, the panel also recommended that such private UFO groups as the Civilian Flying Saucer Investigators in Los Angeles and the Aerial Phenomena Research Organization in Wisconsin be monitored for subversive activities.

> "The Robertson panel's conclusions were strikingly similar to those of the earlier Air Force project reports on SIGN and GRUDGE and to those of the CIA's own OSI Study Group. All investigative groups found that UFO reports indicated no direct threat to national security and no evidence of visits by extraterrestrials."

So, what were/are they? Surely, "the agency" knows more that it shares on its public website, such as all the goodies in its compartmentalized and "need to know" levels of classification.

In my CSETI PR role, I had predictable run-ins with journalists who were naturally and professionally skeptical, curious, mocking and downright insulting. A few were interested in doing stories, including Twin Cities ABC affiliate KSTP-TV, which actually flew a reporter to Seattle for two days to shadow Greer during a lecture and night-sky activity with a CSETI group.

When CSETI got wind that Larry King was going to do a two-hour special on UFOs live from the desert near the infamous Area 51 in 1994, I pitched King's producer to include Greer. And I got lucky! He appeared on what was then King's highest-rated special ever, sharing air time with one of the oldest UFO researchers on the circuit—and the only one with a degree in nuclear physics—Stanton Friedman, as well as Area 51 researcher Glenn Campbell who lived on the rim of Area 51 and knew the area around it well. Other marquee names, from Bob Dean to Jacques Vallee, Kevin Randle (who wrote a Roswell book), Carl Sagan and former Senator Goldwater appeared in pre-taped interviews.

I'd been a junkie for UFO news since the early '90s. But I'd read very little in the common press and broadcast media because those news channels rarely ask the right questions and seem unwilling to do the tenacious work required to get answers and an understanding of "the phenomenon" even at a simple historical level. Perhaps one of the best things I've ever read was a brief column in the *Irish Times* newspaper while traveling the emerald isle. With no condescension or agenda, the writer put forth the idea that with all the reports of UFO sightings and the plethora of visual descriptions about people seeing "the grays"—the squat, chalky figures with the big hollow eyes who communicate mind-to-mind—maybe, just *maybe* extraterrestrials were visiting earth. And guess what? This is what they looked like—squat, chalky figures with big hollow eyes who communicate mind-to-mind.

For every well-intentioned program or comment on the topic, there were many more that used the subject to deride it, just like the Robertson Panel had prescribed before I was born, as if it were strapped to a whipping post to return to and flog when the news cycle dimmed and reporters or columnists needed to off-gas on, you know, "some really out there UFO stories" like the *Washington Post* columnist from a couple decades ago who wrote utter nonsense about a small UFO group trying to push for government disclosure. I'm sure his uninformed readers were delighted. The piece incensed me so much, I emailed him and pointed out how narrow his sense of journalism seemed and how uninformed his thinking was. I added that his arrogant, trite, stereotypical remarks amounted to little more than "calumny."

His response? He wrote back musing over the use of the word "calumny," riffing on how medieval it sounded and playing cute at being such an entertaining writer serving up such rich, self-satisfied fuckery. Vice Admiral Roscoe H. Hillenkoetter, who was on the Robertson Panel, would have been proud of that boy!

Still, the biggest offender during my time with CSETI was CBS News' *48 Hours* special UFO news show hosted by Dan Rather in April, 1994, which was years before alleged Bushies would do him in for his claim that W. went AWOL while in the Guard. I'd been contacted by the show's executive producer who was interested in what CSETI was doing and wondered if we might want to be on the show.

At the same time, Greer was considering a return RMIT to the volcano zone since sightings were still occurring there regularly. After working out logistics, I provided the producer a detailed rationale about why our group would be going to Mexico. I sent her the report of the first RMIT a year earlier, a summary of all the mainstream Mexican news coverage the sightings were getting, and the videos compiled in *Messengers of Destiny*. A good plan seemed in place to prevent the wheels from coming off—CBS would hire video and audio crews from LA and an interpreter, and reporter Harold Dow and his field producer, Claude Becker, would meet us in Metepec for a day of interviews and two nights of sky work, tones, searchlights, covering the zenith, CTS, the whole CSETI enchilada.

I was able to make the trip along with Wayne from Atlanta (the husband of Grace, the Asian woman who seemed to levitate off her chair at the first CSETI workshop I had attended in Los Angeles) and, of course, Sheri and Steve. I got down to Mexico City a day early (and had to leave a day early), ahead of my fellow CSETI colleagues.

Prior to dinner that night, I strolled the neighborhood of the hotel. Within a block, I saw a large colorful mural on the side of an auto repair lot depicting los Ovnis. It was a big saucer buzzing the capitol city. It seemed like a work of public/folk art that referenced the fact that millions of Mexicans had witnessed the strange crafts in the skies during the UFO wave, not just during the total eclipse but afterwards as well.

The next morning, I hired a cabbie to drive me to the zocalo, the city's central downtown. The driver was a young guy studying part time at university. Along the way, in my broken but usable Spanglish, the cabbie and I talked about los Ovnis and how one of his friends, who was also a college student and cab driver, had been taking a fare someplace when they saw cars and cabs pulled to the side of the road and stopped in the street along with clumps of pedestrians. They were all looking skyward at one in the afternoon at a shiny, spinning object that seemed to hover endlessly overhead about a half-mile up in the cloudless sky.

"It was on the news that night," my driver said. A preview of coming attractions with the CBS news team? We arrived at the central square where the old Metropolitan Cathedral of the Assumption of the Most Blessed Virgin Mary into Heaven stood. Constructed over a span of 250 years, beginning in the 16th century, the cathedral is a massive must-see even for an ex-Catholic like me. I noticed renovation on one side of the structure where digging had exposed an ancient Aztec temple built on the exact spot centuries earlier. It was like the old order trying to emerge from the ground again, resurrecting from a Catholic world order that also was aging but simultaneously timeless.

The cabbie explained that now there was a debate as to whether to preserve the newly exposed ruins or find alternatives. The competing structures looked like two civilizations still in collision. Perhaps there was some new spiritual force that would relegate them both to history, I mused. But what could that be? And what would that look like, even architecturally?

I asked my guy to wait a few minutes and went inside. No matter where I travel, if I encounter a church, I go in and light candles.

There were so many chapels with votive candles inside the beautiful Metropolitan cathedral that it was hard to know where to go. I picked the one nearest the door and lit wicks for Susan and the dogs at home and for safety on the upcoming journey into the volcano zone.

A young woman nearby knelt in prayer in the aisle, but also was *walking* on her knees out of devotion. She moved silently after each prayer, slowly moving toward the main altar, while other tourists milled about the church. It was humbling to witness, this pious and painful show of faith. I lit a candle for her faith to be rewarded somehow, the smell of tapers being lit and extinguished briefly carrying me back to my early years serving mass on the altar. The rest of the day I spent mostly in silence back at the hotel until my team arrived early that evening.

* * *

The massive volcano loomed majestic and mysterious on the landscape, seeming like a science-fiction special-effects image for [name-your-favorite space movie here]. The British novelist Malcolm Lowery wrote his most famous novel about this rugged area. Aptly titled *Under the Volcano*, Lowery's 1947 book was about a tormented British consul laid to waste by booze on the Day of the Dead when Mexico never seems more alive.

We had met the *48 Hours* crew a couple hours earlier before setting out for Metepec. The hired guns from LA were in their own rental car with the equipment while on-air host Dow and his bedraggled producer drove a second vehicle to meet up with us. Once we arrived at the compound—a lovely, brick-walled oasis, complete with a restaurant, a café and a big pool with lots of rooms around it—we checked in at the front desk. The desk person spoke decent English, so once we learned where our rooms were, I casually asked, "Have there been any Ovni sightings lately?" as if I were asking if the big ones were biting at a fishing lodge in northern Minnesota. The reply was just as casual.

"Oh yes, some have been seen earlier this week," as if to say the fish are hungry, use good bait. Shari smiled, perhaps recalling her experiences a year ago, and we moved to our lodging.

After dinner, we scouted locations and decided on a couple that were away from light pollution and off the beaten track. As we assembled our gear to drive with the audio and video crew to the first site, one of them informed us that Dow and Becker were stuck in Puebla, about twenty miles away. Their car had broken down and it was unlikely they could get a new one or get the current one fixed before morning. We all wondered why they didn't hire a car or cab for the short trip to Metepec.

Undaunted, we moved forward with the evening's plans. The sky was clear and the air not too chilly once the sun set behind the volcanos. Occasional smoke rose from the top of Popo, making the night even more tranquil. However, the evening's calm was boisterously interrupted for some ninety minutes by a ruckus from a small village that we could faintly see in the distance. Tex-Mex polkas and rancheros blared into the night, an invasive soundtrack that started to drive Greer nuts.

"Make it stop!" he said to no one in particular.

"It must be a holiday of some sort," I countered. "Maybe it will be over soon. Anyway, it's not that bad, it's their music."

"No, it's not," he snapped back. "It's German music that was forced on native people." He was right and I let it slide, the old music critic put in his place. The oom-pah-pahs and happy accordion tones eventually stopped around eleven and we were about to plunge into a CTS. The TV crew was about thirty feet from us comfortably set up on a shelf of rocks that we shared and which looked down into the dark stillness of the valley of the volcanos. Wayne was just about to turn on the tape recorder that held the woo-woo tones when I looked to the east over my shoulder and saw a glowing amber light coming in our direction at a good pace some two miles away—and closing.

"There's an object at one o'clock behind us," I said excitedly. I glanced at the film crew. "Are you guys rolling? Roll tape!" The sound guy said they were on it. Greer clicked on his high-powered light as the silent object moved closer. It was hard to discern if the object had structure and the amber glow was now hot white light as it drew closer. Steven signaled it twice and the object signaled back twice. As it returned the signal, you could make out an oval shape that seemed translucent at the center, especially as it filled with light as it signaled. But after it signaled, it seemed as if there was nothing at the center. Shari and Wayne quietly tracked it with binoculars.

As the object quickly descended, still a mile or two out from us, Dr. UFO flashed it again and it flashed right back before flying behind a high hillside not unlike the one we were on. It was gone. But the adrenalin rush was not.

"Wow, are we good? We don't even have to engage in the CTS or the tones!" I joked. The news crew assured us they had captured the incident, and someone made a disparaging remark about the "talent" and his producer missing all the action. Now the show would have to be called *24 Hours*, providing that the two absentees would even show up the next day. The night proceeded without incident and around two o'clock we packed it in.

The Rapid Mobilization Investigative Team (RMIT) awaiting breakfast after a CE-5 the night before: Wayne, the author, Steven and Shari. (Photo: Martin Keller)

The next morning, we had breakfast at a little restaurant with bougainvillea everywhere, perched on a pretty hillside overlooking a graveyard and small earth-made homes of campesinos. Steve and Shari had eaten there the year before and were very friendly with the two brothers who ran the place. Both parties were happy to see each other.

As we ate a hearty meal of huevos rancheros, fresh orange juice and strong coffee, Shari shared the stories each brother had shared with her and the previous RMIT group. One had witnessed a saucer-shaped object at night approach the graveyard visible from the restaurant balcony. It hovered and shined a light on the graves, as if it were looking for something—or someone. The younger brother said he was out on the restaurant balcony one time when he had seen an Ovni approach, but then he blacked out. His memory of the event was still foggy, but he was troubled by it and felt he had lost track of time.

Returning to the compound in Metepec, we saw the members of the film crew, who informed us that the rest of their team had arrived. They wondered if Greer would like to do the formal interview that afternoon. I asked if they had reviewed the footage with Dow and his producer from the previous night, but the answer was, "Not yet."

Both Greer and Dow did an interview that lasted more than an hour. Steve stood on a weedy helipad that looked like it had not been used in some time, with the LA guys rolling on every word and the producer taking notes and logging tape breaks. I'd seen the big Jefe give a lot of good interviews in the many years I worked with CSETI. This was by far his best, covering all the key points: the assessment of why the visitors might be here; how they get here; and why we have not kept up our end of the deal. Dow showed little emotion, or maybe it was disinterest that he showed, concerning what Steven had to say, and just plugged away with questions, some prepared, some in response to answers he had just heard.

Not a word of it would make it into the finished program.

We agreed to head to the same site as the previous night once the interview was concluded.

* * *

Our CSETI group was first on the scene approaching twilight. But something was different. No, a lot was different. The air felt charged, and the ground literally seemed to be electric, ethereally juiced with something. Soon we noticed small, fleeting flashes of light here and there on the ground, kind of like the odd light globs we'd seen in Arizona. Shari trained her binoculars on Popo, bathed in a preternatural yellow light from the fading sun. She thought she spied an object near the rim, which was barely pushing out steam compared to yesterday's bigger belches. But when the rest of us stopped to look, there was nothing.

Once the broadcasters arrived, Dow acquired a dour expression. Maybe this was the way he always was when "on assignment." Dressed in more rugged wear for the terrain, he walked out of his car drinking a can of beer as if arriving for some kind of campfire soiree at one of the ends of the earth. I could almost feel Greer's indignation flooding the valley floor. Booze on site is verboten, Herr Dow.

"You tell him we don't allow alcohol on site," he told me. But as I approached the reporter, both of us noticed several flashes of light from the ground, fleeting but clearly visible.

"What the hell was that?" Dow said, stopping in his tracks and looking around.

"I don't know, but we've seen those flashes ever since we got here," I said. "We should try to get some on film." Before I could ask him to put the brewski away, he drained the can in a couple gulps, crushed it and carried it toward the spot where Wayne, Steven and Shari were setting up. The producer and the video guys brought up the rear as the light seemed to disappear quickly in the sky.

At the top of the plateau, we got ready for the night's activities. Greer explained what our team would do that evening and what would happen if there were a repeat of last night's sighting and interaction— or even a possible landing, as with the RMIT group that thought one was imminent last year.

Before Greer could finish or further elaborate, Dow, Shari and others facing Popo, which was still very visible in the fading sunlight, saw what must have been a large object judging from its size and distance from where we were. It moved from behind the rim to the front and then back again.

"What is that?" Dow asked, this time betraying some emotion, as if maybe there was some truth to all this UFO shit. Then the object repeated the same movement as if playing peekaboo with us. For its last maneuver, it rounded to the back of the rim and out of sight just as daylight ended.

We all were fascinated by what we had seen, although I don't think any of it got recorded. It happened too fast and unexpectedly.

"Well," Wayne said with a sigh, "it's not like the experience Steve had on board at least." Dow was now animated as his producer stood looking just as puzzled as her talent and asked Greer what Wayne meant.

"I've got to ask you, Dr. Greer, about what one of your guys said just now." I don't know what transpired next because the two of them stepped away and talked out of ear shot while I elbowed Wayne and whispered, "Man, you can't be saying that stuff around media people no matter what happened." My Atlantean comrade was referring to Greer's alleged on-board CE-4 encounter when he was a young man hiking in the mountains around Asheville.

CBS correspondent Harold Dow prepping with Greer and CBS crew.
(Photo: Martin Keller

The rest of the night went on without anything significant going down, or up, or sideways. No more rim shots from the big volcanic mountain, no more flash-in-the-land outbursts in the dirt. But I could tell both Shari and Steven were not happy with the reporter and producer being with us. Dow had trampled on the no-drinking rules and both were an entire day late for the gig. After several hours, the news team left and we departed "our spot" shortly after them. As we drove back to the compound, the boss made it very clear that we would have a come-to-Jesus meeting with Dow and Becker bright and early the next day and be very clear that CSETI field work was our laboratory, that it was to be taken very seriously and that no matter what they thought of it or the entire UFO topic, they would have to respect it. Or leave.

Turns out Jesus had other things in mind.

Dow and Becker were already gone early the next day. And the LA sound and camera guys were packing up when I left my room. Before sunrise, I had been awakened by the sound of light, soothing music wafting through the area. It sounded like acoustic guitars playing a somber interlude. Was it coming over the PA? I couldn't tell. I drifted back to sleep before finally getting up to give the message to Dow.

Overnight, the soundman told me, the *48 Hours* assets had been dispatched to cover the shocking assassination of Luis Donaldo Colosio, Mexico's leading presidential candidate for the Institutional Revolutionary Party (the PRI), which had been in power for decades. Colosio had been brazenly gunned down with a close shot to the head the day before in Tijuana during a campaign stop. Mexico was in turmoil. Suddenly the cankerous reality of the world intruded on what seemed like the meta-reality of the Ovnis under the volcano.

I exchanged friendly farewells with the guys and told them I would eagerly await to see "that footage" from the first night when the show aired later in April. I knocked on Sheri's door to give her the news. Fresh out of the shower, she was sexily dressed—or undressed— in a towel, with another atop her head. I quickly told her about the assassination. We agreed to meet around ten with Steven and Wayne to plot the day's activities.

Greer seemed relieved to be rid of "the media" for which he'd had a pronounced distaste since the first day I met him. However, before the widespread proliferation of the internet, he needed the fourth estate to help spread word of his mission. He furrowed his brow when told of the killing and shook his head.

The church graveyard near Metepec under the volcano.
(Photo: Martin Keller)

At breakfast, he asked, "Did you hear that gentle music this morning?" Wayne and Shari had not.

"I think it was the ETs," he said matter-of-factly. He'd said a few things like that over the years that could have been easily refuted or challenged, but no one, including me, was up for that discussion. Yes, there was music. No, we didn't know where exactly it had come from.

That morning, we also got word from the two restauranteur brothers that a dentist in the area had a videotape of the huge triangular craft the CSETI team had witnessed the previous year. He was willing to show it to us. We eagerly drove to his house to review it and made plans to scout a new location for that night's work.

The dentist, a young, diminutive man of about thirty-five, was not only happy to show us the video, but he told us to take it! Judging from the time code on the tape, the eerie footage was shot at two-something in the morning under a cloudless sky by a couple of locals doing their own sky watch. The massive triangular object had appeared to be black and moved slowly and silently through the sky not far off the ground. The two guys talked occasionally in Spanish as one of them taped its steady movement.

"What is it?" one of them asked, speculating that it was a true Ovni. The other one quipped, "Es Superman!" and they both chuckled. Perhaps it was some country's stealth aircraft doing test runs over a sparsely populated area, although Puebla was only miles away. Maybe it had been making a pass over a largely populated city as well. Then again, perhaps it was not a secret aerial object at all but something else. But what?

A cylindrical object allegedly going into the volcano, captured by a remote webcam trained on Popo

We all thanked the young dentist for the tape and his hospitality, then headed out into rougher country dotted by small farms and simple dwellings. As we walked over a ridge not far from our original spot, we encountered an old farmer-rancher wearing a cowboy hat, his skin weathered and leathery. I greeted him in my broken Spanish and told him who we were, where we were from and how we were looking for Ovnis at night. The old man grew excited and went on to describe a sighting he'd had in this area when a round-shaped disc with lights around the rim hovered above him in broad daylight.

Gesturing with his index finger, he indicated how the lights were spinning rapidly around the craft as it hovered before rapidly taking off out of sight. We shook his hand and thanked him for his story. I asked if we could use this area for our search that night. He seemed to say it was public land, so no problem. Our scouting mission was over.

It was unusually dark later as we drove the washed-out road leading to the new spot. Suddenly, the headlights lit up a thin man with a long guayabera shirt, thick moustache, worn pants and poor footwear standing in the road with his thumb out. We waved at the hitchhiker but did not stop. The risks were too great.

We had been on our new hillside for less than an hour doing our CSETI thing with our bright searchlight and beeping tones when I caught a glimpse of light from the other side of the hill. I glanced down the way and saw the hitchhiker and another man intently climbing the hill, both with flaming torches in hand. I quickly relayed the info and within minutes we had piled up the gear and frantically scrambled down the other side back to car. I'm quite sure Greer peeled out in the dirt to get us the hell out of there. Ah, the quirks of Space Pen Club membership.

Out of breath and frazzled, we each speculated on what they were doing as we headed to a safer location by an old church near the compound. Like everything in the area, the church was under the watch of the silent volcanic sentinels in the distance. Maybe the men suspected we were drug runners. Maybe they were drug runners. Maybe it was their land and they wanted us off it. Maybe they were merely going to do a controlled burn of the hillside. Maybe they were coming to rob us—or worse. And once again the fear and dangerous reality of the world intruded on what seemed like a mysterious metaphysical landscape in this desolate plot under the volcano.

The silent night by the church ended earlier than the previous ones in "our old spot." In subsequent years, remote web cameras have been placed there, perhaps in this spot or in others. And they have over time captured some startling images of large spherical objects entering and exiting the volcanic cone or flying over it. The clips are so fantastic—even for someone who once saw something moving at the top of Popo with an alleged world-class news crew and his CSETI team members—that it is as easy to dismiss the video as hoaxed as it is to simply say, "What the fuck is that?!"

In the morning after heartfelt goodbyes, I boarded a bus back to Mexico City to catch a flight home. Did I have anything to declare at customs, the Minneapolis agent asked.

Only stories you would probably find hard to believe.

* * *

A couple days before the *48 Hours* special aired, I called a few friends to tell them to watch, previewing it for the few who were really into the subject with descriptions of what we had seen.

No one I knew called or emailed that night—or for days afterward. Perhaps they were too embarrassed for me, and for being my friend. The program not only completely distorted the sequence of events but failed to ask what we were doing in Mexico or mention that there had been an ongoing wave of sightings that Mexico's media was not afraid to report on, however superficially. In short, CBS didn't even practice basic who, what, when, where, why journalism. Instead, in a sloppily written voiceover narrative, they showed our gang of gringos doing a sky watch trying to contact extraterrestrials with primitive tools and our minds.

Scouting an alternative location after a close encounter with two guys bearing torches the night before at the original site. (Photo: Martin Keller)

We might as well have been filmed in Wayne and Grace's backyard in Atlanta except for occasional images of the volcanos. At one point, I can be seen and heard pointing at the object we saw the first night, saying, "There it is," but they cut to an airplane in the vicinity recorded on another night. My BFF Tom, a fellow music writer and the guy who once said I was always looking for signs from the universe, got a good kick out of that part! We looked like a bunch of stupid fools. I was so furious I called the executive producer of the program the next day, and in my anger mispronounced the word "disingenuous," tripping over it like a drunkard, while bashing Dow and company for being a day late to the story. She let me vent. I lambasted them for putting no context whatsoever into why we were there in the first place ("You had the Mexican news stories and those tapes from *Messengers of Destiny*!") and ranted at how poorly they had treated us in the broadcast. When I was done, she said she was sorry I felt that way. And that was that.

Oddly enough, to open our segment, footage of the object was used, including that of the object signaling back at us. But there was no context whatsoever—just the image of the UFO replying to us! Greer called the next day as pissed off as all of us were and said he was seriously considering putting on hold any more media coverage that involved shadowing CSETI in the field. I agreed that might be a good idea. Somebody else called too, some old guy in Massachusetts. A stranger I'd never met told me that he'd had a sighting along some county highway one time, a saucer that had shot straight up out of the ground, like from out of nowhere.

"Do you know what it was?" he asked.

"No, what was it?" I asked curtly, not trying to encourage him.

"It was coming out of a flying saucer nest, somewhere at the intersection of those two roads, blah blah blah, honk honk…. There're references to these in the Bible, check it out."

"Thank you for calling."

Maybe I needed to reassess Greer's snarky assessment of "the media." But when Terry Hansen's brilliant, thoroughly researched book *The Missing Times: News Media Complicity in the UFO Cover-up* came out in 2000, he had done the job for me and anyone else who wondered why this subject always seemed to be served wrapped in tinfoil.

The many jaw-droppers in Hansen's book include:

- "A virtual revolving door exists between the U.S. intelligence community and the news media… As Carl Bernstein explained in his landmark expose on the subject, more than 400 American journalists secretly carried out assignments for the CIA over 35 years, according to CIA documents. Often, these assignments were conducted with the blessing of news organization management."

- Incidents in 1967 of objects interfering with nuclear launch sites at Malmstrom Air Force Base near Great Falls, Montana (similar to the Minot incident) and again in 1975 that were widely reported by the local media but ignored (or censored) by major media and wire services.

- Documentation of how major airline companies in the late '50s "were under pressure from the U.S. Air Force to keep their pilots silent about UFO sightings"—a reality that the contemporary National Aviation Reporting Center on Anomalous Phenomena, NARCAP, has made their mission to change since 2000. The organization is run by my hypnotist and CSETI advisor, Dr. Richard Haines, who has documented more than 3,000 pilot encounters and continues to warn of the international safety hazards these objects frequently present over major airports where such incidents have occurred in the U.S., Russia, China and elsewhere.

* * *

Back in our Minneapolis home, we silently watched *48 Hours* until I started railing about what a travesty it was. Despite Susan feeling like I might be in a UFO cult and not wanting to watch the John Salter story sent by Dr. Joe, she let me engage my passion as long I covered our zenith. In my defense, she even speculated that Greer's long interview with Dow and the images might have been screened by CBS higher-ups or government spooks and that somebody with authority might have squelched a more truthful telling of our experience under the volcano.

One night, over a hot roti dinner at our favorite Ceylonese restaurant a few weeks after I had screened that Salter videotape alone, she kind of joined me in the woo woo dance. She asked if she could tell me something. For as long as I'd known her, Susan had never prefaced anything she was about to tell me with that question—she just flat out told me. So, as I sipped an Indian beer, I waited.

She started kneading her hands again, like a nervous Nellie.

She fidgeted and said, "I had an abduction dream recently,"

CHAPTER EIGHT:
STAR NATIONS AND THE UFO GHETTO, LIVE ON THE RES

"The prophecies of the Lakota/Dakota have
stated that you are the foundation of the thousand years of peace. But first there must be a
spiritual purification of man by fire and water.
With that purification comes truth. In closing,
there are those entities who do not want peace,
there are entities that do not want truth, and
there are those entities who do not want you to
be free. The prophecies have already won."

–Standing Elk, Lakota medicine man, Yankton
Sioux Reservation, South Dakota

Susan's dream was a classic abduction story. I tended to agree with her
that she had dreamt it because she'd heard so many similar accounts
over the early '90s UFO cable shows that I had exposed her to. Or because she'd caught solid glimpses of the dream through occasional story lines once *the X-Files* aired. Or maybe because I had done too much
re-telling of similar stories from the ghetto press like *UFO Magazine*,
to which I gave Zod a subscription every Christmas, 'cuz you know by
now how much Santa Claus loves Martians.

The night of the dream event, she had left our bed to sleep in our
guest bedroom a few steps down the short hallway because she had a
cold and didn't want me to get it. As we ate our Indian rotis chased with
cold beer, she hesitantly relayed that in the dream she had somehow
been taken into a sterile-looking room and placed on an examination

table. She was then inspected and analyzed by strange-looking beings.

"Did you feel any sensations, or do you think it was just something you really did dream about and not a 'real' experience?" I asked, knowing that many encounters in the literature I trusted—and even in those that I didn't—were couched in dream-like scenarios. Maybe the ego state was protecting the psyche from the intrusive experience by giving it a dream coating. Or maybe the "abductors" had created an amnesia-like state to protect them and her, as in the experience of Professor Salter and his son. Or maybe the dream was really an interception of her own consciousness, being somehow manipulated in a shared dream consciousness space by other entities. How would we figure it out? Who could we talk to besides the CSETI people I knew, like Dr. Haines?

Sadly, and gladly, there was no physical proof, just the conscious recall of a dream that obviously troubled her, one that took her some time to share ever since she had refused to watch the Salter TV story from Dr. Joe's care package. That thing was beginning to look more and more like a Pandora's box. But maybe this *dream* had been going on for some time in parallel with my early experiences on the second floor of our house. Maybe, maybe, maybe, maybe... maybe one day we would run out of tin foil. Or no longer need it. Or all of it would one day just be left behind in the rubble of the psyche as an undefined, unfinished part of life.

Finally, I had to remind myself of Herr Freud's classic comment, "Sometimes a cigar is just a cigar."

I didn't push too hard on it. We both accepted it and moved on with our lives, which would quickly change dramatically. As they say in Jamaica, "soon come." We got married and Susan became pregnant.

* * *

In looking through family histories for possible boy or girl names, we discovered that Susan was related to Kenneth Arnold, the pilot who on

June 24, 1947, described a fleet of nine "saucer"-like objects flying in formation near Mt. Rainier where he was airborne. This was just two weeks before the alleged Roswell crash was reported on July 8. Distant cousin Arnold's filed report seized the public's imagination once the story got out with the media landing on the term "flying saucers" to describe Arnold's sighting. Mass consciousness had been changed forever—at least for those paying attention.

Well, well, well, I thought, *another fine coincidence. And the plot thickens, thanks to a distant cousin.*

Oddly, the week of the Arnold report—again, only a couple weeks before Roswell blew up the news cycle—was also the week that "flying saucer" sightings had made front pages news across the country and into Canada. Reports of the incidents in an Associated Press story and other credible news sources like UPI featured good detail, like the account that ran in *The San Francisco Chronicle.*

> "Mysterious 'flying saucers' were reported seen again yesterday in larger numbers across the United States," opens the story from the leading Bay area paper. "Descriptions of the still unexplained phenomena, which have now been reported by hundreds of persons in at least 36 states and in the District of Columbia and Canada since June 25, vary greatly, but generally the informants say the objects appear to be saucer-like and skimming through the skies." Later in the account, a pilot in a P-38 pursuit plane, working for the United States Geodetic Survey, encountered 'eight or nine' at 32,000 feet and 'had to dodge out of their path while trying to photograph them.'

Clearly, the summer of 1947 was the Summer of High Strangeness, while the nation chilled to crooner Perry Como's hit "Chi-Baba, Chi-Baba (My Bambino Go to Sleep)."

Weeks before the Roswell crash, UFO reports flood 38 states and DC!

In the early summer of 1996, I took on two major assignments. The first was writing a feature story for *Rolling Stone* about the *X-Files* album that had been inspired by the television show. Boom! It fulfilled a dream I'd had since I was kid—getting a byline in a favorite national music magazine. The second assignment came from Steve Greer, who asked me to attend the first "Star Knowledge" UFO conference on a Sioux Indian reservation near Yankton, South Dakota, in a town called Marty. He was unable to go but thought I could present the CSETI lecture, hold a short class for teaching the fundamentals for nighttime CE-5 activity, and then hit the field with my group after dark.

I frequently joked that I had heard his speech so often I could give it in my sleep, and now I'd have to give it wide awake. I had done one or two small CSETI presentations to a MUFON (Mutual UFO Network) group in the Twin Cities at the request of Combover Bob. MUFON was a classic hunter-and-gatherer group, a well-established nationwide research organization that investigated sightings and alleged CE-4s or abductions, which seemed to be on most everyone's lips those days. And sure enough, that is all the group of about eight guys with big guts and seed caps of one sort or another—seemingly all retired science teachers—wanted to talk about. The hell with real-time CSETI research or the results from RMIT trips to Mexico and England. It bothered me that so little media exposure on a topic like abductions could dominate and/or shift the discussion so easily.

In reviewing the Star Knowledge gig, Greer was cheerfully adamant that I do it. "This one has your name on it!" he exclaimed, and so it did. I accepted the task in Marty and began planning.

The X Files issue of Rolling Stone came out about two weeks before I headed to South Dakota. My story, including interviews with musicians like The Byrd's Roger McQuinn, Prince B. of P.M. Dawn, Frank Black, Billy Bragg, Perry Farrell, the Troggs' Reg Presley (who even had his own *UFO* cable TV show in England), and others highlighted the release of *Songs in the Key of X: Music from and Inspired by "The X Files."* But I had a lot of room "to stretch out," as they say in jazz. I explored how the rock 'n' roll and flying saucer story lines of the forty years before the millennium shared a kindred place in the orphan corner of Western popular culture.

In the article's opening I wrote, "Rock musicians of the past forty years have fixated on different subjects for songs but the fascination with UFOs, flying saucers, close encounters and space junk always strikes an odd but resonant chord. Indeed, you can virtually read the covert history of Ufology through past and present rock tunes.

"Lost in Space: Rock Stars and UFO"s – My X Files story on the cover of the Rolling Stone came out at the same time as the first Star Knowledge conference on a South Dakota Indian Reservation where my friend Foley and I saw a "UFA" en route

"Today, there's a glut of commercial and cable television programs, books, radio shows, mail-order videotapes and internet sites available about the cosmically controversial issue. With the release of *Songs in the Key of X: Music from and Inspired by 'The X Files,'* the sonic link between rockers and saucers has never been stronger. Now in its third season, *The X Files* claims the UFO issue as its anchor tenet and declares in the greatest marketing slogan for both the series and the ET/UFO phenomena, 'The truth is out there.'"

I closed with an acute observation by Bragg, one of Woody Guthrie's wily musical-activist descendants from the UK, that I whole-heartedly agreed with: "You don't need aliens to explain things like Stonehenge, the Pyramids at Giza or even Chartres Cathedral in France," as Bragg says. "Those magnificent structures simply illustrate the strength of human faith in the unknown and the cosmos." But you do need an explanation for flying objects like the one Bragg's girlfriend, Juliet, had seen. "Besides," he laughs heartily, "it would be a lot more weird if we were the only ones in the universe and they aren't there."

I needed a companion to make the trek to the res' and called Kevin Foley, whom I'd met at the Horst fundraising event, although I'd really met him after a friend of his—a County Commissioner—had called about a strange and scary sighting his daughter had experienced. It was a basketball-size oval of white light that appeared over power lines near their house and moved silently along the wires. It sounded like ball lightning, but it started a dialog and friendship between Foley and me that continues to this day.

He was eager to make the trip, and when he asked who else was going to be speaking, I rattled off some names—Whitely Strieber, John Mack (a Harvard prof who had published a popular book on abductees that nearly cost him his tenure at the University), Dr. Richard Boylan (whose credibility always swung wildly from one point to another whenever he published his opinions on the early Internet), the Pope (aka Robert Dean), Chet Snow and Leo Sprinkle (two widely respected hunter-and-gatherer researchers), and others, plus a handful of medicine men from various tribes, including the event coordinator, Lakota medicine man Standing Elk.

There was also an Italian about my age named Giorgio Bongiovonni. Giorgio suffered the stigmata—the bleeding of the hands, feet and forehead like Jesus. Unlike Jesus, though, GB linked his manifestation/suffering to UFO cosmology and some high strangeness experiences he had in Italy. As a fallen away Catholic, I was blown away by his tale, and remembered the many news stories from my youth about another famous Italian stigmatist Padre Pio. He was later canonized by the church, his open and bleeding wounds very similar to Bongiovonni's. I later took umbrage with a reporter in Arizona who wrote about him in an alternative weekly paper, calling his wounds fake and his whole modus operandi a fraud. I had met Bongiovonni earlier in LA at a conference and perceived that the bandages around his hands where the pieced flesh lay open were genuine and at times caused him great pain. And I took great delight in how he reacted to a female Los Angeles CSETI member who was drop-dead stunning, flirting with her and being kinda caddy, stigmata or no stigmata!

Standing Elk, or Hehaka Inazin in Lakota, organized the conference after having a self-professed vision to share with the world the First Nation's "Star Knowledge" of Star Visitors who came to Earth. When told of the lineup for the weekend event, to be followed by a traditional annual Sun Dance (in which we would not be participating), Foley was impressed.

"Wow, the big hitters," he cracked.

"Yeah, almost all of the UFO ghetto—at least the US branch—right there on the res," I shot back. Truth was, I was frightfully nervous about my speech. The polished, award-winning public-speaking skills I'd honed in high school had long lost their shine.

I wrote my speech and rehearsed it a few times at home. And along with all my CSETI field gear and clothes for the weekend, I packed a couple of Greer lectures on cassette tape and listened to them as we drove southwest through the farm country that ran to the horizon. Foley dozed in the shotgun seat while I drove and absorbed the audio.

After lunch, outside of Worthington, Minnesota, either reality or the boys upstairs pulled another fast one. Worthington was a place I previously had known only by name since it had produced two of the toughest women my high school team ever debated at a tri-state tournament. As we slipped over the state line into South Dakota cruising at about 70 mph, I don't remember who saw it first, but once we both locked on it, we nearly went off the road!

Out the driver's side of the windshield, perhaps 400 feet in the air and parallel to the car, was a simply drawn arrow in the sky as if somebody had used chalk. The arrowhead at the end of a white shaft stood etched in the cloudless sky, seemingly pointing toward the Star Knowledge event ninety minutes away. We hooted and hollered, blinked hard and blinked again to be sure we were really seeing what we were seeing. Even though we had two cameras and a video recorder with us, we were too shocked to document it. We didn't even think of doing so, we were in such a state of intrigue and disbelief.

Here's another fine rabbit warren I've driven myself and a companion into. So, we saw an UFA—unidentified flying arrow—on our way to a First Nation conference about what the Native Americans knew about the Ovnis.

We got into Marty by mid-afternoon, checked into one of two modest motels and saw Strieber, his lovely wife Anne and their son coming out of the room next to us. We unloaded gear and went to a nearby grade school where the conference was held, checked in, then hung out. I was introduced to Standing Elk and felt an immediate bond I think he shared. He was a big, sturdy man with long black braids and a big smile and laugh that reminded me of Dr. K from the Space Pen Club. When I saw him the next day, he greeted me by picking me up from behind and lifting me into the air, laughing and cajoling before setting me back on my feet.

Standing Elk, one of the Star Knowledge organizers, who also was amused by CSETI's contact methods, especially the use of high-powered lights. (Photo: Giorgio Bongiovonni)

He joked with me about CSETI's use of lights, as if they were some archaic tools and said there was no need for them. "You just call to the visitors," he said. I was hoping he would show me how to do it.

His written message announcing the conference is still online, but excerpts from it are worth sharing, if only for the deeply profound thoughts and beliefs he hoped to share during the event:

> "My hand is open to all those Elders of the Turtle Island who wish to share their message, dream and vision with the people of the world, for I cannot do it alone. Through our teachings, we know that not one individual holds the knowledge and mysteries of life; we were all given a piece of the puzzle. We are all a part of the Sacred Hoop that needs to be mended, and we must make a humble effort in this task, if the seventh generation, our grandchildren and unborn are to survive this next awareness.

> "The Medicine Men and Pipe Carriers have the ability to communicate with all that moved with the spirit of Mother Earth. Many spiritual entities such as the Eagle, Hawk, Owl, Horse, Elk, Deer, Wolves, Coyotes, and the Star Nations, etc., are utilized in the ceremonial system of the Lakota/Dakota.

> "The Star Nations were the most crucial of all entities, because the thought of other races communicating with the grassroots people would create a major threat to the religious systems, the economy and educational system of any government," he continued, explaining why and how the Lakota and other tribes were forbidden by law to practice their ceremonies and hold their beliefs throughout the brutal conquest of "the West."

"The greatest fear in the governmental structures was the knowledge that all forms of 'Star Governments' had no monetary systems within their governing structures," he wrote. "Their system was based on the mental, spiritual and universal laws with which they were too mentally and spiritually intelligent to break. The collapse of the monetary system within the United States Government and the Religious Denominations became a National Security issue, and so it became an easier task to make the Lakota/Dakota belief system illegal to participate [in] and practice."

"The thousand years of peace" in the quote that opens this chapter, which is taken from Standing Elk's written remarks, sounded like prophecy right out of the Edgar Casey canon of prophetic readings, as well as that of the Bahá'í Faith. And again, I wondered, as I did when the strangeness in the house began, if this was really about a deeper and more enigmatic spiritual reality rather than an odyssey built on consciousness to connect with ET—"the next awareness," as Standing Elk so eloquently expressed it. Or were they one and the same? And how far down the path of purification by fire and water were we? Maybe I didn't really want to know all the answers.

Despite the array of native speakers, I was going to have to settle for glimpses of knowledge from teachers like him in what was really a drive-by situation. I didn't have time to ponder much at the conference. There was too much to do and a lot of schmoozing ahead. But I did hear a bit of Standing Elk's speech about the significance of the symbols allegedly found on the debris of the Roswell crash. Each cryptic image stood for various universal principles of Star Nation beings and Earth beings. The symbols represented Free Will, Spiritual Freedom, the Four Seasons of Earth and other life meanings.

While there have been other alleged crashes of hardware and occupants, Roswell has become the Rosetta Stone of Ufology in pop culture. The July 6, 1947 headline of the *Roswell Daily Record* read: "RAAF Captures Flying Saucer on Ranch in Roswell Region"—on the heels of the massive sightings in North America just days earlier. After it was first reported that debris had been recovered (and later bodies), the US government—facing a PR problem called "Crisis Communications"—went into spin mode. The next day it quickly issued a new explanation of what had crashed. It was a weather balloon, complete with some symbols on its side.

In 1994, the story changed. The weather balloon was really remnants of a different kind of balloon attributed to the top-secret Project Mogul that was used as an upper atmospheric device to detect Soviet nuclear detonations. And the "symbols" were really decorative images that came from a toy manufacturer who supplied the tape, since there was a shortage of "real" tape just after WW II.

Then, in 1997, to account for the stories of recovered ET bodies at the crash sites in Roswell (although it doesn't address another crash in the same period at Corona), the story changed again. Or mutated. The US Air Force issued *The Roswell Report: Case Closed,* a 231-page summary claiming the ET bodies were really crash-test dummies that had been dropped in parachutes from a very high altitude to test if pilots and astronauts could safely return to earth from those heights.

I called my brother when this news broke and asked him, "What do you think that Air Force officer dude did to deserve the assignment of going on national TV and talking about crash test dummies crashing at Roswell?"

Stationed in Roswell, Major Jesse Marcel became part of the history and lore of the incident and is pictured in a famous photo with Brigadier General Roger Ramey, Commanding General of the 8th Army Air Force, holding fragments from the crash, er, weather balloon. But the night before the photo was taken Marcel reportedly brought some of the wreckage home to share with his wife and young Jesse Jr. Anyone who ever met Jesse Jr. will tell you what an outstanding human he was. As you'll read in the next chapter, I met him briefly in California and was struck by his unassuming nature and humility.

A Naval officer and doctor who served until 1996, he was eventually appointed State Surgeon of Montana. But in the first Iraq war, he voluntarily served again for thirteen months in theatre, as the military likes to say, as a flight surgeon with the 189th Helicopter Battalion in Iraq. He later reached the rank of colonel. When he died in 2013, an account of his death and the Roswell incident was covered even-handedly by many news services, including *The Guardian*, which wrote:

> "Marcel's father was an air force intelligence officer and reportedly the first military officer to investigate the wreckage in early July 1947, when Marcel was 10. Marcel said his father brought home some of the debris and woke him up in the middle of the night to look at it, telling him it was something he would never see again. His father maintained that the debris 'was not of this Earth,' Linda Marcel [Marcel Jr.'s wife] said. 'They looked through the pieces, tried to make sense of it. The item that Marcel said fascinated him the most was a small beam with purple-hued hieroglyphics on it,' she said.

> "After an initial report that a flying saucer had been recovered on a ranch near Roswell, the military issued a statement saying the debris was from a weather balloon. 'They were told to keep it quiet, and they did for years and years and years,' Linda Marcel said."

So, who to believe about the purple-hued hieroglyphics? A doctor who returned to active service in a war zone, the staggered reports issued by the military years after the event, or Standing Elk? Frankly, the toy manufacturing kiddie-tape bit really does drive the imagination and a fair amount of indignation.

Student and teacher? Harvard's John Mack, soon to suffer the wrath of the Ivy League university for his "abduction research," and Italy's Giorgio Bongiovonni, suffering stigmata but never vetted by another heavy institution, the Catholic Church. (Photo: Giorgio Bongiovonni)

Aside from parts of Standing Elk's presentation, I didn't see much else, except Bongiovonni's talk. That attractive female CSETI woman from LA was also in the house. I saw Giorgio talking with her during the conference, clearly smitten. The biggest surprise attendees were the Birds from the legendary Aviary in the middle of nowhere South Dakota. Chicadee, a former Naval Intelligence officer, introduced himself and a female companion who was still active in some governmental office. He had written a lot on the UFO topic and was a strong advocate for public disclosure. The other feathered friend, Chicken Little, was also on hand. We were surprised to see each other there. Things were getting "interesting."

Of course, Chicken Little wanted to know everything—why Greer couldn't make it, why I was there. Some believed he relayed it all back to his buddy, the Pelican, at the CIA Weird Desk. Fine, relay away. Foley and I did not share our "floating arrow sighting" with him.

243

On Standing Elk's recommendation, I asked one of the conference helpers, a young native man in his late teens or early twenties, if he could show me some places where we could do the night watch. So, he and Foley and I piled into the car and drove around the countryside looking for a spot. As we found a potential site, two large owls flew up out of the brush, giving the Lakota youth long pause. It meant something to him, but I never found out what it was.

When we finally settled on a more open area, we negotiated a fair price to rent it for a few hours the next night. Back at the school, the crowd had grown to a couple hundred people from all over the country and a few from across the pond. All ages too. I saw John Mack talking with a group of obvious fans, ditto for Pope Bob Dean. Richard Boylan, who appeared to be Standing Elk's liaison to the non-Native UFO speakers, moved through the throng stopping just long enough to greet those he knew before moving on to other tasks.

I practiced my speech again the morning before delivering it later, while my road buddy went to hear other speakers. Once I got to the school, I caught various workshops while mainstage speakers held forth in the auditorium. In one doorway, I stopped briefly to watch the Italian stigmatist lecture to a full house that included Harvard professor Mack who had an intensity I'd rarely seen inside or outside the ghetto. His intellectual prowess and charm offensive included a metaphysical quest for knowledge. I watched him from the doorway as he took copious notes and listened more attentively than anyone else. His deep blue eyes twinkled, and an appreciative smile creased his lips as Giorgio carried on. *He's probably collecting data for the next book*, I surmised before moving on toward the auditorium.

As I paced backstage waiting for the time slot for my speech to arrive, I thought about how far I'd come since my first CSETI conference in LA and the Fort Collins event with all the New Age merch on display, the girl with the weird handwriting, the apparatus to open the third eye. Howard. Shari. Steven. Where was it all going?

My nerves were eating me and my sweat glands were dripping.

Then I was announced. I took a deep breath. I abruptly bent over and picked up a dime that was at my feet 'cuz someone had told me long ago it was good luck. In any case, it took the edge off momentarily ("Whatever gets you through the night," John Lennon once sang). At last, I went out to speak.

I gave Greer's speech, or at least my version of it, quite poorly. My delivery was unpolished and out of key. At least that's what I thought. I hit on the points I felt were worth making, having underlined parts I wanted to emphasize. And I touched on the public-disclosure initiative, Project Starlight (discussed in the next chapter), which was just getting underway. The speech also covered a much discussed, much disputed meeting between Greer and President Clinton's CIA director James Woolsey and his wife, although I didn't mention Woolsey by name in South Dakota.

Quotes from my speech included:

> "When we both heard about this conference, we were very excited to attend given the participation of many notable and venerable Native American elders—and other shaman and medicine men from around the world. Both Dr. Greer and I have Indian blood on our mother's sides—he has Cherokee and I have Potowaname. I think we'll have a very special time this weekend given the fresh perspectives we'll hear from these spiritual teachers and leaders."

> "Recently *Rolling Stone* asked me to write a piece about rock musicians and UFOs as part of its special "X Files" cover story last month. I can assure you the relationship between rock culture and UFOs sheds no new scientific light on our discussions here today—other than the fact that many rock musicians, like many people all over the world, have had real UFO sightings and experienc-

es. So what? What do we do about the fact that it appears we're being visited?"

"I think that CSETI is an honorable research experiment that has generated some very puzzling and exciting results [again, stressing the experimental nature of this work]. We know that CSETI has erroneously been called a cult and other misleading labels by those tradition-bound scientists and detractors whose worldview is shaped by rather worn-out models of reductionist, empirical science and 18th century Newtonian physics." "Point in fact, I came to CSETI in 1992 first as a skeptical freelance journalist, with a modest belief that, yes, there is other life in the universe. But why would it bother to interact with a group of people out under the night sky with high-powered lights, strange beeping tones and an even stranger method of communication using mind— or consciousness—which is what CSETI does."

I tried hard to explain the fundamental communication and more far-out consciousness piece by briefly looking at the two or three exemplary CE-5s in the UFO literature, including the Papua New Guinea event witnessed by a priest and villagers.

"You'll notice that these all share a basic civil attempt at communication by parties who simply wanted to acknowledge each other in a peaceful and non-hostile way. The more important aspect, especially of the last and a bit with the first, are good examples that reflect some ability of the visitors to read thought or brain patterns and anticipate behavior. Now UFO books are full of these cases where the beings appear to have a direct link to the consciousness of those who perceive them through telepathic means or otherwise. One assessment CSETI has made is that these star-ferrying peoples, perhaps hundreds or even thousands of light years advanced beyond our own civilization and its infantile physics and sciences, may indeed possess consciously-assisted technology or technologically-assisted consciousness."

And then, after elaborating on a few points, I was done.

Afterward, a guy about my age from the audience came up to me in the hallway and said he had read the "X Files" piece I'd written and then thanked me for that and the speech. "Best one I've heard at the conference," he said. I thanked him even though I felt I hadn't done my best. But I didn't have time to stand around and beat myself up or take more props, if there were any to be taken. I moved on to the start of the workshop inside a classroom that quickly filled with twenty-five or more mostly young people, along with Chicadee and his companion. Thankfully, Chicken Little was staking out—or stalking—somebody else's workshop.

To start things off, I had people go around the room and state where they were from, what they did and why they had come to the conference. A good number were from California and New Mexico, plus New Hampshire and North Carolina, Florida, Iowa, Horwich and Bolton, England, Ontario, Canada, Georgia and Washington state. As they each spoke up, I started feeling like Richard Dreyfuss' character in *Close Encounters of the Third Kind* as he is somehow compelled to make his way toward the Devil's Tower in South Dakota: Many of these folks also "just felt like they had to be there for some reason," like they had an intuitive sense or calling to make the trip. Among them was a waitress from Nebraska, an older gent from back East and a young buck with a ballcap and long hair who eventually made this comment: "The CIA is at this event." He stared at me as he said this like I was that CIA guy. He wasn't the only suspicious one.

After they'd seen me speak, a forty-something British couple Foley and I met the next day admitted that when they first saw us, the husband whispered to his wife, "These two guys don't belong here! They look like agents of some kind!" We all had a good laugh at that as I told the male Brit it was good to know that paranoia among UFO people didn't only exist in the US. Later, I saw the long-haired kid and asked him who he thought the CIA person was. He grinned sheepishly and avoided looking me in the eye, confessing it was just something he'd heard.

The whole exchange reminded me of another lifetime when I had been the only white teaching assistant on a staff of about twenty African-Americans who ran an alternative high school for the Urban League in Minneapolis called the Street Academy. My boss, the principal, confided during a large gathering of the League that he was sure there was at least one FBI informant in the local Urban League. "You don't have this many black folks in one organization that isn't being watched by somebody on the inside," he explained.

Later, one of Foley's contacts in DC who worked at one of the intelligence agencies confirmed that they "monitored UFO groups" all the time, more than a hundred of them in the '90s. "As long as these groups are above board," the source said, "and don't engage in any kind of secrecy, we don't have any problems with them."

Greer was convinced his phone was tapped, and for a time I felt mine was too. I would pick it up when it rang, and no one would be there. "That's what initiates the tap," Dr. Haines explained at one point. Fine, let the tap dance go on. I filed this info away as a nuisance item in the tin-foil archives.

The workshop went off without a hitch as did the night exercise. The night was cloudless and warm. Including Chicadee and his pal, the group started out with thirty or more people but dwindled as the night wore on with no results. At one point, there was a golden flash of light in the sky and the participants got as excited as grade schoolers at recess. I had grown up in North Dakota not far from Yankton and thought this had all the earmarks of heat lightning so I said that, throwing water on the campfires of the ET-expectant minds.

At the end of the night, I asked if anyone from the workshop wanted to lead the last CTS of the night. A woman about my age volunteered and I let her have at it. She started what sounded like praying to get the Star visitors to appear. She kept at it, hitting some of the right ideas in the CTS protocols but wrapping her words in a religiosity that wasn't right. She was one student I had failed to reach correctly. After she finished and we carried out the customary silent sky watch for another half hour, I called time.

"Did anyone in the remote-viewing group get anything just now?" I asked as we ended our star vigil. No one offered much, but Chicadee approached and said, "At one point I felt as if I had lock on with a commander in a ship who relayed, 'We are well documented.'"

I didn't understand Chicadee at first and asked him to repeat himself, so he said, "We are well documented."

I said that sounded like a good hit and I would put it in my notes. He agreed. But maybe he was playing to both sides too. Such a statement could just as well mean the CSETI group was well documented by the intel agencies.

The next morning, at a local breakfast café with Foley, the Pope and his wife, and one or two others, I noticed Chicken Little in a booth by himself. He motioned me over. I sat down and exchanged pleasantries, then asked him what he thought of the Star Knowledge Conference.

"It's an interesting mix of people, but it's always the same people—you know, the same audiences coming to these things," he sniffed. "It's really not reaching others outside the envelope."

"You mean the mainstream, the majority?"

"Yes!" Chicken seemed tasked to put a larger disclosure effort in play, perhaps by Pelican at the CIA Weird Desk, perhaps not. Maybe it was just his own agenda, which is explored in more detail in the next chapter. Or maybe he was just lonely for company and wanted to make small talk. Then he threw me a high, fast curveball, the kind I used to love to swing at as a kid.

"Tell me about that story in *Rolling Stone* you wrote." For a moment I was speechless. This guy doesn't miss much, I thought to myself. This was the last thing I expected to hear from him, but judging by the way he'd said it, this was the main thing he wanted to talk about. He went on about how well done it was and how much ground it covered for just one story. "You know stuff like that and a skill like yours can be very useful," he finished.

I thanked him for his compliment and headed back to my table where the waitress was beginning to serve. The people there looked up at me, like, "Well?"

"Damn, I think I was being recruited for something," I said, and then laughed self-consciously.

"Of course," said the Pope, implying that the temptations of the so-called "dark side" were always in play and he'd had similar experiences.

"Well, what'd you tell him, Marty?" Foley smiled as he started in on his eggs and hash browns.

"I told him I was *hungry* and had to get back to *my* people," I said, deliberately trying to be enigmatic and play to both sides as well.

Once breakfast broke up, Kevin and I headed back to the conference for a couple more lectures. In the early afternoon, a group of participants and perhaps one or two shamans held a drumming and chanting ceremony that Foley sat in on with everyone in a big circle. He soon came in looking for me and said I needed to come outside because a circle—or hoop—had formed in the sky, much like the arrow we'd seen. A simple, chalk-like circle over the circle of participants on the lawn.

"You gotta see this!" he yelled over his shoulder as he darted through the crowd, which was also getting wind of the strange but fitting appearance. The doorways were blocked, so I waited for people to pile through. By the time I got outside, the circle overhead had vanished. And then it occurred to me, I had not really heard or learned anything of substance from the Native American elders and medicine men at the conference. I was too busy executing CSETI duties.

To make up for my lack of engagement, I hopefully bought a couple books, including Wallace Black Elk's autobiography, which I later read. It blew my mind. I'd studied a semester's worth of Native American literature in college and read *Black Elk Speaks* a couple times, which carried a fair amount of indigenous mysticism in it. I was deeply moved by the part where Black Elk, now aging and nearing his physical death, prayed to a cloudless blue sky to see some evidence, some affirmative manifestation again from the Creator. Moments later, a small rain cloud appeared and sprinkled its holy medicine on him. Wallace's book went even deeper, exploring the many healings he'd participated in, and into what many would consider magic. Or miraculous.

That night, Foley and I joined the British couple, a number of Lakota and many others at a sweat-lodge prayer ceremony in four or five lodges—a first for me, but not for my companion, who was well versed in these experiences. I forget who led the ceremony, but as each "door"—or section of the ceremony—finished and another began, it got hotter and hotter in the domed space. As more wood was added to the lodge's fire, it felt like all the oxygen had been consumed and all our personal karma, juju, mojo or whatever you want to call it was being sucked up into sacred nothingness.

Purged.

The "doors" signified the time segments of each phase of the ceremony, and the leader would open the door to the sweat lodge momentarily to let anyone out who needed to exit. Near the end of the final door, a young boy of eight or nine voiced what we were all feeling, especially neophytes like me.

"Man, it is soooo hot in here!" His mother hushed him and a few people, including the master of ceremony, smiled in the dark. The young boy exited before the final door. When we all emerged at the end of the ceremony, I watched as other First Nation men gathered from their lodges and talked about meeting again the following weekend. They weren't planning on getting together for BBQ or beers, or to watch the game—they were going to pray together again for the healing of Mother Earth—to mend the sacred hoop.

After goodbyes at the school, Foley and I headed out. Many at the conference would be staying for the traditional Sun Dance. But we had to return to our White Man worlds 300 miles away. Not far from the reservation, the clouds built into a massive, dull-gray canopy, blotting out sky and stars, arrows and circles. We drove silently through a hard, steady rain all the way back to Minneapolis.

Cleansed.

CHAPTER NINE:
THE ROAD TO DISCLOSURE, THE BARRIERS TO TRUTH

"It [the UFO matter] will be a case where the cover-up is the disclosure, and the disclosure is the cover-up. Deny everything, but let the public sentiment takes its course. Let skepticism do our work for us until the truth becomes common acceptance."

–General Nathan Twining, former Chairman, Joint Chief Chiefs of Staff (1957-1960), reported by Lt. Co. Phil Corso and co-author William Birne in *The Day After Roswell*

Every year inside CSETI and the UFO ghetto, and every year since I "opted out" of both—as *out* as one could opt—there have been so many claims that "This is the year when we're going to have disclosure about UFOs and ET!" Usually these unsupported proclamations and tea-leaf readings occur as a year ended or began, hope and rumor running rampantly among hunters, gatherers, remote viewers, abductees, sky watchers, star geezers and other flying-saucer partisans. Myself included.

In the new century, more than fifteen nations have opened their UFO files, including the US with thousands of CIA files that offer practically nothing new or revelatory. But there have never been any official government decrees establishing the facts as they are known, nor an acknowledgement that the Ovnis originate from Planet So-and-So, or an official statement on what their intentions were/are. And—in the case of CSETI's mission—no government-sanctioned outreach to establish interstellar diplomatic relations between them and this planet and its inhabitants without secrecy or subterfuge. Those in the ghetto and thousands of others across the planet wanted to see an introduction to the boys and girls upstairs on *Washington This Week* or the late-night talk shows, and so did I.

Then, on December 16, 2017—about the time holiday cards and disclosure rumors start flooding mailboxes, emails and internet sites—*The New York Times* published the first of four watershed stories. The first story was "Glowing Auras and 'Black Money': The Pentagon's Mysterious U.F.O. Program," and the second one, containing interviews with two Naval pilots, was "Navy Airmen and an Object That 'Accelerated Like Nothing I've Ever Seen.'" The stories even featured video evidence supplied by the Department of Defense (DOD) to illustrate the objects' dazzling aerodynamic capabilities if nothing else. The Advanced Aerospace Threat Identification Program, as the secret program was called, studied Unidentified Aerial Phenomena (UAP) through a third party in the private sector headed by Robert Bigelow, a Las Vegas real-estate tycoon with a lifelong interest in space and ETs.

A subsequent January 2019 story in the *Times* ("Project Blue Book is Based on a True U.F.O. Story. Here It Is.") by the intrepid Leslie Kean and Ralph Blumenthal (who wrote the first one along with Helene Cooper) briefly outlined how the secrecy, in part, operated under the Robertson Panel guidelines from the early '50s. Another piece by Kean, Blumenthal and Cooper, followed in May called "'Wow, What Is That?' Navy Pilots Report Unexplained Flying Objects."

More mainstream stories followed in 2020, though they were seemingly obscured by the global health and economic impacts of Covid-19, and the post-George Floyd social justice movements that began near my neighborhood in south Minneapolis during May and extended into the rest of the summer. (We live within a mile of the Floyd murder/ memorial site and eight minutes from the Third Precinct headquarters, where a protest was hijacked by certain "elements" and turned into a riot with numerous arson events that destroyed many storefronts and other buildings and created almost a half billion dollars in damage, much of it minority-owned and small businesses).

The 2017 *Times* stories, however, blew up the confusing, contradictory and long-running story line that the UFO subject —or UAP, if you must—isn't real. (Apparently, UAP is the current polite-society term replacing UFO, but who dictates such judgements?) Moreover, the old Grey Lady delivered the news it finally saw fit to print without once using the derisive terms "conspiracy theory" or "conspiracy theorist," which have been employed often to hijack the reputation of anyone who ventures into the arena. The December 2017 news story seemed to contain the disclosure everyone had been waiting for, at least in the media, and by implication as a primary source, the Pentagon/DOD!

Hallelujah!!

Everybody in the ghetto had their hair on fire. I called Zod to compare notes. He was as shocked as everyone else, and we both agreed it raised a ton of questions as to timing, who now owned "the narrative," and where the hell the Executive and Congressional levels of our government were on this news.

A few days later, at an annual holiday charity event in Minneapolis with the popular Kinks tribute band, Kinda Kinky, I sat with rocker Curtiss A (profiled in Chapter 4), who was guesting on the show and tried to size up the information. Besides feeling vilified for all the shit he had taken through the years for his UFO views and his personal sighting and possible abduction story, the typically verbose rocker seemed uncharacteristically reticent and surprisingly reserved. He was more interested in the recently discovered Oumuamua (meaning "scout" in Hawaiian), an unusual and fast-moving interstellar object that was detected passing through our solar system in October 2017, and which Avi Loeb at Harvard would later declare as "alien technology." I admitted I had not been closely following that new thread in Ufology. Leave it to Curt to be way out in front of it. And everybody else.

Loeb wasn't just another Harvard professor with a wild new claim to make like John Mack from the university's psychiatry department.

Eventually, his 2021 book, *Extraterrestrial: The First Sign of Intelligent Life Beyond Earth*, was published. According to *The Japan Times* report, "Loeb's stellar credentials—he was the longest-serving chair of astronomy at Harvard, has published hundreds of pioneering papers, and has collaborated with greats like the late Stephen Hawking—make him difficult to dismiss outright."

The Japanese account continues, "There are two shapes that fit the peculiarities observed—long and thin like a cigar [I've lost track of how many "cigar-shaped UFOs" have been reported over the decades), or flat and round like a pancake, almost razor thin. Loeb says simulations favor the latter and believes the object was deliberately crafted as a light sail propelled by stellar radiation."

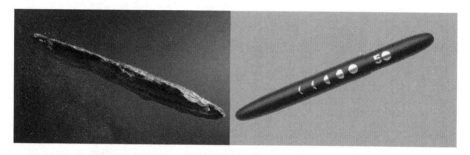

An artist's rendering of the Oumuamua ("scout") object detected in deep space in 2017 by Avi Loeb, Harvard Chair of Astronomy, resembling (it seems) the 400B 50th Anniversary edition of the 1998 Fisher Bullet Space Pen

The well-known artist's depiction of the long, rocky-looking, cigar-shaped cosmic traveler has circulated frequently around the globe since 2017. Oddly enough, it is shaped a lot like the sleek, 1998 400B 50th Anniversary edition of the Fisher Bullet Space Pen—the original design from 1948—the pen that "Goes Anywhere, Writes Anywhere," and is now featured in the permanent collection of the New York Museum of Modern Art as an outstanding example of "industrial art." The anniversary pen even includes beautiful "geometric moon-cycle engraving." It's too bad a "customer sample" wasn't included in the goods that shipped out on the original Voyager I explorer that was launched in 1977 and is still sending data from deep space because it looks like it belongs there, a simple and sophisticated tool of communication, an artifact of consciousness for space probes, astronauts and aliens alike to share.

When that *New York Times* news broke, though, I thought about calling John P., my coworker from the college grounds crew and fellow Space Pen participant, who, during a college reunion event, had poo-pooed any inclinations I might have to write about the subject. But I laid that thought aside. I had enough trouble convincing members of my own family that the topic was worth pursuing intellectually and "live under the stars with Steve Greer and CSETI."

The December 2017 bombshell reported that a secretly funded $22,000,000 "black budget" project originated by Senator Harry Reid (D-Nevada) lasted several years and was shut down in 2012 (although, as you'll see, it wasn't really shut down). To date, in support of the big disclosure, three videotapes have been released by the Department of Defense. The Pentagon officially sanctioned them in 2020, but never could—or never did—say what they were.

But why was the DOD now releasing vetted UFO footage as if it were the alleged Stormy Daniels/Donald Trump sex photos discussed in 2018? And which would the American public want to watch? Judging by the reaction of the general public after rounds of interviews with Kean and her colleagues on broadcast news, talk shows, blogs and websites, the cynical answer would be the latter.

The study was executed in large part by a research team headed by the billionaire Bigelow, who told CBS' *60 Minutes* in 2017, "There has been and is an existing presence, an ET presence." I've never met the man, but I briefly interacted with members of one of his organizations called NIDS, the National Institute for Discovery Science, founded in 1995 and disbanded in 2004. In 2000, after leaving CSETI behind, I tried to create a part-time gig at NIDS offering PR services for its activities, which included studying cattle mutilations and the many reported "black triangles"—similar to the one the CSETI RMIT crew saw in

Mexico and the one on the video that the dentist supplied a year later on the ill-fated CBS *48 Hours* debacle. It would be a rare niche—this sidewinding side hustle—in the other practice areas of my small consulting firm Media Savant Communications.

NIDS employed a small but high-powered staff that included one of the Aviary birds, Penguin, and Dr. Colm Kelleher, Ph.D., a native Irishman with impeccable academic credentials, plus Eric W. Davis, an astrophysicist, who would later show up in *The New York Times* stories. I reached out to Kelleher via email and offered to pay my own way to Vegas to meet with him a couple weeks before Christmas to discuss their public relations needs. He agreed, and NIDS put me up at the Luxor, that buggy-looking pyramid hotel that squats in Casinoland like something the Egyptians built with glass and steel in another desert. As an icebreaker, I gave Kelleher my annual "Christmas mix tape," a compilation CD of broadly defined holiday music I curated every year and gave to family, friends, colleagues and the occasional stranger. It was a seasonal tiding that many had looked forward to for twenty-nine years. The 2000 collection was one of my best and included John Prine's classic "Christmas in Prison." As Kelleher perused the titles on my makeshift album cover, he expressed fondness for Prine. Of course, he would. The late sing-songwriter is practically a saint in Ireland.

After a routine discussion at the NIDS office at which he, Davis, another NIDs staffer, and I talked about our mutual work—plus the usual UFO scuttlebutt shared among parties—Kelleher and I headed out for dinner. As we drove to the restaurant, he made a wrong turn and within seconds we were out in the desert, which was black and foreboding, especially against the neon reflection of sin city in the distance.

"Great," I thought, "Here's where we both—or one of us—gets left to lie face down with the scorpions." Too much UFO ghetto paranoia ran in my blood. However, the good man quickly rerouted us and before long we were each nursing a Guinness while waiting for our meals to arrive. We made small and big talk. I ventured into the sightings I'd had as a kid in North Dakota and talked more about what we saw in Mexico with Geer, Shari and Wayne. That sharing included the little red ball in the park with Zod out on the Great Plains, and the five cherry bombs in the bedroom many years later in the City of Lakes. Those events really got his interest.

Besides cattle mutilations (which Kelleher later wrote about in a best seller, *Brain Trust)* and the numerous sightings of silent triangles that NIDS researched, Bigelow's boys did a few years of hard "paranormal" research at the infamous Skinwalker Ranch in Utah. Alleged to be a hotspot for UFO sightings and other inexplicable phenomena, from energy portals to the appearance of weird sci-fi-like creatures to animal mutilations, the ranch has been written about often in some media. In its storied history, the ranch was avoided by the indigenous tribe that was native to the territory, which claimed it was cursed, a no-man's land—or perhaps it was a psychically-charged nomad's land not to be messed with. Ironically, the ranch was located near Vernal City, a small town I had lived in as a child for a couple years just after my dad got out of the Air Force.

With Vegas investigative reporter and media personality George Knapp, who seems to have done more UFO and paranormal reporting than any mainstream reporter on the planet, Kelleher wrote a book about the ranch in 2005 (which I didn't read until the completion of this one) entitled *Hunt for the Skinwalker*. Publisher Simon & Schuster describes the book in its marketing materials like this:

> The author of the controversial bestseller Brain Trust brings his scientific expertise to the chilling true story of unexplained phenomena on Utah's Skinwalker Ranch—and challenges us with a new vision of reality. For more than fifty years, the bizarre events at a remote Utah ranch have ranged from the perplexing to the wholly terrifying. Vanishing and mutilated cattle. Unidentified Flying Objects. The appearance of huge, otherworldly

creatures. Invisible objects emitting magnetic fields with the power to spark a cattle stampede. Flying orbs of light with dazzling maneuverability and lethal consequences. For one family, life on the Skinwalker Ranch had become a life under siege by an unknown enemy or enemies. Nothing else could explain the horrors that surrounded them— perhaps science could.

Leading a first-class team of research scientists on a disturbing odyssey into the unknown, Colm Kelleher spent hundreds of days and nights on the Skinwalker property and experienced firsthand many of its haunting mysteries. With investigative reporter George Knapp—the only journalist allowed to witness and document the team's work—Kelleher chronicles in superb detail the spectacular happenings the team observed personally, and the theories of modern physics behind the phenomena. Far from the coldly detached findings one might expect, their conclusions are utterly hair-raising in their implications. Opening a door to the unseen world around us, *Hunt for the Skinwalker* is a clarion call to expand our vision far beyond what we know.

As I discussed the after-effects of the five red spheres in my bedroom, he said that they had seen similar, red-colored orbs at the ranch and the orbs had spooked the horses.

"What do you think they are?" I asked earnestly, still trying to complete the puzzle of my lifetime.

He said simply, "We're not sure. But I don't think they're benign."

Not really the answer I wanted to hear, but I filed it away in that foil depository I was beginning to despise. In the morning, I would head back home to the cold and the coming holidays. But back in my

Luxor room that night, I woke up half-asleep and heard what sounded like someone trying to break in through the security-coded door. I
cowered in bed, then fell asleep again. But half an hour later, or maybe
longer, I sensed a large presence in the room but could not bring myself to face it in a wakeful state. Today, I write it off as a tired imagination, "the noisy confusion of life" and the "many fears" born of fatigue
that were articulated so well in the "Desiderata" poem that my college
roommate and Space Pen bro, GhoulDog, liked to quote whenever real
answers could not be found, or tested.

In a follow-up call a few weeks later, Kelleher warned me that no
real decision had been made as to whether NIDS would engage me, but
that Mr. Bigelow doesn't like to pay for such services. So, there was my
answer. About a month later, Colm surprised me with a call inquiring
if I knew how to put out of news release.

"Of course," I told him.

"Oh," he replied, "I see. You'd like to get paid." Or words to that
effect.

Of course, I would, I thought, hanging up the phone. *Aren't you
getting paid?*

* * *

I was as surprised as anyone in 2017 when Bigelow's name appeared in
the covert UAP study and subsequent media stories, and how millions
of taxpayer dollars allegedly had been paid to his team during its time
on the program. But the whole thing raised more obvious and downstream questions than answers—like the ones italicized below. The covert study highlights included:

> "The program produced documents that describe
> sightings of aircraft that seemed to move at very
> high velocities with no visible signs of propulsion,
> or that hovered with no apparent means of lift." *So,
> where are they from and who makes them?*

"Under Mr. Bigelow's direction, the company modified buildings in Las Vegas for the storage of metal alloys and other materials that Mr. Elizondo [the former military intelligence officer who led the secret Pentagon study] and program contractors said had been recovered from unidentified aerial phenomena." *You mean, there are recovered parts from these "phenomena" lying around in a Vegas warehouse like banged up auto parts at Stan's junkyard?*

"Researchers also studied people who said they had experienced physical effects from encounters with the objects and examined them for any physiological changes." *By "encounters with the objects," are they talking about the so-called abduction phenomenon, or in polite speak, Close Encounters of the Fourth Kind (CE-4), a term used by scientific researcher and writer Jacques Vallee in the* Journal of Scientific Exploration *that built on Dr. Allen Hynek's Close Encounter terminology, the same Professor Hynek who went from being a professed "UFO" skeptic to a firm proponent that "there is an embarrassment of riches" when it comes to evidence on topic?*

In a March 2018 *New York Magazine* interview, Nevada Senator Reid expressed the same perplexed reaction that Zod and I and others had to what seemed to be a giant public and governmental shrug of indifference about the news. He asked why the media at large and the *New York* magazine reporter in particular are not doing its job? "Let me give you something that the press has totally failed and conjured," Reid said. "We have hundreds and hundreds of papers, pages of paper, that have been available since this was completed. Most all of it, 80 percent at least, is public. You know something? The press has never even looked at it. Not once. That's where we are. I wanted it public, it was made public, and you guys have not even looked at it."

So, now what?

At the time of the story, Greer sensibly tweeted, "Note that the recent *NY Times* story is couched from a threat office of the Pentagon: This is a clear ramp up to False Flag FAKE disclosure designed to prepare people for a threat from outer space—so the War Mongers and War Profiteers have a new, bigger enemy. BEWARE."

His 2018 tweet shared glimpses of his longer essay (which is still online)—written in 1999! —"When Disclosure Serves Secrecy." It was so prescient that it seems incredible it could have been written twenty years earlier! But this was just part of Steven's brilliance, and I saw it repeatedly alongside his equally noticeable foibles and the mountainous ego that often came off as colossal arrogance. I actually didn't mind that, although I worried this Achilles heel could trip him up even as others were doing their best to do so. And I also watched with concern two scenes from two of the three films he has released in the last few years in which he's pictured with a bodyguard. Even more troubling is a ten-second on-screen interview with him (looking like it was crudely spliced into the section for impact) in which he said, "...And if you're seeing this, it's because I'm either dead, or have been entrapped, or have disappeared."

But I wondered how he really felt under that public-policy pose of the tweet he proffered. After all, he initially set out with an ambitious CSETI disclosure effort beginning in 1993 and peaking in April 2001 with his major Disclosure event in Washington DC at the National Press Club. Here, he and his team were being upstaged by a powerful military institution that routinely hid obscene sums of money in deep black budgets for any number of covert issues with no congressional or presidential oversight. At least he had achieved one of his goals—seeing the UFO subject moved from the grocery-store tabloids to the front page of *The New York Times*.

In 2021, other major media are rapidly hurtling toward a more open, less uninformed view of "the phenomenon," including Jeff Bezos' *Washington Post*, perhaps atoning for running crap columns about UFOs like the one I'd referenced earlier, ridiculing those who wanted an official disclosure by our government. In an April 1, 2021 guest column, written by Daniel W. Drezner is a professor of international politics at the Fletcher School of Law and Diplomacy at Tufts University, Drezner insightfully writes:

> "The U.S. government continues to tiptoe toward the normalization of the idea of unidentified flying objects (UFOs).… The Pentagon went further in August 2020, announcing the establishment of an Unidentified Aerial Phenomena (UAP) Task Force… It is increasingly respectable to acknowledge that unidentified aerial phenomena are a thing. But this leads to a few follow-up questions. Does this evidence point toward the prospect of extraterrestrial observation of our planet? If so, how should we feel about that?

> "I am not going to speculate on the first question beyond noting that if Harvard astrophysicists [implying Avi Loeb at Harvard] are making that suggestion about interstellar phenomena, perhaps we need at least to consider the possibility that these UAPs might also be extraterrestrial in origin.

> "If UAPs are extraterrestrials, however, this is a different scenario: It is not humans contacting

extraterrestrials but rather those extraterrestrials actively observing us. Furthermore, they seem to be doing so in a way that is not destructive. That is promising! Observation without the intent to destroy suggests a civilization that is much less violent than, say, Spanish conquistadors…

"I get the concern from physicists that technologically advanced extraterrestrials might behave as powerful human civilizations have in the past. But maybe the concerned physicists should engage a little more with social scientists. The assumption is that powerful, technologically advanced civilizations will act in a destructive manner. That is possible, but perhaps civilizations that reward destructive entrepreneurship are less likely to generate the technological wherewithal for interstellar travel. And if those UAPs are ETs, maybe there is more hope for interstellar relations than either scientists or science fiction envision."

That is now (and it has to give the Greers of the realm hope). But with the *Times* breakthrough then in 2018, through the holidays and into early January of that year, I tried to fathom why the public reaction was ultimately such a buzzkill. Putting on my publicist's hat, I reasoned that maybe the Pentagon documents had not been summarized properly so as to make it easier for media and others to wade into deeper waters. Maybe the right reporters had not been contacted. Maybe Bigelow hadn't hired a good PR firm to help with the fallout of the *Times* headlines. (I didn't bother to check if he had.)

But the most nagging question—like the one Senator Reid raised—was, "For subsequent stories, why wasn't the *Times* looking into all the available detail in the Pentagon report including information not made available in the overall document? Later stories could have gone beyond the referenced pilot sightings and reactions to the

"Tic Tac UFO" as it came to be called. That first *Times* piece got more than a million hits online! It made me and my fellow UFO/UAP paranoiacs suspect that this was a controlled news event from one of the most influential papers on the planet.

Or maybe we were just overthinking it. Perhaps the answer was simpler. Maybe the level of cultural denial about the topic was so deep as to be blinding, the layers of tin foil too dense to peel back and seem relevant to the "average American" who had more challenges to face like how to make a living. The public's "mute" button had pushed in deep and was not going to be released any time soon, especially as the era of Fake News—pathologically ushered in by Trump and the reported widespread interference of Russian hackers and others online—became more culturally pronounced.

In his early lectures, Greer liked to tell the story of how, when the indigenous people of the Americas first saw the gigantic, militarized ships approaching their shores, they were unable to find a cultural context for them. These kinds of "boats" simply were not a reality in their world view, and so things eventually turned out very badly. European conquerors came ashore to claim new lands and practice genocide in the names of European "Christian" countries, often with the official blessing of the Vatican under the "Doctrine of Discovery" from 1493, justifying the killing, torture and enslavement of indigenous people and the taking of their lands. The thought of space ships from distant planets, galaxies or other dimensions visiting Earth might be too much for modern humans to process ("humankind cannot bear very much reality," the poet T.S. Eliot writes), despite all the polls saying how many people believed there was life on other planets and that UFOs were indeed a "thing," as Drezner wrote above.

Not long after the *Times* 2017 story, a relatively new and befuddling for-profit, crowd-funded entity called To the Stars Academy of Arts & Science appeared and took a seat near the head of the table inside the insular UFO community. It was set up by a rock star, former Blink-182 guitarist and singer Tom DeLonge. The Overview page of its website says, "To the Stars Academy of Arts & Science has mobilized a team of the most experienced, connected and passionately curious minds from the US intelligence community, including the CIA and Department of Defense, that have been operating under the shadows of top-secrecy for decades. The team members all share a common thread of frustration and determination to disrupt the status quo, wanting to use their expertise and credibility to bring transformative science and engineering out of the shadows and collaborate with global citizens to apply that knowledge in a way that benefits humanity. ***Without the restrictions of government priorities*** [their bold italics].

Although the site never says ET, UFO, UAP, or Whatever U Want to Call It, in so many words, Stars Academy has its wonky interstellar, beam-us-up mojo working. I hoped they would succeed in some fashion until I realized it looked like an extension of the intel and DOD agencies into the private sector, given its roster of men who used to work in those agencies. The Academy signed power hitters from Spooksville, academia, the medical industry and the US diplomatic corps to be on its team. They seemed to want disclosure as bad as the rest of us. But one must be circumspect of who they might ultimately be working for, and what motivates their disclosure efforts.

As I followed the rollout of the Stars Academy operation and kept tabs on their media hits, I remembered the night DeLonge had called me out of the blue in the late '90s just as CSETI was ramping up its disclosure efforts. Of course, he was looking for Greer. I told him I would have to call him back. And when I did a few days later, he ignored the call. No big deal. Rock stars are as busy as emergency-room doctors trying to get ET to call them too.

In truth, when the organization announced its plans to launch late in 2017, Delonge's Stars Academy grabbed almost as much attention as the initial *Times* headline. However, its online funding seemed to have stalled out in 2018 even though they produced a History Channel series in 2019 called *Unidentified: Inside America's UFO Investigation*. To me, it looked like a response to Greer's second 2017 documentary film

Unacknowledged: An Exposé of the World's Greatest Secret, in which he identifies a cause of the secrecy around the subject—to protect the national security policy around energy systems, from the trillion-dollar, heavily subsidized fossil-fuel industries that threaten to fry the planet to the alleged zero-point energy systems (drawing energy from space) that appear to drive extraterrestrial vehicles—and maybe some of our own as well.

But I doubt that DeLonge's Academy is going the way of many UFO groups—quietly into the annals of Ufology. My belief lies, in part, with Chicken Little and the contorted pretzel-logic chronology that pervades this trying subject.

* * *

Not long after my first child was born in 1993, Greer called to run down a public-disclosure project CSETI would spearhead that was initially called "The Best Available Evidence" (BAE) and included vetted film, video, pilot testimony, government documents, insider testimonials, astronaut statements, etc. Later, it would become part of The Project Starlight Coalition briefing package used to brief Congress and the president to leverage national hearings and end what "exopolitics" activist Stephen Bassett (Executive Director of the Paradigm Research Group) liked to call "the Truth Embargo" on the UFO subject. Eventually, Bassett became the only official lobbyist on the Hill to talk about ET to lawmakers, a lonely job in the nation's capital.

The BAE was a sound idea. However, there were no Whistleblower laws in place then to protect witnesses from the military and intelligence agencies. So, any individuals who came forward ran the risk of prosecution and the loss of their pensions—and/or the risk of real jail time —if they broke secrecy oaths. The deck was stacked against us. Was I in? Greer wanted to know after congratulating me on the new arrival.

"The train is leaving the station," he said.

"I'm on it," I assured him. I'd come this far, why not go further down the line? Maybe all my questions would get answered. Howard, up in Ottawa, was on board, and Shari was already hard at work on myriad tasks, helping to run the organization on its meager budget plus overseeing her Working Group and holding down her day job as a paralegal in a busy Denver law office. I'd heard rumblings that her health wasn't great. Soon enough, that would be confirmed.

I was "in" because I also felt that having a trove of evidence like that to share with media would make my PR job easier, smarter and more efficient. Plus, it aligned with similar historical efforts by Donald Keyhoe in the '50s and '60s. Keyhoe was a former Marine aviator who later cofounded and served as the director of the National Investigations Committee on Aerial Phenomena (NICAP), one of the era's more prominent civilian UFO groups that consistently pestered the Air Force and Congress to hold public hearings on the issue. He published several popular books on the topic and, more tellingly, was censored on a live CBS show in 1958 when the audio was suddenly silenced. Shades of CSETI's experience with the CBS 48 Hours program. Keyhoe never succeeded in getting the hearings. Greer was determined to do so. The last time Congress had even come close to moving on the issue was after the notorious "swamp gas" sightings in Michigan in 1966. Then, Michigan congressman Gerald Ford called for hearings, but they never materialized.

CSETI's BAE was inspired, in small part, by Chicken Little who had contacted Greer and told him that the climate was right to bring this subject out into the open. If done properly, assets would become available to make public sharing happen—more clear-cut evidence and most likely financial resources. At least that was what was understood from Little's conversations. Anyone who ever talked to the man knew that if you were talking to Chicken Little you were likely talking to Pelican at the CIA Weird Desk too, and if he were talking to you, he was probably talking for his buddy inside the agency. Or so the cat, mouse and chicken game went.

Little seemed to have a lot of time on his hands and could bounce from the UFO issue to eschatology—"end times" stuff he seemed to revel in. And he called Greer often, to the point where the conversations were interrupting his hospital and CSETI work and family life. Greer asked if I would become the main contact between him and the guy with the floppy gums. I hesitantly obliged. After all, when I had first met Greer, this same guy was allegedly spreading falsehoods about him in the media. Now I had to deal with him on a semi-regular basis. And he did ramble on all over the place, one time talking for almost an hour about trying to get hold of "the Red Book," which was separate from "the Green Book." I never did know if there were real evidentiary documents or just more pungent fertilizer self-produced in the ghetto.

Through many conversations, I got the sense that Chicken Little was deliberately feeding carrots not only to CSEIT but one or two other groups around the country to see who would get the job done. As Greer and Chicken Little liked to remind anyone interested in disclosure, there is no department in the U.S. government that "has agency"— an entrusted duty and the authority—to make any information public about the subject. In most federal government quarters, it wasn't even a "real" topic. Disclosure would have to come from a citizen's group in a strategic fashion. There was more than a little irony wrapped up in this effort. The birds from The Aviary were always tainted somewhat as being "the bad guys." Now, at least one or two of them were working toward the same goals as most others in the UFO arena.

On "World UFO Day" 2020, ABC News ran a story that seemed to indicate that the US Senate was creating agency to deal with what could look like an official US government disclosure. In part, the article said:

> "Two weeks ago, the Senate Intelligence Committee included language in the annual Intelligence authorization bill that would require US intelligence agencies and the Pentagon to put together a detailed unclassified analysis of all the data they have collected on 'unidentified aerial phenomenon.'

"The Committee remains concerned that there is no unified, comprehensive process within the federal government for collecting and analyzing intelligence on unidentified aerial phenomena, despite the potential threat," (my italics) the committee said in a description of the bill entitled 'advanced aerial threats.'

"The Committee understands that the relevant intelligence may be sensitive; nevertheless, the Committee finds that the information sharing and coordination across the Intelligence Community has been inconsistent, and this issue has lacked attention from senior leaders,"

A July 2020 story in *The New York Times,* again by Kean and Blumenthal—the Woodward and Bernstein of UFO reporting—confirmed that development. And it confirmed what many in the UFO community felt or knew to be true all along. The military had never really given up their study of the phenomenon, as the *Times* had initially reported in 2017. Its 2020 updated story said as much: "Despite Pentagon statements that it disbanded a once-covert program to investigate unidentified flying objects, the effort remains underway — renamed and tucked inside the Office of Naval Intelligence, where officials continue to study mystifying encounters between military pilots and unidentified aerial vehicles."

I thought their choice of the adjective "mystifying," was intriguing because I knew that at least Kean had a deep cache of UFO information at her disposal—including most likely so-called abduction or CE-4 insights or cases (since she was close with abduction researcher and hypnotist Budd Hopkins).She knew many cases inside out, including the truly baffling ones that showed how some anomalous craft had defied the laws of physics and science as we knew them.

The report said the program—the Unidentified Aerial Phenomenon Task Force—was "to standardize collection and reporting" on sightings of unexplained aerial vehicles and was to report at least some of its findings to the public within 180 days after passage of the intelligence authorization act.

You don't have to look hard for historical parallels suggesting the government has kept secrets on such sensitive subjects even in the face of outside pressure from informed and concerned private individuals and citizen groups. In the '50s and subsequent decades, citizen groups challenged official denials that testing of atomic bomb radiation effects on American soldiers—and radiation experiments on private citizens including children with Down syndrome (!)—harmed and killed. That is, until the Department of Energy under the Secretary for the department, fellow Minnesotan Hazel O'Leary, finally admitted these heinous actions in 1994 by opening and disclosing government's files.

"Here's a good rationale and defense against anyone saying that there was no precedent to disclosing a government cover-up, which, by extension, could also include UFO secrecy," I told Greer when that story broke nationally. He agreed.

I also tried to help again with fundraising and evidence gathering whenever I could. I'd come up with contact info for Dan Aykroyd from Pat Hayes, the leader of Minnesota's legendary blues-rock band Lamont Cranston, which I had covered for years. Aykroyd was also a Cranston fan. I wrote a formal letter to the head Conehead, whose interests in Ufology and the paranormal were well-known. Enclosing some of CSETI's RMIT reports from Mexico and England, plus other materials, I sent a package to him. About three weeks later, I got a very brief, kinda comic reply that said, more or less: "Thank you for the information you sent about CSETI. I appreciate it." Then he skipped down a few spaces as if indicating a dramatic pause: "Be careful." Signed, Dan Aykroyd.

I didn't doubt that Dr. UFO could collect the necessary evidentiary goods and make approaches to big office holders in DC. He already had inroads to Laurence Rockefeller in New York, who agreed to fund some of the briefing expenses for the BAE since the elder Rockefeller had a deep interest in the subject. Before long, Greer had networked through Rockefeller's office, primarily interacting with Rockefeller's attorney, Henry Diamond, into the first Clinton administration to create a channel to President Clinton's Science Advisor, Dr. Jack Gibbons.

But at roughly the same time, Chickadee (who was also at the Star Knowledge conference) was likewise setting things in motion. He was president of the Human Potential Foundation in DC and also pursuing similar goals through Rockefeller and ultimately the Clinton White House, working in concert with investigative journalist Richard Farley, whose name Chicken Little occasionally raised. According to FOIA-researched docs posted on a website called *The Presidents UFO* operated by Canadian writer and Ufologist Grant Cameron, Farley had spent "years" crafting a nine-page briefing paper titled the *Matrix of UFO Beliefs*:

> "Farley referred to the paper as 'an investigative and analytical tool… reflecting primary categories into which beliefs about UFOs seem to fall, when allowing for the broadest range of reported phenomena and perceptions…' *The Matrix of UFO Beliefs* was not designed to suggest to the president or his advisors what 'all the UFOs might be.' And the paper reflects my assumption that, for at least some publicly perceived 'UFOs,' various of our government's branches would be expected to know very well what may have been witnessed.

> "Primarily, the *Matrix of UFO Beliefs* was to serve us as our outline for a briefing of the President and his senior advisors on the range of public opinions and beliefs about UFOs as had been determined from: the popular literature; activity at UFO conferences; and throughout respective UFO venues into which beliefs evolved or had been seeded,

manipulated or reinforced."

Cameron writes that Farley eventually resigned from that disclosure group in 1994, objecting to "the timing and dynamics of 'what to push and when.'" Further, Farley had a serious concern that UFOs were being used as "camouflage for exotic aerospace and directed energy technologies"—something the CIA has admitted in recent time. A similar belief was held by my friend Tom Tulien who researched the Minot case, explored in Chapter Five. He said that realization sent him into a three-month depression: *It's not ET, it's all US.*

As persuasive as his arguments have been over the years, he has yet to convince me. Still, I often ponder if it's true, which would lead you down another dark, tight alley aboard the side hustle bus on the unchartered tour. If the UFO technology is all terrestrial, then—as the storyline goes in the ghetto—there would be "a breakaway civilization" consisting of those "insiders" among us, hiding in plain sight, and perhaps even going off planet whenever they desired for whatever purposes on their hidden agenda.

Many who believed or knew that "UFOs/UAPs" are real, subsequently thought "we"—the government personnel, military units and corporate government subcontractors privy to the truth—had reverse-engineered interstellar spacecraft decades ago and could now become interstellar ourselves. And these same individuals would, almost by rote, trot out the famous quote by Ben Rich, the former CEO of Skunk Works (Lockheed Martin's Advanced Development Programs) to describe their set of beliefs: "We already have the means to travel among the stars, but these technologies are locked up in black projects and it would take an act of God to ever get them out to benefit humanity... Anything you can imagine, we already know how to do." But put in the other context—that the spaceships are not interstellar vehicles, but domestic hardware made by human hands and minds to traverse the stars—Rich's quote takes on an entirely different meaning.

"Tom's dilemma," as I called it—and the dilemma underlying the whole UFO topic—reminded me of the probing questions posed in *Haunted Mesa,* a book written by a highly prolific and successful North Dakota native, Louis L 'Amour. The story was set in Arizona's back country where the Navajo, Paiute, the lost tribe—the Anasazi—and others lived and held fast to mysterious views of reality that readily conflicted with our conventional viewpoints. Here is a relevant passage from *Haunted Mesa*:

> "Each year our knowledge progresses, each year we push back the curtain of ignorance, but there remains so much to learn. Our theories are only dancing shadows against a hard wall of reality. How few answers do we possess! How many phenomena are ignored because they do not fall into accepted categories? Ours is a world that has developed along materialistic, mechanistic lines, but might there not be other ways? Might there not be dozens of other ways, unknown and unguessed because of the one we found worked?"

As I ambled through the paces of the early CSETI disclosure process, it became increasingly clear that the barriers to proof were fraught with personal agendas out of step with each other and that the Truth might be found in thousands of half-truths, like shards of a mirror reflecting only what one wanted to see, or could see, in each fragment but never in the whole.

Cameron also went on to disclose that the information requested by the CIA was written by the Aviary's Sea Gull, a well-known UFO researcher who specialized in optics analysis. He had a "long career at the Naval Surface Warfare Center, presently headquartered at Dahlgren, Virginia," according to his online bio. "He has worked on optical data processing, generation of underwater sound with lasers and various aspects of the Strategic Defense Initiative (SDI) and Ballistic Missile Defense (BMD) using high power lasers."

Cameron indicates that "the CIA had been contacted by the White House to provide a briefing for Dr. Gibbons, to prepare him and provide background information for his upcoming UFO meeting with Laurence Rockefeller." It was titled, "Briefing on the U.S. Government Approach to the UFO Problem as Determined by Civilian Researchers During the Last Twenty Years." Cameron adds, "It arrived just after Rockefeller's UFO briefing was completed and was not presented."

Where were the "boys upstairs" in all this? Would they have their own disclosure agenda once they recognized that humans were getting their act together? Did they even know about it? Did they get the memo? Or were they immune and also prohibited from interfering directly in human affairs. I know, it's one of the more salient story lines—and rules of the cosmos—in *Star Trek*.

As things started to be collected for the BAE, Greer continued to collect important contacts he assumed would be strong allies in the quest. He was good at it. He could win friends and out-influence people forty times better than Dale Carnegie. It was second nature to him, given his depth of knowledge, his flawless articulation of CSETI's goals and assumptions and the genuine charisma he wielded like a surgeon's scalpel.

One of those he won over was John Petersen, a futurist who ran a smallish national security think tank in Washington focused on possible future events, technologies and wild cards. Petersen had written a book in 1994 called *The Road to 2015: Profiles of the Future,* which Greer had read. Because one of Petersen's wild cards was a scenario in which we make contact with ET, Greer invited him to one of his lectures. Soon, Petersen was trying to raise funds for the BAE and playing a somewhat active role in the organization, even coming to a few key meetings in Asheville.

Greer and I also met with him later in New York City where the three of us compared notes. We became convinced Chicken Little had tapped our phones, given that he seemed to know what we were doing before the three of us knew it collectively. I think it was this same Big Apple trip where Greer had arranged a meeting with Ingo Swann, the famed psychic/remote viewer, artist, author and self-described "consciousness researcher" who had worked on the Stanford Research Institute's "Project Stargate" and had ties to the CIA and US Army. The movie, *The Men Who Stare at Goats*, is broadly based on this period and program in Swann's life. Unfortunately, the visit was the same night that I got two last-minute free tickets to see Bob Dylan and his band do their MTV "Unplugged" session at a mid-town studio. I felt like this was a decision where I had to pick between two masters, my lifelong passion for Dylan's music and my emerging passion for understanding more about remote viewing, the whole psychic and science of consciousness shooting match.

Had I gone to see Ingo, I would have asked him about the time he remote-viewed an ET base on the back side of the moon, and how I might better fine tune my nascent remote viewing abilities without doing it occasionally and rarely in my sleep. After all, this was the guy who created structure, protocols and processes around remote viewing at Stanford for the spooks at the CIA. The Dylan show, on the other hand, was only "pretty good." Our seats were on the back side of the stage, forcing us—me and my old pal and publisher of *The New York Rocker*, Andy Schwartz—to stare at the back of Bob's head all night and make disparaging cracks about the drummer, who was the closest performer to us. Neither of us cared much for him, and neither of us could count all the live Dylan shows we'd seen to that point. I should have gone to see Swann.

* * *

If you view the Amazon page for John Peterson's book, you'll find his bio: "John L. Petersen, a leading futurist, founded and presently heads The Arlington Institute, a Washington, DC-area think tank that studies global futures. He is the editor of *FUTUREdition* and the author of *Out of the Blue: Anticipating Wild Cards and Other Future Surprises*, and *The Road to 2015: Profiles of the Future*. His often-unconventional perspectives on what lies ahead are the product of having worked in the military, for the National Security Council at the White House, in business, real estate development, advertising, marketing, and the non-profit world."

One of the book's other wild cards was that the world's poor would finally realize how poor they really are and take measures to change their situation. Peterson got that right. The Exodus-like migrations of millions of impoverished and threatened people from war-torn and failed nations is sadly a grim feature of the early 21st century. Stories and images of central and south America refugees surging to the US, and thousands of Syrian refugees and others in the Mideast, are a clear example of a prediction Peterson made twenty-five years ago that has become a stark, depressing reality.

During a discussion with Peterson in Asheville on how to package the BAE, we worked on strategic messaging much like one would do for a product roll out or a political campaign, which the BAE resembled. I suggested that a successful disclosure effort would inspire people "to rethink their place in the universe and that of the Earth"—the planet is actually part of a larger, inhabited universe. And this revelation might change how we behave and interact with one another and the environment. It wasn't an original idea, but it was one that I held fast as a kid, wondering how one could positively change the thinking of the masses; perhaps it could be through a disclosure of this nature. Peterson liked the idea, as did Steven and the others in the room—Shari, Dr. Joe, Howard and a few new volunteers from the area.

Greer especially liked when Petersen offered to get a meeting with then-Director of the CIA James Woolsey, whom Petersen had known prior to Clinton having appointed him to head the agency. It would be a quiet, informal dinner with wives since a formal meeting in agency quarters or anywhere else "official" would be off limits given the dicey subject matter. As Petersen liked to point out, this topic isn't even considered a serious subject in DC. Years of marginalizing it in various (mostly) media channels were toxically effective.

Much was made in the ghetto about this dinner party—and occasionally in mainstream news and online forums—once word of it leaked out via the internet in 1998. Many disavowed it ever happened, including Petersen—under pressure from Woolsey, most likely—until confronted with written emails and a letter Woolsey had written to Greer outlining the December 13, 1993 event plans. The controversy heated up so much five years after the tête-à-tête that CSETI decided to put out an official news release to set the record straight:

FOR IMMEDIATE RELEASE

FORMER DIRECTOR OF CIA JAMES WOOLSEY DISCUSSED UFO/ET ISSUES IN DECEMBER 1993 WITH DR. STEVEN M. GREER, DIRECTOR OF THE CENTER FOR THE STUDY OF EXTRATERRESTRIAL INTELLIGENCE (CSETI) WHILE HE WAS IN OFFICE

GREER ALSO NOTES SERIOUS CLINTON INTEREST ON SUBJECT WHILE CSETI CONTINUES TO COLLECT MORE THAN 150 WITNESSES TO UFO/ ET EVENTS, PROGRAMS & KNOWLEDGE VIA ITS PUBLIC DISCLOSURE EFFORT

ASHEVILLE, NO. CAROLINA — February 24, 1998 — The former director of the CIA, James Woolsey, met for nearly three hours in December 1993 while he was in office to discuss the subject of UFOs and the geopolitical, scientific and other implications of the extraterrestrial presence with Dr. Steven M. Greer, Founder and International Director of The Center for the Study of Extraterrestrial Intelligence (CSETI), Greer said today, after revealing the information publicly last month over several national radio programs including the nationally syndicated "Art Bell Show."

Among other related topics, the candid meeting between the two men touched on the necessity to

279

establish concrete evidence of the ET issue and
how to begin to make this subject an informed reality for the American people and its leaders, "who
have no serious information about the issue or how
it's managed through Unacknowledged Special
Access Projects (USAPs)," Greer noted, "residing
in often above-top-secret contract work between
leading high-tech private industry companies and
select branches of the government, intelligence and
military." Similar claims were recently made by
retired Lt. Colonel Philip Corso in his revelatory
book "The Day After Roswell," where the former
NSA officer under Eisenhower says he helped seed
the technologies gleaned from the Roswell crash
to private enterprise to develop among other things
the laser particle beam weapon, the integrated circuit and other technologies.

Greer also admitted recently that President Clinton was given a packet of briefing materials and
evidentiary pieces prepared by CSETI's Project
Starlight effort (a public disclosure program) by
Laurence Rockefeller in the summer of 1994 while
the Clinton family vacationed at Rockefeller's
ranch in the Grand Tetons. Greer says this is not the
first time the president has taken an interest in the
subject. According to a recent New York Post article, Clinton asked embattled aide and friend Webb
Hubbell to look into the UFO subject when Clinton
first came into office. The anecdote is related in
Hubbell's new book *Friends in High Places*.

"Clinton had said, 'If I put you over at Justice, I
want you to find the answers to questions for me.
One, who killed JFK. And two, are there UFOs.'

Clinton was dead serious. I looked into both but wasn't satisfied with the answers I was getting," Hubbell says in the book.

Last April 9, the Project Starlight effort presented its case with 15 military, aerospace and civilian witnesses and hundreds of pages documents and a related video summary to more than 24 congressional offices in Washington along with former Apollo Astronaut Edgar Mitchell who supports a complete disclosure on the issue. Says Greer, "We now have identified more than 150 witnesses in our evidence pool who are ready to testify. But we need to continue to make the public aware of our leaders' accountability in this matter; we urge all citizens to contact their congressional representatives by writing them and urging open hearings on the matter."

Sample copies of a congressional letter and other Project Starlight information is available at the CSETI website.

The news release leapfrogs over the stylized chronology of this book, including the discovery of the Unacknowledged Special Access Projects [USAP), a secrecy mechanism within the federal government/military and select corporations (which was part of the content for the first disclosure mission in Washington explored briefly in the final chapter). Suffice to say, the Woolsey-Greer dinner was a three-plus hour affair in which Greer had shared the CSETI mission and best evidence.

At some point, Woolsey and his better half purportedly admitted to a UFO sighting of some kind in New Hampshire when they were younger. The issue of compartmentalized secrecy came up, and Greer told Woolsey to ask for certain documents from such and such departments. Woolsey agreed to, although he was never able to locate said paperwork. Barriers to truth were everywhere, even if you were the head of the Central Intelligence Agency. How deep they went —and how the secrecy worked—neither Greer nor I nor the rest of our group would find out until several years later.

With the Rockefeller/Project Starlight Initiative came two players who would shepherd the process and see that Rocky's money, reportedly $30,000, would be spent wisely. These players were New York socialites Marie Galbraith and Sandra Wright. At the same time, Rockefeller allegedly was funding John Mack's organization in Cambridge, Massachusetts—the Center for Psychology and Social Change. One source reported that Mack had received a quarter of a million dollars for his work related to so-called abductions, which also powers his books on the topic. This really burned Greer, who couldn't stand to play second violin to any other hunters, gatherers or visionaries in the UFO orchestra. He had a bad habit of denouncing others around CSETI's leadership team, often trotting out what he perceived to be the culprit's blatant weaknesses or shortcomings. In the case of Mack, Greer attacked his confessed use of psychedelics. That would be perceived in The Space Pen Club as not-so-cool for those who found self-discovery and realization in their exploratory use of substances as one gateway into deeper consciousness.

Galbraith, who everyone called "Bootsie," and "Sandy" were tasked with helping to create the BAE with CSETI and freelance contributors from the ghetto. Greer suggested they hire me to help write case studies of well-known historical incidents. But as I soon figured out, he also tried to put me in that role so as to help keep his influence elevated in the process. He knew where all the pieces on the chess board were. So, I got on a plane to New York City for a day before flying the next day to an annual UFO Congress in Laughlin, Nevada, where researchers from around the world were participating. The mission? Try to get conference participants involved as part of the Project Starlight..

Sandy, Bootsie and I met in an office in midtown, perhaps at Sandy's BSW Foundation (which might loosely be described as a "New Age" organization), which advocated for the "principles of balance, spirit and wisdom," according to Sandy's 2009 *New York Times* obituary. Wright served as BSW's president. Bootsie, an attractive, middle-aged New Yorker dressed as you'd imagine the wife of the former U.S. Ambassador to France would dress, occasionally took breaks by the loo where she would smoke a heater like a schoolgirl, waving the smoke away toward the powder room. Her quieter, more casually dressed and mannered counterpart mildly scolded Bootsie, seemingly an old exercise between two longtime friends.

I couldn't tell if they were Space Pen material or not—Sandy, most likely; Bootsie, not so much. Their heads seemed to be in the right place regarding disclosure, as we talked for two-plus hours about Starlight, the work needed to be done and CSETI. Later that night, back in Minneapolis, I called Greer and told him I thought it had gone well. He said it did. Bootsie had called him and said the job was mine if I wanted it. Finally, a paid gig in Ufoland, however small!

That may have been what the many researchers gathered in Laughlin the next day were thinking too. Word of the Rockefeller money had leaked and spread among the gathered international group. Those buzzing the hive sensed real money and real opportunity. And who could blame them? This group was different, and yet, in many ways, the same as the Star Knowledge gathering on the res' and included some of the folks who seemed to show up at every major UFO program.

Before the formal presentations began, I circulated inside someone's crowded and dark hotel room in which the curtains were half drawn at midday. Rocky's dough was on everyone's lips like some kind of UFO mark of Cain. I started making the rounds, letting the air out of balloons as gently as I could by describing what the BAE and Starlight were, and also getting a feel for whether participants would like to be part of it by bringing disclosure through official channels beginning at the Clinton White House. Without saying as much, I pretty much indicated the funding would come through Greer's organization, not directly to them individually.

I talked to A.J. Gevaerd from Brazil, who I'd met previously at a similar event and who was very excited by the news. Then I spoke with a known researcher from Britain who sadly reeked of booze before noon, then with Dr. Richard Boylan, Ph.D., who was dubious of Starlight's potential for success. "You know, Chicken Little's here at this conference," he warned. I did know that. I had seen him checking in and said hello.

I spoke to Jorge Martin from Puerto Rico, who enjoined Sun Shu Li from China in the conversation, since Sun spoke fluent Spanish and lived in Mexico part of the year. So, word of Starlight went from English to Spanish to Sun's Chinese brain. In his later public comments during the confab, Sun proudly exclaimed that the UFO organization he belonged to included more than 30,000 members across China and discussed some his country's more viable cases. In private, though, he was stoic but friendly and seemingly interested in participating.

By the end of the unplanned social hour, most everyone knew they might get expenses covered for evidence and that they could send their best-case studies, which somehow would reach the Clinton White House. Jorge Martin lingered awhile as others trickled out and we started comparing notes. I told him of my personal experience with the five red spheres in my room, still casting about for a plausible explanation. Without missing a beat, he replied, "It's the Grays! They're shape shifters." That's one for the Grays on my personal scorecard.

In what was the event's biggest surprise (at least for me), the famous public interest lawyer Dan Sheehan was also in Laughlin. I had greatly admired Sheehan's work during Iran Contra, the Karen Silkwood case and the Pentagon Papers, and his help with my 1960s heroes, the priests Dan and Phil Berrigan. He was also involved in Watergate, Wounded Knee and other high profile, highly politicized legal affairs involving the US government and many social justice issues. Most controversial and high profile national or international headlines involving misdeeds or unfair treatment of a group of people or individuals were often connected to Sheehan's name. His expertise would be highly valued in any situation. But what was he doing here in the desert with the rest of us?

It turns out he had a lifelong interest in the subject, an interest re-affirmed during a deep conversation with Greer on Facebook in spring of 2020 in the social media ramp-up to the *Close Encounters of the Fifth Kind* movie. Sheehan's headline-studded resumé included his stint as legal counsel for the Jesuits in DC, which required trips to Rome. While President Jimmy Carter was in office, he helped prepare a Top-Secret UFO study. But in Nevada, he explained that, while working with the Jesuit order, he learned that the Vatican allegedly had a secret depository of UFO/ETI material. He tried to access it only to be told he would never be allowed into that area. Fresh into our first conversation, I talked with him at length about Project Starlight, Rockefeller's interest and CSETI.

The more he talked, the more he started sounding like Steven Greer! He didn't think disclosure should be left to the government—it was too important and would never happen. At least not in a way that would benefit the people or the planet. I told him why I was in Laughlin and suggested he join the Project Starlight group. I didn't know at the time, but he was already engaged in forming a group with the same objectives as CSETI's Starlight project. That group included Bob and Cecilia Dean, Air Force Colonels Wendelle Stevens and Donald Ware, Jorge Martin from MUFON in Puerto Rico, A.J. Rivard from Brazil, Michael Hessemann of Germany, Tony Dodd from the UK and Professor Sun Shi Li from China.

Given his credentials, Sheehan would bring a ton of credibility and much needed legal insight to bear on the disclosure effort. He said he wanted to talk to Greer, and we walked immediately to my hotel room to make the call. Chicken Little saw us from across the way, but I paid him no mind. I called Greer and made quick introductions. Pretty soon the two were name dropping with each other to establish their bona fides, but more importantly to underscore that Starlight—and

Sheehan's interest in the topic—were substantial. Dan had mentioned Woolsey, so Greer was sharing that story.

Then came a knock on the door. I opened it to see the diminutive, nebbish Chicken Little standing there, raising his pointed little head to peer over me as he spied Sheehan sprawled on the bed, freely talking to Dr. UFO. Sheehan glanced at the door and kept talking. Little's tiny proboscis went into the air under a set of black framed glasses and a short crop of brown hair. It reminded me of the scene in the movie *Chinatown* right before Jack Nicholson gets his nose sliced up.

"Listen," I said to the pest at the door, "I'll catch you later, we're busy right now." He continued to eye the scene and tried to catch bits of the conversation, which had dwindled down to a few words such as "yes," "that's right," and "let's discuss that more," as Sheehan guarded his comments in front of the notorious bird man. Chicken left. The next day, a small group of us were finishing lunch, including Sheehan, Boylan and a couple of others. Chicken walked over and asked if he could join us. Bad move.

We made room for Chicken Little at the table before the high-profile attorney tore into him. Questions flew out of Sheehan's mouth like flames on a char broiler lacerating a piece of tender meat. As Sheehan cocked his head of curly dark hair in the direction of the alleged CIA interloper, lunch conversation screeched to a halt.

"Who are you working for, the agency? Are you on contract? Why don't you guys get your act together?" Sheehan barely let Chicken Little answer before another barbed insinuation wrapped in a question or comment came his way. Chicken folded. I thought he would lose it in front of us. We quietly paid our bills and left the restaurant.

The next day, while having a word with Boylan, Chicken Little sheepishly came up to us and replayed the ugly scene at yesterday's lunch wondering why "Danny Sheehan" had laid into him so hard, as if he and "Danny" were old buddies. Boylan, another ex-Catholic and a one-time priest, offered some genuine consolation, saying something like, "Oh don't take it personally, man, he was just fucking with you," and put his arm halfway around Little's humbled shoulders. I half-heartedly gave him a back pat and went on my way.

As I approached my room, another attendee (let's call him Stan) walked with me for a while and discussed what might happen with Project Starlight. Seemingly a ghetto lifer, he'd written an opinionated self-published book of fifty pages or so. It talked about the deceptive nature of the phenomenon, aligning with the demonic-forces camp, a strain of Ufology rooted among Christian fundamentalists who saw the work of the devil in things out of their purview, often including early rock 'n' roll. He lamented how it tore friendships and families apart. And yet, he was still at a UFO convention.

In response, I opined that Starlight was a good strategy and the right people were involved, especially Greer, who could get things done. Stan eyeballed me hard, saying (paraphrasing here) "A lot of people here at this conference have a lot of strange ideas about this whole subject, but your guy, I gotta tell ya, your guy, he's at the top of the heap!" He also warned about doing too much stargazing in the desert at night, which puzzled me. Nonetheless, his words threw me back twenty-five yards from the line of scrimmage. Somehow the way he said this—or perhaps the way I heard it for the first time—jilted my whole perspective of CSETI. Had I hitched my wagon to a dark star? Was I just another hunter and gatherer following a self-proclaimed pied piper visionary who cannily tried to distance himself from the rest?"

The man's comment reminded me of a favorite quote learned in my college William Blake seminar: "He became what he beheld."

There was another favorite Blake quote that seemed to apply to "my guy" too. It was an artistic statement about Blake's metaphysical vision and dense cosmological view to set the poet engraver apart from his peers: 'I must create a system or be enslaved by another man's." Greer had done that in large part. But suddenly, CSETI seemed as ghetto blasted as everything else, its own visionary construct of the non-locality of consciousness nothing more than a construct, even though I had experienced it firsthand through the precognitive dream set in

Boston harbor and other episodes. I paused and nodded. It was a good flush of cold water right in the third eye. It momentarily blasted the air out of my own balloon and, frankly, made the call I would get the next day somewhat more palatable.

Home in Minneapolis, as I proceeded to get back to the real world to tackle writing assignments and/or new PR clients, Ms. Galbraith called on my home line instead of my work number and left a message. Playing it back, I could hear a bunch of ambient, bar-like noise in the background. Later, she admitted she'd been at her hair salon getting boofed.

"We've decided we're going with someone else to work on the BAE pieces," the message said. "I'm sorry if there's any inconvenience. I hope you understand. I know we'll see you again as we move forward with this wonderful project."

I've always hated that kiss-off phrase, "I hope you understand." What if I didn't understand? And from her hair salon? I thought she was a classier broad than that. Old Bootsie just pulled a surprise move on the chess board. One of many, along with Greer. Often, I would get conflicting messages to share with Sheehan from both of them, which eventually pissed him off, and I think he blamed me for dictating them, even though I was just the messenger. Once I had moved on from CSE-TI, I heard that Sheehan and Bootsie had reportedly suffered a falling out over a remark Dan had made about her alleged good friend, Henry Kissinger. I can only imagine what it was over, given Kissinger's many imperial moves on the global chess board, some not so pretty.

Greer was as disappointed as I was over the failed assignment and later said he'd learned she had changed her mind after talking to J. Antonio Hunees and Don Berliner, writers who were better-known players in the arena. Maybe she just didn't want a Greer ally in her orbit on top of having to deal with the good doctor. However, if you check out the bio of Hunees online at *Open Minds: Credible UFO News and Information* and catch another good whiff of the ghetto's sometimes tainted aroma, you would discover that, "he was the co-author of the

Laurence Rockefeller-funded *UFO Briefing Document—The Best Available Evidence.*" Sure, he may have rewritten materials and interjected new pieces into the package. Fair enough! But I can still smell it from here today.

On the flight home from Laughlin and over the weeks ahead, I thought about Stan's biting remarks again. Still, I had some victories to celebrate. I'd done what I had set out to do at the annual UFO Congress—getting the global researchers on board and landing superstar Daniel Sheehan on the Project Starlight roster. Later, he put together a January 31, 1995, memorandum of Understanding (MOU) to codify the creation of The Starlight Coalition, which was sent out to the basic Project Starlight team at CSETI, Bob and Cecilia Dean, Kevin Foley, Jacqui Dunne and me, and now also Bootise, Sandy and attorney George Lamb. In it, Sheehan stated that between September and December of 1994 he learned of "at least five separate and distinct individual efforts being advocated to gather together, evaluate, and then to present to the world, in an authoritative manner, the 'best available evidence' establishing the bona fides of the related phenomena of Extra-Terrestrial (sic) Intelligence; Unidentified Flying Objects; the World Wide Government Cover Up of these Phenomena—and the possible Abduction of Human Beings (and other life forms) from Earth by Aliens."

Sheehan's MOU went on to outline the five groups that he was initially exposed to who would break this enigmatic subject out of its contrived and controlled cave environment into the bright sunshine of disclosure and truth. The groups included John Mack at Harvard Medical School, Lawrence Rockefeller, Bob Dean and his military and UFO researcher colleagues, CSETI, "and finally one was desired by a number of the personnel at the United Nations (perhaps including both Madame and Secretary General Bhoutris-Ghalli)."

Sheehan highlighted that with each group there "were consistently missing from every one of these several independent efforts two essential 'needs.'" They were one, a "certain Authoritative Forum" in which all the data could be evaluated, assembled and presented to the world. And two, "<u>certain</u> Financing necessary" to pay for this daunting process (all Sheehan underlines). Reading this section, I could hear Motown's first hit on its Tamala label from 1959, "Money (That's What I Want)," being sung aggressively by Barrett Strong, although Curtiss A and many others have since done their own stellar versions.

Our Starlight Coalition group first convened that last day in January in 1995 in Midtown at Sandy's spacious apartment for what turned into an eight-hour nighttime meeting. I remember it well because I walked in my cowboy boots from lower Manhattan's East Village where I was staying with Andy Schwartz to Sandy's address and worked up a good set of blisters, a Midday space cowboy hobbling into one of New York's high-rent districts. The other thing that sticks in the head was what looked like a small film crew perched on a rooftop about three buildings away and looking in the direction of where I stood on Sandy's small balcony. I verbally pointed it out to her and perhaps within earshot of the others back in the meeting. She abruptly put both hands on my shoulders, spun me around and walked me back into the room. I often have wondered if they were spooks eavesdropping on our planning session.

* * *

Having Sheehan join our efforts was as a good get, or better. And it was comparable to the night later in Minneapolis where I helped introduce Apollo Astronaut Edgar Mitchell—the sixth man to walk on the moon—to Greer after Ed had given a lecture about consciousness for the Continuum Center, run by my friend Jane Barrash, one of the Twin Cities' most inspired "out there" and "down-to-earth" intellectuals.

Greer had flown in especially for Mitchell's speech and knew that there would be a small party at Jane's house after the event. Mitchell had experienced a cosmic epiphany while hurtling back from the moon in which he felt that everything was connected—the rare, elusive "Oneness" —and sensed the universe itself was conscious. He writes eloquently about it in his book, *The Way of the Explorer: An Apollo As-*

tronaut's Journey Through the Material and Mystical Worlds.

Apollo 14 astronaut Ed Mitchell experienced a cosmic epiphany on his way back from the moon

Perhaps the best summary of the book is the July 2020 lead Amazon review: "Among authors trying to bridge the gap between science and spirit, former astronaut Mitchell brings unique credentials. Originally scheduled for the ill-fated Apollo 13 mission, Mitchell, as told in this smooth blend of autobiography and exegesis, journeyed to the Moon in 1971 (and generated great controversy over ESP experiments he conducted on the flight). As he gazed on Earth, surrounded by blackness and an unfathomable number of stars, he experienced 'an overwhelming sense of universal connectedness' that was to change his life. Within a few years, he had left NASA and founded the Institute of Noetic Sciences aimed at the systematic study of the nature of consciousness. At the institute, he came to some fascinating conclusions, detailed here and based on principles of resonance, regarding a possible natural explanation for psychic powers."

Despite his interest in consciousness studies that he shared with Greer, once they met, Mitchell made a beeline for the outdoors after something Steven had said. I casually trailed him, nursing a beer, while Ed held court for a couple of women as he drank red wine and smoked a cigarette. I listened to him telling stories and began mentally revamping my boyhood fascination with astronauts. I would have to make room for ciggie-smoking astronauts and this consciousness business.

Mitchell wasn't the only astronaut I'd excitedly encountered during this period and who were among the autographed photos I'd gotten from NASA as a kid. And I slowly realized that even those who had set foot on the moon had done so with clay feet too, just like some of the idolized rock artists I'd interviewed in my other lifetime—Dylan, McCartney, Bob Marley and many others. In 1997, I met Buzz Aldrin while doing publicity for the second annual Starkey Hearing Foundation Gala in Minneapolis (Starkey travels the world giving hearing aids to children in poor countries). Aldrin was the second man to hoof it on la luna after Neil Armstrong, In a quiet moment during the cocktail hour, I approached Aldrin and asked about some of the more stunning allegations regarding captured ET technology allegedly being funneled into private enterprise. These charges had been made by Colonel Philip J. Corso in his controversial book *The Day After Roswell.*

Apollo Astronaut Buzz Aldrin: Don't ever ask him about the faked moon landing!

Buzz looked me hard in the eye, his hands clasped tightly together as he sat on a chair, and said, "Son, I don't know anything about that," as if to say, "Don't ever ask me another question like that again!" A few weeks later, I saw that he made the news again, not for moon walking or charitable good works, but for slugging a guy who confronted him about "the fake moon landings."

As Project Starlight progressed, I heard many compelling and comic stories from Mitchell, such as the time Uri Geller retrieved a pin from one of Ed's cameras that had accidentally been left on the moon. Uri somehow had retrieved it by teleporting it with his mind! I also heard about the line Mitchell often used for people who asked him what he really saw on the moon. Mitchell would pull them aside, saying, "Yeah, I can tell you what I really saw, but you'll have to step over here away from these other people." Then he would lean in slightly and in hushed tones say, "Here's what I saw on the moon. A big buttload of rocks!"

He admitted he didn't like talking about his time on the lunar surface; it was much more prosaic than his cosmic views of things. Greer and the astronaut exchanged numbers that night and it wasn't long before Mitchell was being copied on Starlight email updates, including one that would convene the Starlight team in Asilomar, California, at a conference center about ninety minutes from San Francisco. Set on a beach, the location was beautiful and comfortable. Here the team would listen and film testimonies of key witnesses, including those of two Russian military officers that the well-known Russian researcher Valery Uvarov had lined up. It was all going on Uncle Laurence's tab, which meant Bootsie, Sandy and Rockefeller's attorney would be coming in for the event along with a couple other facilitators.

Also attending was Bob Dean, who again shared his "Assessment" story, noting how he had at the time of reading the report "a Cosmic" security clearance while at SHAPE in Europe. And how the report emphasized that Earth had been under surveillance for a long time by ETs; how the best minds at MIT, Oxford, the Sorbonne and Cambridge had contributed to the study; and how it had "changed my life forever" and launched him on a "thirty-year search in my life to make sense of this." He closed out his interview comments with the passionate belief that "people have the right to know" while also suggesting that the constitutional process was in danger, given how the subject has been managed and kept from the government's chain of command all the way to the president.

Even more passionate but in a very understated fashion were the comments of Jesse Marcel, Jr., the son of the Roswell officer who allegedly handled the Roswell craft debris and had brought home pieces of it to show his son and wife in the wee hours of the morning after the crash in 1947. The 12-year-old boy had seen his father produce the thin but impenetrable skin of the craft and an I-beam covered in what looked like Egyptian hieroglyphics. Jesse had brought a replica of it to share with the team. And he avowed that the materials from the crash that his dad and General Ramey could be seen holding in a nationally syndicated photograph the next day clearly were not the same materials he'd been shown at three o'clock in the morning. That photograph, now on media's radar across the country, was just part of the cover-up, Jesse said. It was the day the original flying saucer crash story became the downed weather balloon tale in what the newspaper world calls a "day two story."

Kent Randle, who had been doing more latter-day Roswell research, presented a highly articulated update of his findings and had us all sign a petition that was later sent to the Clinton White House urging a full disclosure on Roswell and the UFO issue in general. Mitchell and fellow astronaut Brian O'Leary, whom I'd met at the New Science confab in Ft. Collins early on my side hustle sojourn, shared their more academic views on the subject. Both agreed in an open discussion that the unified field theory—the holy grail of the post-Einstein world— would never prove satisfactory until the integer of consciousness was added to the equation. They talked about it casually, as if it were a given, even though "modern" science has yet to embrace it.

Man, I thought, sitting just a few feet away from them, I was out in the deep water now, trying to learn and understand concepts never broached before in my formal education or personal reading. Was it too late to program Mr. Peabody's WABAC time machine from *The Adventures of Rocky and Bullwinkle and Friends* cartoon show back in the 1960s so I could switch my major from English to Astrophysics?

I had two designated roles for the Project Starlight gathering. One was to help conduct interviews. The other was to pick up the Russian brass—one during the day, the other that same night—from the San Francisco International Airport, about a four-hour round trip each time. I'd be driving Magazali Endreev, the First Deputy Minister of Internal Affairs of Kabardino-Balkaria republic, and Valery Dvuzhikny, a UFO expert from Far East of Russia (Vladivostok). He was the one who was investigating a UFO crash case near Dalnegorsk. Unofficially, he was working in the air defense system with forces of Far East Russia, according to Uvarov.

Thank God for FM radio, especially left of the dial, which is often full of musical program surprises. Since the arriving Russians didn't speak English, I had to hold a sign with their names in Russian. On the final day, I put down the car keys, took up the pen and asked questions on camera of the visiting generals.

I had flown into San Francisco a day early and rendezvoused with my buddy Kevin Foley who was serving as a Starlight liaison to key people in Clinton's Washington because he had done advance work for the President's first term and knew Al Gore and some of the support staff. Foley was staying with researcher and CSETI supporter Jacqui Dunne whose good friends and Starlight facilitators for the weekend included Ralph Steiner and Dan Drasin, a media producer and documentary filmmaker.

I first met Drasin early on when the world of Ufology and high strangeness seemed to be a diversion from another dimension. I'd heard him give a funny but insightful paper in Ft. Collins, Colorado, about debunking UFO debunkers. That was before I fully understood what a "debunker" was. Steiner was close with reporter Leslie Kean and introduced me to her. Along with Shari, they had helped put the San Francisco event together and handled on-site logistics. They tried in vain to get participation from Mercury astronaut Gordon Cooper who lived in the area, but not even Ed Mitchell's presence, nor O'Leary's, the one-time astronaut designated for Mars missions, nor Dan Sheehan's, could persuade him to join the "Starlight Coalition."

The well-spoken Russian, Valery Uvarov, was about the same age as those on the San Francisco team, mid-to-late 30s and good-looking with fluent English. He reminded me of a Brit rocker I couldn't quite put my finger on, with his stylish haircut, pierced ear and cool demeanor. He also liked to bash Boris Yeltsin, then-president of Russia, for being a sloppy drunk who couldn't even speak good Russian. Uvarov had taken a train across America and marveled at how beautiful and expansive the country was.

All things considered, like the rest of us, Uvarov had UFO cred. His views were summarized in part by the ExoNews website run by another deep ghetto researcher and writer, Michael Salla: "According to Mr. Uvarov, ET craft are abundant around the world, manifest at specific cyclical times and for the most part (unless having technical difficulties) just travel too fast or at a time rate that renders them normally invisible to the naked eye [a view Standing Elk claimed as well back on the res']. Some of the pyramids built in Russia would have already attracted them but they can only be seen if filmed at high speeds and then by slowing down the video. Apparently, in order to 'travel' from one place to another, ET civilizations would make transitions between 'chrono fields' (time-space fields) using crossing points between 'time corridors.'"

Greer also held a deeply established theory about the crossing point—the point where hyper-space melds into 3D time-space materiality (he even used Crossing Point as the name of his self-publishing entity). In 2020, in the last film of his trilogy, *Close Encounters of the Fifth Kind*, Greer clearly articulates what and how the crossing point is and how it "functions"—and what the implications are—much better than I ever could.

According to Valary, however, these "time corridors" would be policed by a neutral exopolitical force. Some of this account can be read in Uvarov's reply to General Alexey Savin's comment about why extraterrestrials do not openly contact humanity, as explained in ExoNews in which Uvarov also proclaimed "the Russian government doesn't have an official information suppression policy [on the UFO subject] and has never told him to stop researching. Moreover, issues such as 'extraterrestrials' and 'pyramid power' seem to be less of a taboo among formal Russian institutions."

One was tempted to quip, "Fascinating," like Spock, when encountering yet another viewpoint, especially from a citizen of our once avowed enemies in the former USSR.

As things got underway on the coast, the New Yorkers arrived at Asilomar attired in expensive Western wear. They looked smart, even if slightly overdressed. Knowing that I still carried some resentment for Bootsie's handling of the BAE writing assignment, Foley went up to greet her as I stood within earshot. He inhaled the air around her and said, "God, you smell good!"

I don't know who was more taken aback, me because Foley's crack was so brazen and put me off my grudge, or Bootsie, who seemed genuinely flattered. The next day I set out on my first roundtrip to the airport while the team filmed a couple of witnesses, including Stephen Lovekin, reportedly a Brigadier General who claimed he had served in a secret cryptology department of the Pentagon in the radio frequency office and briefed President Eisenhower on the efforts to decipher the symbols found on the Roswell wreckage, which looked like hieroglyphics. He also noted that Eisenhower had a deep interest in the topic and wanted as much UFO information as he could get. That flow of info eventually slowed to a trickle by the end of Ike's term, and by the time Kennedy took office was non-existent, he noted.

Lovekin's credibility was later rigorously attacked by Penguin from the Aviary flock, who pointed out in his book that there was no military record of Lovekin's that could be found! Only some expert sleuthing by Kevin Randle, a well-respected UFO researcher and author who also served in both the Army and Air Force, finally established where Lovekin served. In his February 2006 blog, Randle writes: "He was not a brigadier general on active duty with the Army, he was not a member and brigadier general in the North Carolina National Guard and he was not a brigadier general in the Army Reserve. He is, as I speculated, a brigadier general in the State Guard of North Carolina Association, a volunteer civilian organization."

Still, I "enjoyed" his story, even if it wasn't true. Perhaps I was becoming a mere woozy spectator to the parade of characters and their unwieldy tales, intoxicated by their detail and the alluring patina of authenticity. UFO lore could knock you out! With Lovekin, it was the less overt UFO details of his tale that made it attractive. Because of his involvement in this alleged secret military enterprise at the Eisenhauer White House, even after his hitch in the service, Lovekin said he knew that he was routinely surveilled over the years with anonymous checks of his bank accounts and other "reminders." It he was making it all up, he was pretty convincing. But why would he? Did he want to be a spolier?

Lovekin's testimony wasn't on a par with Bob Dean's story about "The Assessment." But since I had no ultimate way of verifying either, I found some value in taking it all in with both. But I had to be careful; I was becoming more like Combover Bob from my Minneapolis Working Group, who made room for everything he heard at UFO conventions and confabs. Unfortunately, I eventually gave up on my Minneapolis group with Bob, Jesse Taylor and company. It was just too hard to participate in as the '90s inched toward the aughts and kids started coming.

I picked up Endreev in the late afternoon. As we drove back to the conference center, I played a college radio station and hoped my guest liked what he was hearing. I then got a quick download on who had been filmed that day and if there had been any surprises (none, Foley advised). I grabbed a quick bite and a new sign with Valery Dvuzhikny's name on it and headed back to the airport.

It was stone-cold dark by the time I got my fare. He smiled when he saw my sign. The general firmly shook my hand and said hello in a thick Russian accent, which seemed to be the only word in English he knew. Once we cleared the Bay-area sprawl, traffic all but vanished as we pushed south toward the Monterey Peninsula. I don't know if the good general slept in the back seat as I drove because it was pitch black back there. I couldn't even sense he was *in* the car. A good place for an abduction/close encounter/cosmic interlude I thought at one point. I had the same college station dialed in, which was now featuring a folk and blues show.

After a cut by John Lee Hooker, I tried to break the ice. "Blues," I said to the invisible stranger in the vacant backseat. "Blues music. Good stuff, right?"

Silence as thick as the darkness. Maybe he was just too tired to mutter, "Dah."

We drove on toward midnight. Then out of the darkness, some old friends emerged from the radio in the dashboard—Koerner, Ray and Glover, the legendary Minneapolis folk-blues trio whose records were in the collections of the Stones, John Lennon, Dylan, Jim Morrison, Bonnie Raitt and others. I knew them well—John, Dave and Tony. Now they were rescuing me from my own fatigue, singing about an old mill that burned down in the Muddy Waters' song "Can't Get No Grindin.'"

The universe may well be a conscious organism, or a complex matrix-like construct, or, as a recent Microsoft research team reported, a machine-learning algorithm "that's continuously learning about itself." Or an infinite superstructure built on quantum building blocks that allows for personal synchronicities, precognition, universal consciousness and the like, and the universal non-locality of consciousness. And maybe, if you're lucky, this same uncharted universe might even allow for the ability to remote view. It might likewise be conducive to creating a CE-5, the vectoring of space-ferrying travelers to Earth from distant galaxies at subluminal speeds as the boys upstairs reach the crossing point of the third dimension and manifest in space-time-Earth. But that night, the universe just gave me a simple juke-joint feeling from a familiar tune via old-fashioned radio signals along a dark, lonely highway under the lost light of ancient stars. Call it a small comfort along the cluttered Cosmic Highway.

At the conclusion of the briefings with our Starlight group, a letter to President Bill Clinton was set after being signed by all participants asking for a meeting with his administration to discuss disclosure and requesting two executive orders to release U.S. government witnesses from their national security oaths, and to declassify and release related

evidence. Of course, that never happened. If it had, this paragraph—
and maybe even this book—might not have been written.

THE PROJECT STARLIGHT COALITION

June 4, 1995

William Jefferson Clinton
President of the United States
The White House
Washington, D.C.

Confidential

Dear Mr. President:

We, the members of the Project Starlight Coalition, a group of American and international citizens working to effect a public disclosure on the UFO/extraterrestrial issue, respectfully request the following:

That appropriate members of the administration meet with members of the Project Starlight Coalition to review significant evidence and witness testimony related to the subject.

That the President issue an executive order to release U.S. government witnesses from their national security obligations/oaths related to the subject so that they may provide public testimony.

That the President issue an executive order to declassify and release currently classified materials, documents and evidence related to the subject.

We feel that these requests are consistent with recent administration actions which resulted in the release of classified information related to the Department of Energy, intelligence satellite photographs, and other documents. We recommend that this matter be handled expeditiously and we respectfully look forward to your reply.

Sincerely,

Steven M. Greer, M.D.

Brian O'Leary

Edgar Mitchell

Kevin Foley

George Lamb

Sandy Wright

Marie "Bootsie" Galbraith

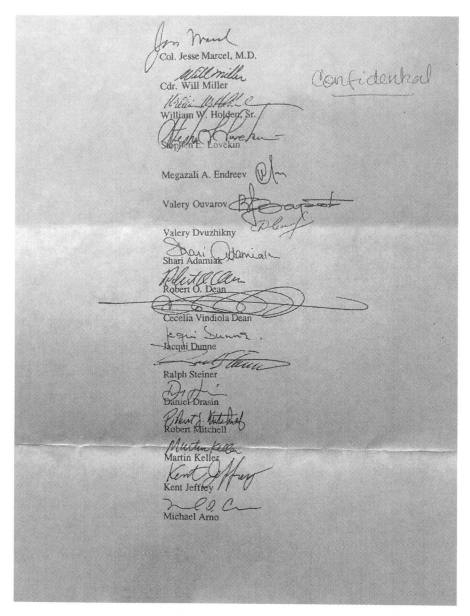

Col. Jesse Marcel, M.D.

Cdr. Will Miller

William W. Holden, Sr.

Stephen L. Lovekin

Megazali A. Endreev

Valery Ouvarov

Valery Dvuzhikny

Shari Adamiak

Robert O. Dean

Cecelia Vindiola Dean

Jacqui Dunne

Ralph Steiner

Daniel Drasin

Robert Mitchell

Martin Keller

Kent Jeffrey

Michael Arno

Confidential

Letter to President Clinton signed by members of The Starlight Coalition

Then Bootsie thought it would be a wonderful departing gesture to "our new Russian friends" to give them a collective donation. They were preparing to spend a long weekend in San Francisco before heading back to motherland Russia. So, everyone in the room reached into their wallets and forked over cash like we were stepping up to help our broken one-time enemies with some good old American goodwill and Yankee dollars.

I forget which general took our money, but he reached into his pants pocket and pulled out a big wad of cash that he already had. It was folded over and latched with a thick rubber band. It had to be at least four-inches thick! A few of us smiled at the Russian's display of US greenbacks. I looked over at Shari with her big, brown eyes. She was trying to suppress a laugh. Foley poked me in the ribs as if to say, "How 'bout that!" Sincerely issuing thank you's in his Russian accent, the dude tucked our bills into his fat stash, perhaps thinking of how they would spend it all in the Bay Area.

Somehow, it oddly and more than a little darkly reminded me of another pop culture moment from my OK Boomer youth—that scene in the 1964 classic *Dr. Strangelove* where Slim Pickens as the B52 pilot Major T. J. "King" Kong is commandeering his squad to go bomb Moscow. He breaks out the crew's survival kit and meticulously surveys its contents over his radio.

In a delectable Texas drawl, Pickens enumerates all the items: "One forty-five caliber automatic; two boxes of ammunition; four days' concentrated emergency rations; one drug issue containing antibiotics, morphine, vitamin pills, pep pills, sleeping pills, tranquilizer pills; one miniature combination Russian phrase book and Bible; one hundred dollars in rubles; one hundred dollars in gold; nine packs of chewing gum; one issue of prophylactics; three lipsticks; three pairs of nylon stockings. Shoot, a fella could have a pretty good weekend in Vegas with all that stuff."

CHAPTER TEN:
ASSESSING THE JOURNEY, HOLDING THE MISSION?

"The border of our minds are ever shifting, and...many minds can flow into one another... and create or reveal a single mind, a single energy.... The borders of our memories...are shifting, and ...our memories are part of one great memory."

–William Butler Yeats

Shari was dead. The Big C.

Her health had begun to rapidly deteriorate a year or so prior to her passing in mid-January 1998. Even while attending CSETI events outside of Denver, when she probably should have stayed home, she suffered quietly and with grace. And then she was gone—a lamp darkened on Earth, a star overhead made infinite. It devasted the doctor and deeply saddened many of us in CSETI. And as the years crumbled forward, others from both the UFO community and the Space Pen Club took their inevitable last flights beyond the blue horizon.

Greer's eulogy for her posted online at CSETI's website still moves me twenty-eight years later. Part of it reads:

"Since 1991, when we first met at a lecture in Los Angeles, Shari has been a pillar of strength and support, an indefatigable colleague, a true friend, an intrepid fellow explorer, an irreplaceable confidant and a fearless lioness without whose dedication CSETI could not have realized its many historic achievements.

"She has been my right hand and trusted assistant for over six years. Whether braving the dangers of the remotest parts of Latin America or assisting with meetings at the offices of the Joint Chiefs of Staff in the Pentagon, Shari was there with me—and for all of us. She never faltered and she never gave up. Unphased by the barbs of critics or the machinations of relentless covert operations, she resolutely worked for a time of peace—a peace universal, for the earth and for countless worlds beyond.

"How many wonders did we witness together? From walking in the shadow of some of this world's largest volcanoes with extraterrestrial spacecraft floating silently above us, to watching a dozen top-secret military witnesses tell an assemblage of Congressmen the truth about UFOs, Shari and I saw events unfold of such great significance that only the passage of time will reveal their true and ultimate significance."

About the same time that she was diagnosed with a carcinoma cancer, the Doc was also diagnosed with melanoma. He had it removed from his shoulder area, I believe. Shari wasn't so fortunate. Some in the community believed she had been covertly killed to weaken the progress the organization was making. One person went so far even as to identify a company that specialized in producing viruses that could cause cancer. And Greer suggests as much in an emotional interview on camera in his *Close Encounters of the Fifth Kind* movie of 2020, grimacing and choking back tears as he speaks of "members of my team" who killed themselves or "were assassinated." Was it purely speculative? Watch the film and decide for yourself.

By the time Shari passed, I was of the mind that nothing would surprise me in this realm anymore, nothing physical nor psychic, metaphysical or synchronistic, nothing in consciousness or submerged deep in the collective unconscious. Nothing glimpsed in dreams, nor seen under star fields in deserts, near mountains nor on the prairies and near many lakes across the Great Plains.

Shari lived long enough to contribute to the unpredictable and often astonishing achievements made with very few resources and more chutzpah than one small non-profit was entitled to. Greer admitted more than once during the '90s that the speed at which the organization grew and became a leading resource far exceeded the sixty-year timeframe in which he expected that to happen.

At Asilomar, where she and Greer were at the top of their game for as long as I was in it, the two seemed inseparable in their passion for what they were doing. And they were happy to be doing it, despite the overwhelming challenges. Shortly after that excursion in Monterey, she and Dr. UFO exhausted themselves in the run-up to the first Project Starlight disclosure event in Washington, DC at the Westin Hotel in April 1997. With just days until the event, along with Emily Greer and a few others in Asheville, they prepared reams of information for the Best Available Evidence (BAE) package that a group of volunteers in another part of the country had been asked but failed to assemble.

Shari lived long enough to see that event come to fruition, but not the much bigger and more substantial 2001 disclosure session at the National Press Club that drew a good cross section of national and international media. That event, now 20 years old, had been slated for broadcast over the web, but the server crashed before the event had begun. I wasted an hour trying to log in to see what the old country Dr. had cooked up this time. In a 2004 white paper called "Media Play," Greer blamed the inability to access the broadcast on outside forces: "Sources later confirmed that this was an electronic warfare jamming of the broadcast." Today, the historical event is available as both a DVD and a book full of witnesses from aerospace, the intel agencies, the military and other related industries.

At the first disclosure in 1997, we each had tasks to execute before we traveled to Washington. Foley was to muscle as many Clinton and congressional contacts as he could for the briefing. According to Greer's CSETI summary dispatch on July 4,1997 (reproduced on the Zeta/Troubled Times website), "Nearly 30 congressional offices were represented by either members of congress or staff members. Also present were VIPs from the executive branch, foreign embassy staff, government scientists, representatives sent to the briefing by 2 state governors' offices, and many other dignitaries."

Media fell to me. Dr. Joe from LA was there for moral support. He chose to fast, as he had done during Vietnam protests in the nation's capital in his younger days. Ed Mitchell also was there for support, comment and credibility. The day before the event, a couple of us picked up Donna Hare at the airport, one of about fifteen witnesses who were participating.

As we drove toward the beltline, Hare began recounting her time as a subcontractor in the photo labs of NASA's Johnson Space Center in Houston inside Building 8, in which she witnessed how UFO objects "disappeared" from satellite photographs. Hare said she had seen one NASA technician air brush a UFO out of a space satellite photo, which was "done routinely" according to a colleague. I'd heard her story before and momentarily tuned it out as I glimpsed the nation's capital in the distance, the flag flying majestically above it. It looked like a commercial for the 4th of July!

Suddenly, I felt a surge of national pride like I had never felt before nor since, not even when attending Boys Nation in DC back in 1970 as a junior in high school. That event was run by the American Legion, which also sponsored Boys State. Even then, among a hundred of us from fifty states, the stark political and ideological divisions were as deep and well defined as they are currently (although not nearly as craven, uncivil and seething). The more conservative candidate—short-cropped hair and pro status quo on 'Nam, Nixon and other issues of the day—that we elected as our fearless high school leader won by only two votes.

That week, I was in a photograph with my fellow Boy Staters published on the front page of the *Washington Post,* standing in the Rose Garden with President Nixon at the height of the Vietnam War. On the White House lawn! That convenient place where all the naïve naysayers, skeptics and cynics wanted ETs to land as proof that they were real. But it seems the "boys upstairs" had already done their version of that —three times!—on July 19, 20 and again on July 26, 1952, with flyovers in the DC area of several bogeys.

"Some of the objects had appeared over the restricted air corridors above the White House and the Capitol," according to David Michael Jacobs' straightforward historical accounts in *The UFO Controversy in America* (published in 1975, and a must-read). Caught on radar and ranted about in the press nationwide, the incidents readily flummoxed the Pentagon and President Truman. The Air Force again got tagged with damage control to manage the dramatic—and seemingly deliberate and defiant display of UFO/UAP flight superiority and shenanigans. On July 29, 1952, the Air Force held "the longest and largest press conference since World War II" to "allay fears and rumors," Jacobs writes.

Washington Post photo of "me and the boys" of Boys Nation on the White House lawn in the Rose Garden with Nixon (see arrow.)

But in DC 18 years later many of us gathered to play at government leadership sported long hair, which the Legion veterans who ran the program wanted us to cut. We refused. One of my fellow longhairs from Colorado tried to organize a boycott of the White House visit since we had press following us everywhere we went, including places like the FBI where we saw agents poking at various captured, herbal substances like hashish and pot. A lot of us already knew what those mind zoomers were even as one FBI man mouthed the words "hash" while staring at us and flicking through the confiscated goods. Looking back, I wish I had supported the Colorado kid and the others in that failed anti-Vietnam/boycott Nixon effort. But I thought my dad would kill me. Just like I thought he would when I told him I was going to apply for conscientious objector status when the 'Nam draft intruded into the lives of all the young dudes and their families everywhere.

Back in Washington many decades later, I was rooming in a hotel with Foley, who had accompanied me to South Dakota, even though Greer wanted us to try and stay with friends to save money. I talked him out of that, arguing that this would be a reward for all our pro bono work. Every time we left our room, Foley insisted on putting a small piece of paper in the door so that if anyone entered while we were out, the paper would fall to the floor signaling an intrusion. Coming back to the room the first morning of the event, we saw a man and a woman—nicely dressed professionals about our age—walking toward the elevators. When we opened our door, the slip of paper was not in the lock, but on the floor.

"See, Marty?" Foley said with a smile, "Somebody's been sleeping in our beds!" We shrugged it off.

My list of media contacts was sprawled across the desk, but nothing seemed to have been disturbed. So, what if they got a copy of the media list? It wouldn't matter much. We weren't going to see much coverage, mostly because—unbeknownst to us—the annual White House Correspondents Dinner was on the second night when we would have prime witnesses giving testimony. Timing truly was everything. One producer at CSPAN gave his regrets, saying that they might have considered it. Most of his colleagues would be out of commission that night, but—"Good luck!"

One print reporter on my list was coming from the DC weekly *City Paper*, whose editor, David Carr, was an old colleague and friend from my work at the Minneapolis alternative weekly *The Twin Cities Reader*. Dave would go on to become the brilliant, much admired media columnist and culture reporter for *The New York Times*. He seemed neutral to dubious on the whole UFO issue. But he was happy to assign a story, especially given the witnesses, which included a former Apollo astronaut riding shotgun.

"I'm sending you an alien to cover it," he said with a laugh over coffee before the event. "He's an odd kid, but he knows the subject and he's a pretty damn good writer too." When I finally met the guy, I don't think I got more than ten words out of him.

Prior to the disclosure activities, Greer, Mitchell and Shari had been making the rounds trying to drum up more support. They met with a writer from *USA Today* and a high-ranking military official who invited a producer from CBS' *60 Minute* to a private meeting. It was most likely Howard Rosenberg. But there's a remote chance it was Ira Rosen, whose own compelling 2021 memoir about this massively influential news organization conveniently takes a shot at Greer. The producer's only comment after listening to the pitch in DC about the testifying witnesses, the evidence, pilot sightings and so on, was telling on a couple levels: How could this be true in this town and I don't know about it?

How indeed?

Greer was on the verge of solving that riddle but wasn't about to share it with anyone yet, not at that meeting nor during the two-day 1997 disclosure events. Perhaps an even bigger question about whether interstellar life forms have been visiting Earth is/was reflected in that producer's comment: If this were true, how could it be kept secret for so long?

At an earlier CSETI meeting in Asheville, my Arizona hypnotist, Dr. Haines, casually gave us copies of a list of ten levels of secret classification that allegedly existed above Top Secret. He wouldn't say where he got it, nor if it were authentic. The list topped out with "Umbra." Another part showed "Top Secret Crypto" levels and positioned the President at level 18 out of 28 levels of uber secrecy. He just thought it was "interesting."

Haines also shared a belief he had developed while working at NASA Ames that there were two space programs, a public one that thrilled the world in the '60s and '70s with "man's" early trips into space, and a secret, purely military program that was way more advanced. It would not surprise me if there were two programs, and still are, given recent developments.

To wit, in 2002, a high-profile arrest of a young British hacker, Gary McKinnon, provided insight into that secret space force possibility when McKinnon said he discovered an off-planet space deployment. If you're not familiar, the Wikipedia entry about McKinnon's alleged crimes is worth reading beyond the following sentence: "McKinnon was accused of hacking into 97 United States military and NASA computers over a 13-month period between February 2001 and March 2002." (The short Q&A with him in *Wired News (WN)* is also worth checking out, if only to get a sense of his motivation.)

Since then, the U.S. government has been trying to extradite McKinnon, not unlike they have been trying to extradite Edward Snowden from Russia for blowing the whistle on the high-tech spying the NSA and other intel agencies do routinely on US citizens, a charge that was rightfully torpedoed in 2020 by a U.S. Appeals Court: "Seven years after former National Security Agency contractor Edward Snowden blew the whistle on the mass surveillance of Americans' telephone records, an appeals court has found the program was unlawful—and that the US intelligence leaders who publicly defended it were not telling the truth [Reuters]." Gee, a secretive agency that won't tell the truth. Where had I heard this before, besides on the *X-Files* and a hundred UFO websites?

While no court in the US or UK has ruled in a similar fashion for McKinnon, supporters big and small—including many with no UFO interests or agendas—have rallied for his protection. A prominent group of British artists, writers and entertainers, from Sting and Peter Gabriel to Julie Christie, Stephen Fry and others, have lobbied against his extradition to America, where he would face decades in prison and a huge fine.

The 2006 *Wired* interview (and other media sources) indicates that McKinnon, who also has Asperger's syndrome, was inspired to go hunting for proof of ET after becoming aware of the testimony in CSETI's Disclosure Project:

McKinnon: I knew that governments suppressed antigravity, UFO-related technologies, free energy or what they call zero-point energy. This should not be kept hidden from the public when pensioners can't pay their fuel bills.

WN: Did you find anything in your search for evidence of UFOs?

McKinnon: Certainly did. There is The Disclosure Project. This is a book with 400 testimonials from everyone from air traffic controllers to those responsible for launching nuclear missiles. Very credible witnesses. They talk about reverse-(engineered) technology taken from captured or destroyed alien craft.

Later, McKinnon said he also found an alleged space-based contingent that was already operational: "I also got access to Excel spreadsheets. One was titled 'Non-Terrestrial Officers.' It contained names and ranks of US Air Force personnel who are not registered anywhere else. It also contained information about ship-to-ship transfers, but I've never seen the names of these ships noted anywhere else."

Although I've never seen public comments by Greer about McKinnon's alleged "inspiration" for his hacking exploits, it's worth noting that when Trump announced the formation of his much lampooned

"Space Force" in 2018—just six months after *The New York Times* UAPs study reveal—Greer publicly opined that one has existed since the '60s, although little known to anyone even inside government.

Back at the April 1997 disclosure, the first night's program featured a presentation by Greer of a thesis intended more for congressional types. The speech was surprisingly focused on the planetary destruction of our ecosystems from the heavy, oil-driven industrial base that was eroding and reshaping climate and enslaving populations.

Hyper-advanced technologies the ETs might possess, the speech suggested, could rid us of our additive oil dependencies and begin to provide a more decent way of life for those without clean water and other basic necessities. Although it was insightful and well-researched, I wasn't sure it was an appropriate opening speech. But looking back now, it was probably *the* speech to give. It didn't shed light on the more dramatic details of CSETI field work but was focused more on pragmatic problems that people in Washington were elected to solve, or at least manage responsibly. However, Greer was so exhausted from prepping for the two-day even that his speech lacked the charisma, sense of humor and grandiloquence he was known for and the night seemed flat, considering the often compelling and confusing witness testimonies that would follow the next evening.

Despite the traditional press event across town, stray reporters from *The Washington Post Writers Group, US News & World Report, The Boston Globe,* The British Broadcasting Corporation (BBC), an ABC affiliate in New Haven, CT, United Press International, Strange Universe TV and other invited guests did turn out for the briefing. A good publicist, though, is never satisfied getting *some* media coverage. You want it *all.* So, with many media folks out of the mix for the second evening because of the media dinner, another unexpected job fell to me prior to starting the introductions for the program—remove Phillip Klass, the biggest UFO debunker the community had ever faced.

Somehow, Klass had gotten wind of the event. He was there with his pen and pad and a tape-recorder slung around his shoulder like an unholstered pistol. A career journalist and author reporting on aero-space and aviation issues, Klass also had an abiding and dissenting interest in Ufology. He had published an assortment of books on the topic, mostly to counter others in the field. He had a reputation as long as his detailed, heavily annotated Wikipedia entry for allegedly —pick a card, any card—attacking, smearing, denouncing, arguing with and playing the contrarian to just about everyone in the UFO communi-ty at one time or another. He was also a cofounder of the Committee for the Scientific Investigation of Claims of the Paranormal (CSICOP), now called the Committee for Skeptical Inquiry (CSI), which generally goes after any claims of paranormal or psychic activities. At one point, Klass allegedly even put a curse on all "UFO believers," which I had to admire in some ways because a guy that tries that hard obviously knows more about the ET/UFO matrix and has more telling facts in his own tin foil files than he will ever admit to himself, let alone anyone else.

But in 1997, seven years before his death, Klass was a stocky, shuf-fling old man of seventy-nine who looked like a shrunken version of Matt Drudge complete with the fedora. But he was crashing the party before it began. Generally, he was seen then by Ufologists as one of the best overt nuisances "the opposition" could provide. Falcon from the Aviary was the other one (although he was not in attendance at the Washington event).

Falcon did turn up in a 1994 Larry King special about UFOs, a show that I managed to get Greer on after exchanging emails and Greer's bona fides with a top CNN producer. Along with this Czar of Disinformation, other usual suspects also appeared on the program—Bob "the Pope" Dean," Jacques Valle, Stanton Friedman and even Wil-liam Shatner (beamed onto tape)!

The bulk of the show was shot live near Area 51. Falcon was openly identified on King's show as a covert specialist who went to great lengths to misinform, deceive, divert, hoax, mislead—again, pick any card—well-meaning and fair-minded hunters and gath-ers. In other words, he and Klass came with the UFO territory. But you never thought you would have an up-close-and-impersonal ma-no-a-mano with either one. Nevertheless, here Klass was at the DC Westin loaded for bear.

"Get him out of here!" Greer demanded through clenched teeth via a burst of anger I had rarely seen. He was pink-red with steam. So, I took Mr. Klass by the arm and asked him to walk out of the room with me since this was an invitation-only event. He protested, looking shocked and outraged. "I have a right to be here," he cried, claiming freedom of the press and demanding my name and address. I freely gave both to his recorder's mic, which ran from a cord to his shoulder pack as we waltzed toward the exit and I showed him the door. As I slowly moved him to the exit, I felt like Robin on orders from Batman leading the Penguin away. Klass really did remind me of Burgess Meredith in that role from the *Batman* TV show from the '60s. KOW! KABLAM!! He was out of there! I don't know if I ever made it into Klass' skeptics newsletter, but I'd be honored if I did.

Another unexpected media person showed up as well—Jeff Rense, who looked like a rock star with his feathery shoulder-length hair, brushy moustache and nice suit of light mauve threads. Rense had an escalating reputation for his wide-ranging radio program and then-nascent website that aggregated news, opinion and columns from all over and included UFO stuff. His radio show didn't have the later firepower of Art Bell's paranormal and occult rollercoaster of a program, *Coast to Coast,* which debuted in the late '80s and became exceedingly popular when it went national in 1992 with more than 300 stations at its peak. For better and worse, Bell was a true American original who opened Pandora's "paranormal" box nightly from ten o'clock to two in the morning Pacific Coast interstellar time.

By contrast, the current Rense.com is a lot like a Drudge Report for those looking for alternative news sources and commentary on the "phenomenon," plus analysis of more mainstream daily world news stories. But the headlines, mocking political cartoons and photo distortions ultimately reflect the sensibilities and character of the name it bears. Unfortunately, Rense.com also provides a platform for many questionable, soiled outliers on the socio-political spectrum, avowed anti-Semites and racists like David Duke and a handful of others, creating an occasional sewer as much as a reliable alt news site. Upon meeting the doctor, Rense hovered and circled Greer, sizing him up like a dog sniffs a stranger.

Without warning, Randle, our alleged Roswell-related witness bolted right before his part of the disclosure event commenced (after a rumored phone call from one of the alphabet-intel agencies warning him not to attend). But other witness testimony poured forth throughout the morning and into the afternoon. You can find highlights online from the 1997 event, but I thought a soft-spoken Virginia serviceman named Merle Shane McDow topped them all.

Shane described in chilling detail an October 1981 event that had the US Atlantic Fleet (CINCLANTFLT) Command Center "in chaos." An object, estimated at 300 feet in diameter and disc-shaped, was able to rapidly move in one radar sweep from an area off the coast of Newfoundland to the coast of Norfolk, Virginia. During this daylight event, the US Atlantic Fleet Command Center went to Condition Zebra alert and orders were given by NORAD to the CINC, Admiral Harry Trane, to identify the object and force it down if necessary.

Fighters were scrambled from land- and sea-based forces. While one fighter got close enough to photograph the object, it moved in the span of one radar sweep from the coast of Norfolk to an area in the Atlantic near the Canary Islands, then turned upward at a 60-degree angle and appeared to leave the earth's atmosphere.

Other witnesses described events at select Air Force bases, including one sensational report of "an alien being shot at the end of the runway at McGuire AFB and later removed by a C141 transport plane flown in from Wright Patterson AFB to retrieve the body"—the same AFB to which the bodies from the alleged 1947 Roswell crash were sent. All participating witnesses during the Project Starlight event in Washington signed legally binding oaths under penalty of perjury that what they shared was true. So, was an alien really shot dead on an Air Force base?

Hillary Clinton Likens Focus On Whitewater to U.F.O. Fad

By JAMES BENNET

WASHINGTON, April 10 — With a note of weary exasperation, Hillary Rodham Clinton today dismissed Whitewater as a "never-ending fictional conspiracy that honest-to-goodness reminds me of some people's obsession with U.F.O.'s and the Hale-Bopp comet some days."

Mrs. Clinton denied that White House aides had solicited jobs for her old friend and law partner Webster L. Hubbell, a central figure in the Whitewater investigation, to keep him quiet about the case.

"There isn't anything to be hushed up about that," Mrs. Clinton said today in the first of two broadcast interviews in which she sounded tired but philosophical — even resigned — whenever the conversation turned to the charges that have been directed at her and President Clinton over the last four years.

Mr. Clinton said today that he accepted the apology Mr. Hubbell made on Sunday on the CBS News program "60 Minutes" for having deceived him and his wife about overbilling the law firm in Little Rock, Ark.

Speaking to reporters at the start of the first Cabinet meeting of his second term, Mr. Clinton said: "Let me remind you that everybody pays in life. Somehow we all wind up paying for whatever we do, and he paid a very high price. And he's apologized, and I accept his apology."

But Mrs. Clinton sounded less forgiving. She expressed astonishment that her friend of 20 years would mislead her, and pointed out that he had, in effect, stolen from her when he overbilled the firm where they were both partners.

"The money he went to prison for having misused was partly my money," she said in the first interview, this morning on WAMU, a public radio station here. "I feel particularly bad about this because I believed him absolutely — you know, I had

Continued on Page A26, Column 1

Hillary Clinton in the April 10, 1996 *New York Times*: Using the "UFO Fad" to deflect Whitewater before teasing UFO disclosure in the media during her 2016 presidential run.

While Foley's attempt to get the Clintons or their close aides directly involved didn't succeed, it was made clear as fogged glass that they—or at least Hillary—were well aware of the event even as they fended off persistent Whitewater allegations being made against them during that period. On the day of the witness testimonies, Hillary Rodham Clinton made the following widely quoted statement, first on the Diane Rehm Radio Talk Show and then a variation of it on in print: "That's part of the continuing saga of Whitewater," said Clinton, "the never-ending fictional conspiracy that honest-to-goodness reminds me of some people's obsessions with UFOs and the Hale-Bopp comet." Her reference was to the southern California cult, Heaven's Gate, whose members committed mass suicide in anticipation of a collective rendezvous with a spaceship they believed to be trailing the big Bopper.

Maybe Clinton was just trying to send Project Starlight a signal while throwing off decades-old Whitewater affairs. Years later, in 2016, her teases on the national talk shows—along with those of her presidential campaign Chair, John Podesta—about disclosing the truth about UFOs, or UAPs, during her presidential bid, were always eagerly scooped up by online UFO sites. It's important to note, however, that CSETI's website back then reported semi-regular to heavy traffic from various military and government agencies and a White House server address, according to its then-webmaster Tony Craddock.

Not long after Shari's passing, Greer dug in deeper on the secrecy issue, which often is a deal breaker for people who believe there might be other beings like us, or unlike us, in the universe. What they don't believe is that the subject could ever be kept a secret so well for so long. Still, the military always has protected its knowledge with compartmentalization of information and need-to-know classifications compounded by covert funding and additional cover in black budgets that elected and appointed officials have no access to, including POTUS. Protecting national secrets is done all the time.

The Manhattan Project that produced the A-bomb in WWII is a case in point. While thousands worked on it, only a handful of people actually knew what was being built and how. Was that a conspiracy theory, a conspiracy fact, or just a smart, cohesive, top-secret-project management strategy?

My father, a lowly Air Force staff sergeant in the late '50s, had a specialized security clearance for a task that he refused to share with me until much later in his life. It was related to nuclear weapons codes, so I knew a little bit about the opaque mechanisms employed by the military to shut people up. But how could this topic be so well-guarded that even four- and five-star generals and a big cat like Woolsey at the CIA couldn't penetrate where the "there" was?

Greer searched long and hard to come up with the answer. When he did, I initially was skeptical, thinking he had gone so far into the netherworld, that he had become what he beheld in the UFO community and turned into another true "conspiracy theorist," a term I detest. After many insider interviews including multiple confirmations, Greer believed the UFO topic was managed through Special Access Projects (SAPs) and another more complicated, also off-the-books category, Unacknowledged Special Access Projects (USAPs). These designations often were found within the above-top-secret contract work between leading high-tech private industry companies and select branches of the government, intelligence and military sectors. Even the CIA director was not able to get at the truth because the subject matter was not available within the regular channels of government. Moreover, no one was formally assigned to the teams playing in the USAP world in which ET allegedly roamed. You had to be verbally "read into" the program by a colleague already working in this deepest black arena. No paper trail is no trail at all.

Although Greer's insights into this secrecy realm were still in their formative stages at the time my *X Files* story was published in *Rolling Stone*, he and Shari occasionally pestered me to write about SAPs/USAPs for the magazine, or to convince an editor it was a story worth assigning to someone. But I never pitched it because it seemed it could do more damage than good for CSETI, especially if there were no sources other than Greer and one or two others to corroborate the goods. So, he wrote one of many white papers on the subject, including a description of it as a threat to national and world security. Here is a quote from one of them:

> "Key military and national security leaders have been inadequately informed on the UFO/ETI subject due to its management under Unacknowledged Special Access Projects (USAPS). This lack of information has resulted in substantial national security risks. The risk of inadequate and/or dangerous actions by uninformed or misinformed leaders is greatly increased by the lack of indepth briefings and discussions on this subject. Key areas of operational readiness are thus placed 'at risk' by these leaders being dangerously uninformed or misinformed."

Greer says "this unusual USAP" has the following characteristics:

- it's global in scope;
- it has multiple levels of subcompartmentalization;
- it is primarily based in the civilian, privatized contracting/work-for-others sectors;
- it runs parallel to and generally separate from conventional government, military and intelligence programs, including other sensitive USAPs/black projects;
- it exists as a hybrid entity which draws from high technology corporations and compartmented, government, intelligence and military operations, but which in effect function as an independent, separate entity;
- it apparently is controlled by no single branch of conventional government, military service or agency;
- access to this project generally is by project-controlled inclusion and access has little to do with an individual's position in government, military rank or position in the traditional (constitutional) chain of command;

- after nearly 60 years of studying advanced extraterrestrial technologies from retrieved ET devices, the group which controls this USAP possesses substantial technologies which may present a threat to conventional military assets and to world security in general;

- funding for these operations is derived both from the so-called black budget and from 'creative,' nongovernmental sources; and

- maintenance of secrecy/control over this project has been at all costs and has consistently violated legal, constitutional oversight and checks and balances and the rights of U.S. citizens."

One critical aspect of the ET/UFO-USAP was that any and perhaps all such assets were, as Greer maintained, like the formula for Coca Cola—they were deeply-held business trade secrets not even the US government could obtain. The same sentiments were later echoed in Colonel Philip Corso's controversial book *The Day After Roswell*, which contended that his commanding officer at the "Foreign Technology Desk," Lt. General Arthur Trudeau, instructed him to seed technology recovered from the Roswell crash into private enterprise so that big corporations would then hold the patents on it—and keep the secret.

Years later, I found convincing corroboration of the USAP mechanism while writing another UFO story for a national publication and reading a book by Seymour Hersh, the esteemed investigative journalist who broke stories like the My Lai massacre in Vietnam. Hersh's late-'90s book was completely unrelated to the UFO issue but mentioned the USAP function. By then I had washed out of Steve's World, mostly because I needed to make a more decent living for a growing family while increasingly working in public relations for clients who weren't literally reaching for the distant stars. Nevertheless, like Michael Corleone, the Godfather's favorite son, even if I wanted out, I kept getting pulled back in. I couldn't shake it.

A UFO piece I wrote was finally published in the 2006 November/ December *Utne Reader,* then produced in Minneapolis and one of the few national print publications with the intellectual integrity and journalistic cojones to broach the topic thanks in part to its editor at the time, Dave Schimke. I took Dave out for what we in the PR biz call a "pitch lunch" to sell the story idea, then followed up later with lengthy emails and short phone conversations. Eventually, he came around, packaging my piece with other stories about space.

The story was called "Life in the Stars: Whether the existence of extraterrestrials is an irrefutable fact or just a compelling theory, the media would do well to start telling the story." The story touched on the USAP reality that I had become convinced was true largely due to the work of one of the last true lions of American journalism, Hersch. His affirmation—and a couple supporting observations—were all I needed to build my case into a short article that drove home many of the key elements in this book.

As my *Utne* piece revealed, the role of secret military affairs was both nauseating and fascinating. Writing on his website (www. ufoskeptic.org), author and astrophysicist Bernard Haisch points out that SAP "is for programs considered to be too sensitive for normal classification measures... They are protected by a security system of great complexity. Many of the SAPs are located within industry funded through special contracts." Much of his analysis is based on "In Search of the Pentagon's Billion Dollar Hidden Budgets," an article by Bill Sweetman in the highly regarded British publication *Jane's International Defence Review.*

"Even members of congress on appropriations committees (the Senate and House committees that allocate budgets) and intelligence committees are not allowed to know anything about these programs," Haisch writes. "Moreover, Freedom of Information Act requests cannot penetrate unacknowledged special access programs."

In Hersh's 2004 book *Chain of Command: The Road from 9/11 to Abu Ghraib* (HarperCollins), the frequent *New Yorker* contributor reports that one SAP used to recruit operatives has been linked to military torture in Iraq. The desired effect is the same—to avoid scrutiny and sidestep opposing elements that exist in the CIA and Pentagon.

My *Utne* story went on: "'The granddaddy of all USAPs is the UFO/ET matter,' writes Steve Greer in his book *Extraterrestrial Contact: The Evidence and Implications* (Crossing Point, 1999). Greer says USAPs are a top secret, compartmentalized project that not even the commander-in-chief has the power to access."

Steven would go on to write more books after 1999, often assembling small volunteer CSETI teams at his home. There he would dictate chapter content, provide research references, documents and the like where needed, and then have volunteers convert everything to finished chapters, to which he would make corrections and tweaks.

He and sometimes Shari and astronaut Ed Mitchell, as well as Naval Commander William Miller (who seemed to have access to Pentagon brass including flag officers), held a series of briefings with Pentagon officials and others in the DC area for several years. As part of his congressional briefings, with the aim of getting government to do its own hearings and ultimately offer an official disclosure, Greer flew into Minneapolis to brief Minnesota US Representative Martin Sabo, along with Jacqui Dunn from the Bay Area, Kevin Foley and me. Sabo had committee ties to both Homeland Security and the Department of Defense and was a notorious chain smoker.

In Sabo's government office in downtown Minneapolis, his deep blue eyes sparkled as Greer showed footage from the BAE package including a video sequence of objects seemingly multiplying from just one or two objects against a bright blue sky, like a hatch of celestial Mayflies. There were several similar instances of these "multiple releases" from single objects in different parts of the country going back to the '50s. Could they have been secret launches of military satellites that one sees today with similar commercialized space business launches of satellites? It's possible. But the way the little silvery dots split apart from each other in the video we showed Sabo reminded me of the way cells subdivide and multiply. Inscrutable during and after the meeting, Marty Sabo took it all in, huffing several heaters throughout the presentation but without offering much comment or insight. He took Greer's card and that was that.

If only to set the record straight, it's important to state that these CSETI briefings were decades before *The New York Times* reported in 2020 that Eric Davis from Bigelow's old NIDS organization in Las Vegas was doing the same thing. This is the same Davis who, upon my arrival for a PR meeting in Vegas (discussed in the previous chapter), quickly engaged me in a lopsided conversation about "how they can get here from there"—wormholes. He was convinced of it. Now he had become a source in the *Times* story:

> "Mr. Davis, who now works for Aerospace Corporation, a defense contractor, said he gave a classified briefing to a Defense Department agency as recently as March about retrievals from 'off-world vehicles not made on this earth…'

> "Mr. Davis said he also gave classified briefings on retrievals of unexplained objects to staff members of the Senate Armed Services Committee on Oct. 21, 2019, and to staff members of the Senate Intelligence Committee two days later."

I know why Steve Greer was never quoted in this story or others despite the fact that he was way ahead of Davis in informing government personnel and the public about the phenomenon. It was because, as stated much earlier in this book, Kean (who did the *Times* reporting with Ralph Blumenthal) felt Greer had misled her and so she would never trust him again as a source. It was, IMHO, the public's loss.

It was amazing that in 2020—thirty years later—Greer still seemed to be a pariah in the UFO world, just as he was when I met him in the early 1990s. Or maybe he just needed a better publicist.

* * *

Besides the *Close Encounter of the Fifth Kind* film in 2020, Greer also produced two exceptionally well-made film documentaries—*Sirius* (2013) and *Unacknowledged* (2017). Both films relied, in part, on online funding platforms and were based on his books and the Disclosure Project work and documents. The *Close Encounter* movie received harsh reviews in the mainstream press, which predictably tossed around lame conspiracy clichés to besmirch it. But *Sirius* seemed to self-sabotage itself by including a very small, six-inch body known now as the Atacama skeleton from Chile that might be of alien origin.

Sadly, the controversy over the alleged strange humanoid seemingly upstaged the more important messages in the film, such as this one that Greer relates on camera: "Once people understand that classified projects have figured out how UFOs operate, they will realize we no longer need oil, coal and nuclear power. *This is the truth that has driven the secrecy*" (my italics added).

Since 2017, I have been working in communications and doing a lot of media relations with and for the irrepressible "rock star" Winona LaDuke, the Anishinaabe leader, hemp farmer, author and activist, and two-time vice-presidential candidate with Ralph Nader on the Green Party ticket. LaDuke and her non-profit organization, Honor the Earth, co-founded with The Indigo Girls twenty-seven years ago, have been battling the Line 3 pipeline with the Minnesota Department of Commerce and a host of indigenous and other environmental groups and your average citizen, fighting this big, $4 billion Enbridge Energy tar sands oil pipeline in northern Minnesota—the dirtiest, most polluting oil on the planet, and the equivalent of 50 coal burning plants, according to John Abraham, a professor of thermal sciences at the University of St. Thomas in St. Paul, Minnesota.

The award-winning, indigenous novelist, Louise Erdrich (a member of the Turtle Mountain Band of Chippewa, or Ojibwe), called it a "a tar sands climate bomb" and "a breathtaking betrayal of

Minnesota's indigenous communities—and the environment" in an end-of-year 2020 *New York Times* piece condemning Line 3, its Canadian builder, Enbridge, and Minnesota government supporters from the governor on down, even though his lieutenant governor, Peggy Flanagan is a Native and member of the White Earth reservation who opposes the line.

I didn't need convincing of Greer's assessment, which is shared by many in and out of the UFO subculture. The pipeline is emblematic of all that is wrong with outdated, early twentieth century national and global energy policy still tied to fossil fuels, and gigantic government subsidies. Especially in the face of the two major 2019 climate change studies from the United Nations—and even the failed Trump administration. Both warn that we have ten years to reduce the carbon-loading of the planet to a manageable level or face dire consequences.

I don't know what Greer and the production team paid for the Atacama oddity that appears in the film. But Greer's post-film defense of it in a lengthy YouTube video concerning its DNA testing does raise serious issues for further discussion. Years before these films were made, however, he mistakenly bought an indiscernible skeletal entity in Mexico that turned out to be a sea-based lifeform. This reach for physical proof initially struck me as quiet desperation, but it also was part of the Disclosure Project's trial-and-error process to find irrefutable evidence. Most likely, the good stuff is kept in the land of USAPs well out of reach of the Steven Greer's of the world. In his written work, Greer indeed catalogs the military installations around the US where UFO/ET assets are kept.

Unacknowledged, his 2017 film, is described on IMDb like this: "Focuses on the historic files of the Disclosure Project and how UFO secrecy has been ruthlessly enforced—and why. The best evidence for extraterrestrial contact, dating back decades, is presented with direct top-secret witness testimony, documents and UFO footage, 80% of which has never been revealed anywhere else." Detractors and critics alike pounced on its claims, questioned the documents cited and lobbed aspersions at some of the characters in the movie, including—SURPRISE—Falcon from the Aviary, the self-proclaimed covert Air Force specialist who appeared on the Larry King UFO program that was the highest rated King special in the '90s. The public's appetite was never sated, and yet they were fed so many empty calories.

Seeing Falcon as a civilian in the Greer documentary begs the question—is he no longer an alleged bad guy but now an ally of the disclosure movement? I'm dubious. This dude was even in a strange artsy film made in part about his involvement in the troubling Paul Bennewitz story, *Mirage Men*. That movie documents a sophisticated disinformation campaign in which Falcon was involved in Albuquerque near Kirtland Air Force Base where the UFO researcher, scientist and entrepreneur lived. That disinformation effort may have literally driven the duped researcher over the edge.

Still, this birdman claims in Greer's *Close Encounters* movie that a specialized unit of the military—through the USAP's (Unacknowledged Special Access Projects)—has been staging false abductions of civilians dating back to the Air Force's Office of Special Investigations (OSI)!. That insight, if true, gave me pause once more... Maybe some of the high strangeness in my bedroom back in the beginning was really the work of our bad guys—the ones belonging to the same mindset, a broken consciousness, that believed it was okay to spray guys like my old rocker pal, Curtiss A, and his classmates with a toxic substance—zinc cadmium sulfide with radioactive particles—when they were kids under the patriotic banner of Cold War protection.

The weird noise in my house, the lights coming on, the dogs' nails prancing on the hardwood floors downstairs —perhaps they were really being held and muzzled by a black ops team member, and later, the flash of light from the ground that made me shoot straight up in bed…were these things the manmade nightmares of the UFO community? How could I, or anyone in similar situations, ever prove it without a thorough reopening of congressional investigations into the 1970's MK-Ultra program again, and then looking hard into the psychotronic claims made by Martin Cannon in Chapter Three? Looking back, the whole sadly begotten notion reminded me of a couple of damning lines from Dylan's "Jokerman"—"Nightsticks and water cannons, tear gas, padlocks/Molotov cocktails and rocks behind every curtain."

Astonishingly, Falcon also asserts that leading mainstream news organizations were paid in cash for their silence—for not digging too deeply into the UFO issue. It sounds like another channel to investigate officially. Or was it just more disinfo?

Although Ed Mitchell was also featured at the 2001 Disclosure event and was allied with CSETI for years, not long before his death in 2016 he seemed to have had a falling out with Greer while the Falcon was flying in. Mitchell complained about Greer to Dr. Jack Sarfatti, who ironically has done a great deal of work on consciousness and quantum physics. He and Greer might have shared a lot of the same points of view on consciousness, subluminal thought and related topics. But in true community fashion and trademark factionalism, Sarfatti accused CSETI of being a "Horse and Pony Disinfo Show & Tell." If it weren't all so infuriating, these feuds would make good spectator sport.

Mitchell said Greer had gone out of bounds. According to the Sarfatti/Mitchell dialogue posted on rense.com, Ed complained that, "I had cooperated with Steve Greer some years ago, but he began to over-reach his data continuously, necessitating a withdrawal by myself, and I believe, several others. I have requested to be removed from any website, announcements, etc., but see that has not taken place… Although I firmly believe it is time for openness and disclosure by government, I object to being misused in this fashion and acquire guilt by association with certain claims that simply are not true."

"Overreaching his data continuously" was an interesting euphemism. I'd seen it before occasionally with the Doc, or variations thereof, but it was not a consistent pattern. In my estimation, Greer's "sins" were venial, not mortal. After my old Canadian pal Howard and I reconnected after many years, he cited why he had quit the organization: "I left CSETI because of an unwillingness to seriously entertain the possibility that what we were encountering via our in-field protocols was not exclusively amenable—if at all—to a 'nuts-and-bolts' understanding of experiences of an apparent Otherness, and whose true nature upon serious self-reflection might—in part or in whole—turn out to be anything but Other."

That was Howard, brainy and academic as ever. But, he continued, "We might be looking unself-reflectively in a mirror, seeing only what our preconceptions permit us to see. Once, when at an Executive Council meeting, I raised this possibility and suggested we take such 'human factors' into account when making sense of CSETI-related 'data' and how they were being 'observed/produced.' The idea was vehemently rejected. It left me wondering about the nature of the nerve I'd just hit."

Although it was not an intellectual opinion that I necessarily shared with him, he had a point. Too much CSETI navel gazing might, indeed, eliminate other explanations of what "the phenomenon" was or wasn't—if there were any ultimate or final determinations that could be made in this field. It was overlaid with so many factors and mind fucks, from the number of ET civilizations outlined in Bob Dean's Assessment document (still MIA) to the rock-solid Rand report to Whitley Strieber's Grays, the Air Force's revisionist accounts of Roswell, John Mack's abduction subjects, and on and on...

At some point on the Side Hustle bus, I just hit the wall with Ufology fatigue and the bottomless pit of UFO porn that littered the information superhighway of the internet.

But for all the good, bad and outrageous "data" I'd encountered on the journey, I'd also seen a great deal personally, as this book will attest—the bedroom cherry bombs, the chalk arrow in the South Dakota sky, the random ability to remote view in dreams, the vast implications of the non-locality of consciousness, the nefarious mind-control voodoo cooked up by mad "scientists," etc. The dreaming part always was intriguing and long after I took the exit ramp, I kept a watchful third eye on what I brought back from dreams, particularly rare, lucid power dreams, as well as the fleeting, meaningless ciphers that roamed like phantoms through the sleep kingdom.

Once, while napping after a hard day's work, I fell into such a deep, restful sleep state that I didn't know what time of day it was when I awoke. But I was convinced the Big One had hit in LA, because I'd seen a huge newspaper headline describing a 7.2 earthquake. The first thing I innocently asked when walking into the kitchen was if there had been an earthquake out west. Maybe it is further on up the road... My limited remote viewing abilities, always in sleep it seemed, produced other, more tangible results, from pre-cognitive images of the woman who would eventually buy our house where the strangeness started, to previewed images of our first-born, bald-as-a cue ball son many months before my wife became pregnant again.

But despite the lack of answers and understandings for much of the really weird stuff, I knew that the side hustle I'd taken in 1990 had set me on a course that would alter my world and my worldview for years to come. And time has proven as much. Case in point, after years of searching for answers about the red spheres in my Minneapolis bedroom and the one red orb that confronted my friend Jim and me in a Dickinson, North Dakota, park, I have reasoned, rationalized, realized—pick any synonym—that they probably are not tied to the UFO/ET issue. They are a separate, paranormal phenomenon, perhaps of an interdimensional nature that manifests in real time and is seemingly under intelligent control. and perhaps capable of harm. Why I have seemingly experienced them twice is unanswerable.

Although I complain at times about the bulging tinfoil file I'd accumulated during this trek, a psychic friend of mine likes to remind me that "You're lucky. Most people don't have these experiences." But I'm not sure "luck" is how I would describe the sheer sum of information, useless and helpful, and experiences, personal or within groups and gleaned from others. But the subject won't leave me alone. Maybe writing this book is as much of a tallyho to the topic, a self-proclaimed, self-indulged exorcism, as it is a kiss-off to the boys upstairs and the UFO community.

But it seems both may be exercises in futility.

On a 2005 winter trip to Tulum, Mexico, with my family, long after I'd set aside all CSETI duties, my son and I were throwing a football on the beach at midday. Suddenly a white object darted in and out of the clouds, playing peekaboo with us, just as I was thinking about some of the stories I'd read the night before in Michael Luckman's wonderful book *Alien Rock: The Rock 'n' Roll Extraterrestrial Connection*, which I'd brought on the trip. The book recounted the UFO stories and "paranormal events" experienced by some of rock's heaviest, from Elvis to John Lennon, David Bowie, Dave Davies, et al. Eventually, my son and I watched the white object trail north along the coastline. When I later relayed the story to Greer in a friendly catch-up email, he called it a CE-5.

A couple of days later, I awoke around four in the morning. Our room faced the sea, and my bed, set back the furthest in the space, faced directly out in the same direction, making it easy to take in the beach and aqua-colored Caribbean just seventy-five feet or so from the shore. The curtains were open on the large, glass windows that faced the same direction. Although the sun had not yet risen, the sky looked milky chartreus with early, dull light emerging. And there, out over the water about a hundred yards from the room, sat a strange object that at first looked like a compressed pirate ship with a dull yellow—or was it orangish in color?—of what seemed to be its center. I didn't stir. And I thought best not to sit up or get out of bed to check it out more closely because I felt like it was watching—that I would be detected even more so if I moved. So, I laid there with my pillow slightly elevated to watch it for another five minutes or so. I felt "it" was not friendly. But I wasn't convinced it was hostile either.

Although my family was sound asleep, I was now consciously awake and troubled. It sat there, motionless and monolithic, this deconstructed vessel over the early morning Caribbean. I felt like it knew I was fully conscious of it and I tried to limit my thoughts to just visual information. There was no inclination to try and signal it to establish contact like any good CSETI member would do. I didn't feel like contact would be mutually beneficial, or a smart idea. So, I laid there and watched. And then I gave up on it, slowly turned over, closed my eyes and went back to sleep.

That night or the next, after another full day in that scenic beach setting, after I'd gone to sleep, a bright shaft of light shot through the roof right over the bed on which my wife and oldest daughter were reading in our beachside cabana. Terrified, my daughter dove under the covers. I don't know what happened next if anything. But I remember during the night a skunk-like stench filled the room, only more pronounced, perhaps like the pungent odors Whitely Strieber described in his early experiences with the visitors in *Communion*. I wrote it off to an odor emanating from deep in the Yucatan jungle where we were mere temporary trespassers in an exotic natural place.

These are the incidents I wonder about occasionally, strange re-*mind*ers that my consciousness has undergone a potent transformation that has reshaped my worldview and inner bearing. But the following event is the best, or worst—or maybe the most comical—depending on what the implications might be.

We moved to a bigger house in 2000, away from the home where it had all begun nearly ten years earlier along Minnehaha Creek. As I was getting ready for bed one cold winter night not long after the move, I jokingly wondered to myself if I should mentally send our new address to the boys upstairs like I had done with utility companies, magazines and newspapers, prior to leaving the old place.

At around three-thirty that morning, the front doorbell began ringing. And it wouldn't stop!

Susan and I searched for possible reasons for the interruption as we hurried to shut it down before it woke everyone else up. I slipped on a heavy coat and a pair of Sorrels and checked out front. The street was dead. Our new neighbors were fast asleep all around us, none stirring. Nothing!

I went to the back door and walked out into the yard to look around the corner of the garage. More nothing. When I came in, my wife was standing on a stepstool trying to dismantle the small box that housed the ringer. Eventually, she managed to take out the battery and the noise ceased. Was it the cosmic welcome wagon? Or yet another suspiciously impeccable major coincidence? Or just one of those things, as the old Cole Porter tune goes?

A couple of days later, I called our hippie handyman Quint, who looked like a younger version of Ron Moony as Fagin in *Oliver*. As I came back from a meeting, he was busy toying with the unit in the hallway ceiling near the kitchen and bedroom, trying to determine how and why it might have been set off. Was it somehow connected to the security system that we never used and had never paid for?

"Well?" I asked him as he stood on the same stepstool and poked with his tiny screwdriver at the offending apparatus. "What do you think?"

"I don't know," he said, as he reassembled the box. "I can't see anything wrong with the wiring or battery. It's screwy, that's for sure. And the security system is not activated. I don't know what would have caused it. Maybe it was aliens."

"Yeah, maybe aliens," I echoed faintly. And maybe not. The Space Pen seesaw never seemed to stop going up and down.

The longer I was away from CSETI, the more I hoped I wouldn't be concerned with all the issues and noise from the community. But the world around me often won't let it be, and I had too much experience to not keep looking. Still, I often had to remind myself that this was only a side hustle (wasn't it?). I could get off the bus (couldn't I?). It was not an avocation or vocation. A side hustle… and nothing more. And that's where I tried to leave it, although it still often fills my waking thoughts and conscious dreams.

* * *

Not so long ago, driving by myself one night through southwestern Minnesota close to the little town of Cosmos again, I took a reckoning of my side hustle and of those in this book whose lives ended, some before I even began working on it. Like Shari, gone from the body and Earth, and many others. Other people were very much alive, however, like the friend who had called me back in the beginning to ask if I'd like to interview this guy, Dr. Steven Greer, about UFOs and Close Encounters of the Fifth Kind. This person asked to remain anonymous in this book after checking in with me because the same person had a dream in which "a couple of low-grade entities" and I were trying to get my friend to join in some unspecified nighttime escapade. This did not make the person happy. It didn't make me happy. It curled the tin foil.

"You looked like you were under some hypnotic spell," the person said. *Great*, I thought, *I have let my parents down and ignored their advice about running with the wrong crowd, this time through the frontiers of consciousness. And I somehow had crossed a boundary with a friend.* I told my friend I was sorry, although I didn't know for what, really. I also told the person I was tiring of the subject and I wanted all the high strangeness to stop. Period.

As I drove toward Cosmos, I listened to a mix tape I'd made and thought about Shari, the angry friend, and the rest. And about the passing cosmic parade of experiences and characters, plus the other certifiably wild stories I'd heard along the way.

The tape featured a collection of novelty songs as well as more straightforward tunes centered around space, ET, and the broad flying saucer rock 'n' roll world. It was a good shield against the black doubt that occasionally crept up on me and pushed against the hope and clarity I thought I had achieved. I didn't care anymore if my zenith was covered.

Once I got to Cosmos, I noticed how the painting on the Lennon Peace House of the lyric from John Lennon's immortal "Imagine" was fading and blistering. I remembered reading in a small history of the community how the town's visionary founder had dreamed one day of making Cosmos a seat of learning only to freeze to death in a punishing Minnesota blizzard. Greer had similar long-range plans to establish a university-like campus someplace in the post-disclosure world where the true knowledge of the universe and its inhabitants would have a free exchange of information and ideas to make the world new again. And to help maintain the peace.

I drove to the open highway again, memory flying, and recalled all the nominally crazy shit I'd heard alongside the handful of valuable lessons in consciousness just as New York folkie (and an early roommate of Bob Dylan's) Dave Von Ronk began singing about swinging on a star. Maybe that's why I had stuck around as long as I did—for all those stories, the wild comments and twisted plot lines that sometimes sounded like A- and B-grade science-fiction plots all wrapped in bright, enticing foil.

One of my favorite stories was about the Bush Senior-Mikhail Gorbachev summit held on ships near Malta that symbolically signaled the end of the Cold War not long after the Berlin Wall had come down. To provide their own input to the détente between the two superpowers, the boys upstairs created rough seas and poor visibility, keeping the media away while a tentative peace deal was put in place.

And another story and another and another: Steve Greer was an ET. Steve Greer was CIA. I was CIA. Fallen angels, the Nephilim, who were still present in the cosmos (and still visiting Earth), reproduced with human women, which resulted in hybrid beings. This one intrigued me, if only because when our required college theology class pressed our monk professor on what the Nephilim were in the Bible section we were reviewing, he didn't seem to know, or dodged our simple question. A big disclosure event, initiated by the boys upstairs, would occur in Cleveland, according to Dr. Richard Boylan, PhD and "Councilor for Earth" who helped put together the Star Knowledge conference); he had many more such whoopee revelations and plausible strange tales to his (dis) credit. And still another scenario… the Earth had been quarantined as a hostile planet by the Galactic Federation.

This one I also fancied, musing that perhaps our planet was an experiment, a robust but very rickety planetary terrarium seeded by the boys upstairs (panspermia in the literature). This spaceship earth was filled with the different races, evolving animal and plant species, with natural laws and quantum principles in play. The talented woman who cuts my hair once suggested that Earth was just somebody's ant farm! And some days when things appear to be falling apart again, it seems that's not a bad look either and echoes the Urantia view of our place in the cosmos. Here on "Maggie's Farm," we have been left to forge our own outcomes as the evolutionary forces of the universe—including the evolution of consciousness itself—take hold. Quarantined indeed.

I pushed on into the night as a thin line of falling light circumscribed the horizon, beckoning the car westward. Graham Parker's "Waiting for the UFOs" jumped out of the sound system, followed by those crazy Brits, The Bonzo Dog Doo-Dah Band, singing about "The Urban Spaceman" (although this one was not about our boys upstairs but about a street-side pharmacologist peddling various Mind Zoomers that anyone might indulge in). Humming along, I took a mental inventory of The Space Pen Club members and other folks from the UFO community I'd interacted with.

By now, the line of Fisher Space Pens had grown exponentially since the company's founder literally dreamed it up. Like most everything, the pens were all for sale online, some nine web pages deep! One former employee of the company called it the last great American pen company, surviving the other more elite pen makers whose high-end pens, now relics from another time, sell today for hundreds of dollars on eBay.

In no particular order, I noted the select journeys of my compatriots in the shorthand that memory and memoir allow.

Of all the nicknamed "dogs" on the fourth floor Tommy dorm at St John's, MurDog, HairDog, GhoulDog, HairDog was the Most Dog. But now, HairDog was dead too, the golden boy who sat butt naked in an autumn tree, who had nicknamed me the Hawk and mentored the Fallen Angel, Morris, in the ways of feminism, the smart as the world, smart at the world young man. He'd become an outstanding doctor like his dad at Mayo, but early in his career, in the service and treatment of a patient with a complicated unknown illness, he contracted it overnight and suddenly passed away. The innovative bong-maker Dr. K also became a real doctor and studied the brain for a time at Tulane University, eventually settling in Kentucky with a general practice, a lovely wife and kids. MurDog dropped out of college, never really claiming Space Pen Club membership. Instead, he successfully made long-term sobriety a goal (Space Pen sybarites be damned!) and married his college sweetheart.

GhoulDog, my old hippie roommate, went on to make an outstanding life with a dedicated wife and two daughters. He developed several diverse businesses, created lots of jobs and became an award-winning vintner and an outstanding contributor to the arts and community life. Along with his wife, they even commissioned a bronze statue of President Barrack Obama in the city filled with statues of all the US presidents not far from Mt. Rushmore sitting on stolen Native land. But despite all of his achievements, he admitted that he was most proud of being against the Vietnam War.

Through a lot of hard work, he'd earned his rich life, including his polo-playing-pony period, when he'd *fly* his horses to matches throughout North America. On a less grandiose note, this electric cowboy drove his Tesla, or rather it drove us, to bid farewell to Queen Mary E. at our Collegeville stomping grounds in the late summer of 2017. Like Shari, she died of cancer, long after her own world travels—including her sighting of a zig-zagging UFO on an Israeli kibbutz—and a career as a teacher at the St. John's prep school, where she became a staff and student favorite.

It was evident by the good number of Space Pen members present and the additional hundred or more friends, former students, teachers and relatives gathered for her service, how much light she'd brought into the world. Even Boston flew in from Massachusetts, where today he is still the keeper of the Space Pen Archive, complete with the flag, memorabilia and a cache of lively "ceremonial" party photos. Her lucky husband, Chuck (a former football ace on the celebrated Johnny football team coached by the legendary John Gagliardi), and their son

337

greeted folks as they filed into the room. I'd been to a lot of funeral services to that point. But the Queen of the Club's service began with the words, "The bar is open." Ah, sweet Mary, even in death… you never missed a beat.

Officiating her service was a younger monk from the Abbey, who admitted to the congregants that he was a former ringmaster in the Ringling Bros. and Barnum & Bailey Circus before joining the monastery. (This intriguing aside made me want to interview him for a magazine profile, the journalist in me still alert and at attention.) I had signed up to speak during the opening comments period of her memorial "as a fellow traveler," but first came the remembrances from fellow teachers and a relative or two, including her brother, tall Steve and sister-in-law, Jolene, both Space Pen revelers. Her brother told how Mary was prohibited by her parents from going to see Jimi Hendrix's debut in Minneapolis. But Mary told her mother she was staying overnight with a girlfriend the night of the concert. There, fifty-five miles from her St. Cloud home, on a rock 'n 'roll lark, she stood up front by the stage. Then Jimi, who may have been a UFO/ ET "experiencer" if you read *Alien Rock*, made intense eye contact with her when he played his elegiac "The Wind Cries Mary." Mary E. believed he was playing it especially for her. And perhaps he was.

Cuing off my "fellow traveler" note, Brother Ringmaster made a somewhat laudatory introduction as I approached the podium. I provided a brief eulogy, noting, "We would be remiss in remembering her many accomplishments and travels if we didn't recognize that M was also a High Priestess in The Space Pen Club, an ad hoc group of seekers, pranksters, fast friends and perfect strangers who celebrated the fall and spring with our own kind of rites, usually at the old chapel on the lake with select beverages and controlled substances. So now the Space Pen members gathered here—and those afar—wish to salute her and properly send her to the stars."

I don't know who they were, but several younger people in the rear, one wearing a tie-dyed t-shirt, made fist pumps into the air as if hailing her and the Club. Maybe they were former students of hers with whom she had shared the stories of the Space Pen Club and its merry members. In my brief eulogy, I wanted to point out that the old chapel and Space Pen Club stomping grounds across the lake—the Stella Maris Chapel ("the star of the sea")—had now been renovated and re-sanctified as a working, prayerful place after a generous gift from an alumni couple years after our spacey revelries. But I left that out. There would be no more REO Speedwagon or Grateful Dead tunes wailing from its quaint brick windows, no more arrivals of costumed students marking time and making pagan whoopee with reefer, 'shrooms, acid, beer and fraternity.

Further on up the road: The Space Pen Club's Fallen Angel became a real mother eventually – and a mother confessor in her sweet little Northeast Minneapolis coffee shop. (Photo: Mike Schroetke)

The other High Priestess, Morris, the Fallen Angel, eventually married a classmate, then got divorced and raised two beautiful daughters. After embracing the close community and fellowship of The Space Club, she recreated a similar one many moons later in "Nordeast" Minneapolis. For a time, she became the morning mayor of Nordeast with a popular coffee shop where she was equal parts matron-proprietor and mother confessor for the many customers, artists, musicians and friends who frequented the place.

My CSETI working crew in Minneapolis with Combover Bob and the rest? Bob, who tried to make gospel of everything he heard at UFO events and his CSETI working group? Sadly, I lost track of them all. But I have fond memories, including the time both Bob and I ran into each other at a Nevada UFO event of some kind. As we were taking a breather, we watched a huge bank of lenticular clouds came swooping in like a fleet of flying saucers doing recon!

The Pleiadeans cloaked in the lenticular clouds? Or a really impressive weather front?!

A woman who'd heard about their arrival raced out of the building, yelling, "Save me!" as if she'd had enough of life on Earth and was ready for her Richard Dreyfus moment at Devil's Tower. Dr. Boylan, the guy who helped orchestrate the Star Knowledge event in South Dakota, and another attendee, relayed that a psychic inside had reported they were really Pleiadeans cloaked inside those big, circular clouds. But I'm pretty sure it was just a massive, impressive weather front. And I'm also fairly certain no one, especially the boys upstairs, are here to save us —even from our miserable and remarkable selves. Although they might be here to awaken us. Or to provide us with true alternative energy. Or to blow our minds with the mere acknowledgement of their existence. Or…

Later, I heard from fellow CSETI members in Minneapolis that Jesse had died. He was the senior member of our local working group. One of the last times I'd seen him, he excitedly gave me a pile of literature about life-after-death contact groups and techniques, pioneering travelers who explored the survival of consciousness, one's eternal stardust essence. In some of the literature were explanations how beyond the physical body there exists the astral and etheric bodies housing one's consciousness and perhaps their past lives data and other soul ephemera. Jesse, a heartsick lonesome widower, had approached one such beyond-the-grave contact group, futilely looking for his lost love so as to communicate with her again from this side of the veil. His recollection of the empty search ripped through me; it was the first emotion I felt again when told of his death. This afterlife contact/communication attempt made Ufology seem a tidy little Netflix series. But there's probably another Space Pen book there.

John Mack, the best-selling Harvard "abduction" author, was gone too. While he was alive, Harvard had threatened to fire him for his abduction work and his side hustles into UFOland. This just wasn't done in the Ivy League. One of his attorneys, the ever-reliable Dan Sheehan, welcomed the threat and was going to defend him and put much of the best UFO evidence into the public record in his defense. Harvard soon dropped its termination plan.

Mack was run over by a drunk driver while on a speaking tour of England in 2004 where he was talking not about ET but about the legendary T.E. Lawrence. Mack had written a celebrated biography of Lawrence that won a Pulitzer Prize many years before he stepped into the UFO/abduction deep end of the pool. Before he died, John was working on a book about the survival of consciousness after death. The "dead" Mack, however, "appeared" at least twice to two colleagues according to a convincing account that was reported in fine detail in *Vanity Fair* —the same publication to which I first had tried to peddle my CSETI story decades earlier. The account seemed almost like something out of the old Lives of the Saints book with classical illustrations my parents had. The story bears quoting for a couple reasons that should be Space Pen clear:

> "[Veronica] Keen [whom Mack had stayed with during his fateful London visit]… who sat with Mack's body at the morgue, said he materialized and told her, 'It was as if I was touched with a feather. I did not feel a thing. I was given a choice: Should I go, or should I stay? I looked down at my broken body and decided to go.'"

The story notes that others also had visits from the late Harvard prof with the intense blue eyes.

> "Roberta Colasanti, one of Mack's research associates, said he communicated to her a cryptic message on the abductions they had been studying: 'It's not what we thought.' Colasanti waited breathlessly for the solution to the mystery, but it didn't come. Mack promised to return with more information. So far he hasn't."

So, the ghost or spirit-based Mack—or Mack's consciousness—reportedly shared that the whole abduction thing was not as it seemed. He fucking materialized like Shatner on *Star Trek*! But he faded out on the astral plane or wherever he was before he could reveal any more detail. At one point, while he was alive, Mack had posited that the abductions his research subjects/patients had shared in his books were quite possibly not physical in nature but played out in consciousness.

This theory and the *Vanity Fair* post-mortem struck a strange chord with me, if only because I had been toying with that idea for years—that many of the abduction stories "experiencers" told were not necessarily physical in nature. And they weren't produced with the psychotronic weapons discussed in Chapter 3 (although there is reliable evidence that they could be). And they were not Close Encounters of the Third and Fourth Kind that were prevalent in the trustworthy literature about on-board experience like those described by Professor John Salter and his son in a previous chapter. Rather, these alleged abduction encounters took place in their heads—only in their consciousness—while they slept. But, of course, such a theory could not explain the physical marks of alleged abductees like Curtiss A, who struggled with Greer's assessment that the boys upstairs were not a threat. He felt they were certainly a personal threat to him and he made it known in many long conversations over time.

The only reason I even had that hypothesis was based on yet another of my experiences that I had almost forgotten about. Reading the 2018 *Vanity Fair* piece and Mack's words—"it's not what we thought"—triggered the recall. It happened just as I was first setting foot in the CSETI universe, and included Howard, Canada Bro.

This "dream experience" didn't take place at the usual four in the morning hour like most of the other incidents explored in this book, but around a quarter past one. I know because when it was over, I "woke up," roused myself from the condition that my condition was in (as the late Kenny Rogers might have said) and looked at the clock. Actually, I looked first at my hand and flexed the fingers to make sure all of me had filled in, right up to my fingertips. I had been power dreaming again, this time in a lucid rendezvous with unseen figures who had a bunch of us fixating on a video screen. If your attention wandered—and mine did—one of them would tap you with a wand or utensil on the top of your head, at the crown chakra, and you'd be glued again to whatever we were watching.

I also recalled that Howard seemed to be there, the way familiar characters in dreams show up in sketchy dream plot lines. And together we had witnessed some kind of giant, thickly-cut crystal shafts in an "engine room" coming together in synchronized fashion from opposing sides of the room, spaced apart so they folded together like two hands clasping. Then they broke apart in a very mechanistic sequence that repeated over and over. I told Howard, or he told me, "This isn't what we thought it was," echoing the words of the late Professor Mack just after crossing the Rubicon of death.

This "dream" concluded with what felt like all the contents of my psyche being poured through the top of my head back into my body, like sand that had been sucked from one side of an hourglass suddenly being returned in full measure. I could actually feel this sensation of "me" —perhaps my ethereal or astral body one reads about in the life-after-death literature—returning to the flesh of the body in an unconscious state, although I had and have a very conscious memory of it even after thirty years. (I can hear the naysayers saying that it was a classic case of sleep paralysis. But I know from sleep paralysis, and this was not it). Mack's comments triggered my working hypothesis, one that I could never prove or disprove.

And what did I have to compare this experience to other than some odd, might-be-related-tale or two I'd come across, like the one about Dave Davies of The Kinks claiming that he had a conscious moment of aliens, or beings of some sort, downloading or cloning the contents of his brain into container of some kind. In an interview with the UFO magazine *Encounters,* the kinda Kinky account was later published in 1996 UK newspaper *The People*, in which Mr. Davies also alleges that "They showed me crystal computers that monitor every single person living on Earth." Of course, the headline screams, "They Really Got Me Says Kinks Star Dave!"

Later in 2021, after the Mack materialization, in a written online summary about the appearance of Mike Damante, a guest on the radio show *Coast to Coast* in 2020, I discovered there were others who shared such off-the-charts notions. *Coast to Coast* generally comes on too late for me, but I've made an occasional habit of looking at guest summaries to see what community noise and news is gurgling to the surface. Damante was on to promote a new book he'd written called *Punk Rock and UFO's*, "a book based around the idea of rebelling against our conventional beliefs, challenging our own inner thought process by examining our cognition, memories, and media literacy." A former writer, editor, web producer and copy editor at the *Houston Chronicle*, Damante and I shared common ground around music scenes we'd witnessed and the machinations of the UFO realms.

The summary of his appearance in early September 2020 reminded me of the things Dr. Haines had shared in an interview discussed earlier about the fallibility of mainstream science as a tool to understand the phenomenon. The *Coast to Coast* summary stated, "Two areas where science falls flat is connecting UFOs to religious texts and consciousness, Damante proposed. Alien beings have figured out consciousness and with it the ability to travel to other universes [hello Steven Greer]. Different states of minds, even death, may one day allow humans to travel to other places in the universe as well, he speculated. Damante also suggested abduction cases involve the transfer of consciousness rather than the abductees physically being taken into mechanical craft." [Paging Dr. John Mack: pick up the white astral courtesy phone for a call].

Mack's statements in *Vanity Fair* and Damante's thinking over the *Coast to Coast* airwaves obviously would be hard to prove "scientifically" or otherwise, just like Bob Dean's "Assessment" claims—unless, of course, someone was to suddenly unearth the Assessment document and dump it all onto the internet, or leak it to a savvy reporter, an even better strategy. But sadly, Bob, ever the Pope of Ufology, was gone too, dying in 2018 and taking the alleged truths he had read in "The Assessment" to his grave after having shared them in public for so many years.

"Teacher of the Star Ways," Standing Elk has been elevated to Chief Golden Light Eagle

Among those in the community who are still among the living was the strange Italian stigmatist, Giorgio Bongiovanni. By all recent accounts, the man whose hands, feet and forehead bled for years while on the cosmic saucer circuit, has become a journalist and publisher back in Italy, dangerously focused on outing the Costa Nostra. And his bleeding has drastically subsided.

Standing Elk, who had the wisdom to call the first Star Knowledge conference, remains on the planet too, and is now Chief Golden Light Eagle, a member of the Nakota Ihunktowan Band of South Dakota and a spiritual advisor. This "teacher of the Star Ways" was now entrusted with being one of the "original code carriers" who understood the Star Laws symbols gleaned from a craft, according to the Star Knowledge website. I hope we see each other again before we depart this world, like so many, including Sandra Wright who passed on also. My old pal Kevin Foley really liked her. He choked up telling me the sad news. But Bootsie is still alive as of this writing in mid-2021.

Thankfully, Sheehan is still with us too. He stayed on as legal counsel for Greer's 2001 Disclosure effort and is prominent and well-spoken (as always) in the last film Greer made—and most likely his signature celluloid statement: *Close Encounters of the Fifth Kind*. In it, Sheehan challenged the imperil power brokers of the UFO Kingdom, who are really "the elites," as he says, who try to run the world to protect themselves and the 1 percent." And he castigates them for their reckless, unconstitutional behavior about all things Ufological and energy-related.

But in a mid-May discussion about the *60 Minutes UFO* story over Grant Cameron's "The Paranormal UFO Consciousness Podcast," Sheehan—like most everyone following the glut of UFO reporting that month in virtually all major and minor media—was at a loss to explain why the military and federal government are just now making this a highly visible subject where was it was previously regarded as indisputable tabloid trash.

Laughingly, he rightfully called the light *60 Minutes* reporting and interviews "a nothing burger." After fifty years of pursuing the facts and truth about what he believes are clearly extraterrestrial vehicles and occupants visiting and/or surveilling the planet, the erudite and outspoken barrister puzzled aloud about the big *WHY NOW?* question.

He went on to underscore how in all the vetted CE-4 cases he had read or investigated, the boys upstairs consistently emphasized two major messages in their close encounters with their subjects—humans must rid themselves of nuclear weapons because they are a threat not just to this planet but to the wider universe; and we must end the profound environmental degradation that we are witnessing across the Earth. As the ninety-minute podcast progressed, he and his fellow panelists continued to toss around the question of the day—*WHY NOW?*—only to come up short as to who was instigating it and promoting this once exotic narrative now made commonplace and served up pretty in prime time.

Perhaps, I offer, it is the ET's themselves who are finally, *finally* pushing this agenda. But, alas, I have no proof, only a futile supposition, intuition, imagination. But that little cynic on my other shoulder counters that if these events were indeed initiated by off-planet players, the humans downstairs—in the basement and hiding covertly in the closets, and in plain sight on the chaise lounge—would surely fuck it up without the proverbial cooler heads prevailing!

Still there may be a more surprisingly prosaic and obvious financial reason it is happening now with a major historical antecedent. The cost of the secrecy is bankrupting the country, just as the arms race and the obscene militarization between the so-called Super Powers, the US and the former Soviet Union, bankrupted and dissolved the latter. In a web-based, May 2021 report and video on something very ghettoish called Forbidden Knowledge TV, "predictive linguistic" expert Clif High believes—and had predicted such an event for years prior—"that a large part of our national debt is connected to the UFO cover-up. As the site's summary explains, 'Because we've had to pay all these corporations to deal with UFO sh*t, because they had to pay them under the table, because they couldn't get the authorization, because they wanted to keep it a secret, so it was the secrecy part that caused all this to happen… it never came up on the books.' A lot of this debt went into maintaining the infrastructure that kept secrets around UFOs for seven decades, at least."

High amusingly calls it the *Woo Deal* (my lilacs)—the deal that the military is making; the controllers are making. "They're going to surrender the woo in order to get a deal that they don't have to pay for the secrecy anymore, because it is a crushing burden and it has crushed them and they've actually come to the end of their ability to deal with it, primarily because of 'wooflation'… His dark, mob-like perspective shared a lot of what the Flacon had offered about paying off media and others in the Greer film.

"We will learn about what our government thinks it knows about the UFOs," High added. "We may learn something that it actually knows about the UFOs but I doubt we're going to learn very much of the UFOs, in terms of their own internal secrets… The Woo Deal is going to… participate in the debt bubble losing air pressure, because they're not going to be able to hyper-inflate through all of these hidden projects anymore, which was an aspect of hyperinflation…The big process kicks off next month, in June, as the secrets start coming out and that's when the debt bubble is going to slowly start deflating.

"All of our economic issues are going to change," High predicts, "The social order is going to change because there won't be people being bribed anymore. They won't have money, they're going to have to find some new line of work, because it won't be necessary to keep those kinds of secrets, etc. Plus, we 're going to learn things about UFOs that are going to change the nature of our thinking about ourselves, about our planet, about our interaction with each other…"

While the June 2021 revelations may be old news by the time you read this, keep in mind this intriguing disclosure analysis because it could lie beneath whatever information—and/or cover stories—are disclosed. We might see a whole lot of zigging going on while the real reason is zagging over here—off to the sidelines and in the bleachers.

* * *

Aside from powerhouses like Sheehan and other "flying saucer lifers," most of the other Birds in the Aviary were still active too, last time I checked, including a couple who had migrated to Tom DeLong's To the Stars Academy. Chicken Little is out there on the web and flying around the chicken coop, cooing about the End Times, with his chicken hat still in the UFO ring, or was that the hall of mirrors? I think Smith was allegedly responsible for setting up some kind of spy bullshit around a project I had started while slowly exiting CSETI.

Near the end of my time in that community, I developed a treatment for a cable TV series called "Cosmic Highway" with an award-winning producer, director, writer and actress from Toronto, Phyllis Ellis, who was married to badass Stewart Gavin, a professional NHL hockey player. I'd mentioned the project off-handedly to Chicken man in one of his frequent check-ins about Greer and company, noting that the show would probably explore a host of "paranormal" subjects for a pilot, including Ufology. And we would be traveling to the International Association for New Science (IANS)—the New Science forum—to vet some of our interview prospects, including a couple of life-after-death researchers who blew our minds. It was being held in Denver this time, and not Ft. Collins where I had first encountered it in my side hustle journey.

The "Cosmic Highway" concept—which never got sold into syndication—was about a year or two ahead of the wave of paranormal shows that eventually fogged up cable television with ghost and UFO hunters, ancient aliens, and all sorts of wacky metaphysical TV. On a nice afternoon, Phyllis and I skipped part of the last day of speakers and headed over to Red Rocks Park and Amphitheater, which she had never seen.

As we took in the view, Phyllis sat about twenty-five feet ahead of where I was perched higher on a slope. She turned around and saw a guy with a camera who was hiding behind a bush and shooting photos from about twenty yards away! She nonchalantly walked toward him to ask what he was doing. He hightailed it back to a car with another guy in it and sped off.

What the hell? I should have known something was askew when I had first checked into my hotel room and on the window, scrawled backwards on the pane, were the words "Help Me!" I guess spooks gonna spook you, or screw with you through character assassination if you try to get to close to the heart of the UFO enigma. My boys and the few gals in the club would never pull that kind of fuckery, I thought to myself while driving through the night, pushing out of Cosmos and toward the West, like the Little General, nearly as cunning as the French Revolutionary War strategist Lafayette in organizing student anti-war protests.

Many years down the road from 'Nam, he elevated his Space Pen Club standing by writing a book called *The Vatican Prophecies: Investigating Supernatural Signs, Apparitions, and Miracles*, which includes an insightful chapter on the Holy See's involvement in the ET discussion. His previous *New York Times* best seller, *The Vatican Diaries*, is an insider's look at the institution's power and political base as well as the characters that people Vatican City's multiverse. It was based on his thirty-plus years as a self-described "Vaticanista" reporting for the Catholic News Service and other media. Having returned to the Twin Cities after his long run in Rome, we occasionally meet up to hear live music (often Curtiss A!) and compare notes on books, the world, our private lives and those of classmates and Space Pen members. Many of the hardcore club members like Chats, Winks, CV, Smithie and a handful of others, still officially reunite occasionally to golf, fish and hang out, the bonds of the Pen strong and certain.

My childhood buddy and now my lawyer (all those high school debate and student congress triumphs really paid off for him) Jim, aka Zod and I still exchange UFO information and links, often via new books at Christmas and on birthdays, just as we have been doing since we were old enough to read the UFO rags in a North Dakota shopping mall. All of our lives are full and meaningful with families, spouses and partners, careers, the futile remedies against time and aging, and the audible ticking of the clocks, like all those noisy time pieces often seen and heard in Bergman films.

The college kid who turned a joke about the pen among friends into "a thing," Dennis the Accidental Founder. (Photo: Mike Schroetke)

More renegade club members, like the "Keis," have managed to lead more alternative lifestyles. Catching up with him not long ago in his Minneapolis apartment, he appeared in good health after being on the brink of the ultimate long, strange trip with a serious infection during which he spent twenty-two days suspended in a medically induced coma. But his spirit was mighty, like Achilles. His old college roommate, Dennis—our de facto Space Pen brother-founder—was less fortunate. He succumbed also from cancer late in 2020, the year of Covid. His former classmates kept up their Space Pen communion with more than sixty Zoom events, not so different really from their late-night Space Pen salons in the dorm that began with the reading of *Alice in Wonderland*.

Almost three quarters of a century ago, modern science split the atom. It sent a space dune buggy called Voyager with Chuck Berry, Beethoven, Bach, a raga from India and other soundtracks into the universe and it's still out there, having dodged how many asteroids, large, small or microscopic? But today, science and all its medicine still cannot kill cancer. May these pages somehow bless our founder's memory, his family and story. Ditto for Queen Mary E., Shari and the rest.

Der Keis, renamed "The Oakman" by The Mendota Mdewakanton Dakota tribe for his miracle of the four oaks. (Photo: Tom Kladek)

Meanwhile, still long-haired and bearded, and looking like Klaus Kinski in Werner Herzog's movie *Aguirre, the Wrath of God*, Keis had an entire room—the largest in the apartment—full of trees and shrubs he was studying. And there were posters of musicians like Frank Zappa, the Grateful Dead, the Allman Brothers and others as well as some of his own compelling art on the walls of his dwelling, memorable stuff that I had never seen during our college capers.

Like the Little General, he had made his own odd niche inside the world. The Mendota Mdewakanton Dakota tribe had adopted him with an Indian name meaning "the Oakman" after he had successfully helped graft four oak trees the tribe considered sacred but were in the way of a Minneapolis highway expansion. The trees nearly had been destroyed after weeks of protests, arrests and sit-ins. But the Keis worked his own true miracle of the oaks many years after mysteriously appearing to transfigure on a hillside in front of a bunch of awe-struck Space Pen day trippers.

I took my mental inventory of the living and the departed as I drove through the dark. In the background played a stirring instrumental pipe organ version of Bowie's "Life on Mars" on the mix tape, a reverent homage by organist Rónán Murray in St. Joseph's church in Glasthule, Dublin, just after Ziggy Stardust died. The gloriously somber notes momentarily turned the car into a church, and I realized some of the comments that classmate club members had made over time about the Space Pen Club could well have described the aspirations of those in CSETI and the wider UFO world who were trying to establish proof and make contact, to encourage disclosure, and, for me personally, to make sense of it all.

"We were in an age of great myths and fables," my old GhoulDog roommate wrote to me about those collegiate times. "Who knows what was true and what wasn't…? I think back on those days as the best of times. The second memory I have that will not be forgotten is sitting away from the party back in the woods. It was the last party I attended."

In the company of a young woman away from the psychedelic din, the two, in his words, "laid down under a canopy of large oak trees and had fallen asleep. What peace, what calm! I remember sitting with her after we awoke and being struck by a melancholy on that perfect fall day with a robin-egg blue sky. We had taken a bit of a nap and cuddle and were just getting ready to join the rest of the party when I felt a sense of loss. I realized that it was over in many ways and my life would never recreate that same time and place. Not really an epiphany but a sense of finality, a growing awareness that our lives were about to change. We had lost that moment and would never be able to go back again."

Driving under the faint canopy of pinholes of light that constitute the heavens from down here on Earth, I now accepted that most of the lessons I had been exposed to and the elusive answers I'd pursued were merely moments fleeting through space, escaping in time, *stuck* in consciousness. They never would be repeated and perhaps never fully understood. Still, I'd earned my hefty participation trophy—this book—a consolation prize that also doubles as a faintly drawn roadmap into this new science of consciousness, a Mind Zoomer as old as the Vedas.

Tony Bennet came up on the mix tape crooning an old Kurt Weill standard. But inside my head, it was the fantasy voice of the severe crew cut-wearing Chris Kraft that I also heard, the TV voice of NASA's Mission Control from the early US space program that dragged my mother and me out of bed at four-thirty some mornings for launch. I invented his reassuring tone, saying aloud into the vehicle with no passengers while reverting back to a favorite grade school expression Zod and I often used to negate homework or other teenage blues, "This is Mission Control in Houston, at T-minus 10:30 p.m. We are putting *the mission* on hold until further notice. Repeat, we are putting the mission on hold."

For me, that was the night the side hustle was really over. The bus stops here.

Or does it?

Or does it perhaps continue moving forward with or without me?

Beneath my mind's chatter and fleeting recollections, Bennett sang Weill: "But I've been walking through the night and the day / Till my eyes get weary and my head turns gray…"

While I drove on, with my thoughts turning down low, the song's lyrics rolled through my disquieted brain pan. I reasoned, *If the boys upstairs (or even the earthly intel agents or their Aviary Birds) wanted to seek me out—and if they finally planned to do a proper disclosure from their side of the universe—I'm pretty sure they know where to find me.* I also imagined that a CSETI Working Group—without but hopefully with Greer who's invested his life — one day would go off planet or have a major CE-5 someplace down here. And if we're lucky, we'll learn of it through the vast media-saturated, hyperlinked world we live in. If we're lucky. Or there will be a disclosure that is truly a disclosure, and a new era of history will dawn with its own problems and perfections.

Hopefully, when that—or some other event like it occurs out in the open—our disjointed tribes and raging, entrenched partisan factions, both domestically and globally, will grasp the significance. We could use a genuinely new perspective, especially after the devastation of the global pandemic, the riveting social uprisings yet again over racial injustice and the seemingly endless murder of so many people of color in 2020 and 2021, and the skull-numbing, soul-stultifying storming of American democracy at the US Capitol early in 2021. Plus, the ever-present dangers of global nuclear war and other natural calamities that threaten "to pick us off," as Boston, my Space Pen brother, noted upon hearing of our accidental founder's death.

Perhaps it will be a realization like the one proffered by theoretical physicist David Bohm, another pioneer in the interwoven worlds of quantum physics and consciousness (and, by default, another emeritus Space Pen Club member), that "Deep down the consciousness of mankind is one. This is a virtual certainty... and if we don't see this, it's because we are blinding ourselves to it." I'm certain that a new perspective, whatever it reveals to the good, will permanently change the mission we're on—if permanence is a domain of Earth.

Through the blackness, Tony Bennett kept singing with such comforting, warm bravura. But also, with joyous, cautionary resignation, serenading the darkness and celebrating the beautiful and troubled blue planet that we journey on, even as it journeys through the cosmos itself. Effortlessly, Tony sings on a compact disc, whose flimsy data will one day fail. Tony sings, and your heart cracks open like a small flower blooming:

> We're lost out here in the stars.
> Little stars, big stars, blowing through the night.
> And we're lost out here in the stars.

ACKNOWLEDGEMENTS

Every book is a long solitary effort, with many collaborators. Heartfelt Thanks to the following:

Buzz Morison for making the first copy edit slog through the manuscript (hopefully it wasn't as fearsome as that stormy night driving the Delaware Water Gap at 3 a.m.). The Kings at Calumet Editions, Gary Lindberg and Ian Graham Leask and their staff, for believing and hand holding. The generosity of Mike Gould, Fred and Sarah Haberman, Jeff Arundel, and Mr. Funkytown, Steven Greenberg, who helped launch this payload. To the Beta Readers – Good Eye: P.D. Larson, Emcye Edwards, The Little General, Gini Dodds and Curtiss A, Milly Mohr and Angela Frucci, Zod, Isak Keller and Susan Hamre.

Picture Makers, Bonnie Butler (whose fitting Curtiss A photo inspired me to put images in the book when none were planned originally); Chuck Statler; Jimmy Steinfeldt; Kathy Chapman; Greg Helgeson; Giorgio Bongiovanni; Cecilia Vindiola; Rachel Schachter; Chuck and Mary Hughes; Der Keis; and Mike Schroetke (who shot pretty damn well for someone using an expensive borrowed camera while looking through a psychedelic lens). Muchas Gracias also to Jane Barrash, Dr. Larry Dossey, MD, Louie Anderson, Owen Husney, Mary Cassidy, Boston, Toni and Handsome Harley Hughes, and Michael Bodine for the miscellaneous blurbs, tips and deep insights.

And finally, a Big Shout Out to Rico Anderson, for hooking me up with Dan Aykroyd. And to Danny, who not only read the tome but gave it a rousing Aykroydian endorsement as only this cherished Soul and Blues Brother could.

ABOUT THE AUTHOR

Martin Keller is a former pop culture journalist, published author and unproduced screenplay writer, whose work has appeared in *Rolling Stone, Leaders, The Washington Post, The Boston Globe, Final Frontier, Billboard, Utne Reader*, Right On! *The Star Tribune*, the *Mpls.-St. Paul Business Journal, City Pages* and others, with appearances on *Today, 48 Hours*, PBS, Public Radio and more. Keller also has written *Hijinx & Hearsay: Scenester Stories from Minnesota's Pop Life* and contributed to The Minnesota Series. For the past 25 years, he has worked as an award-winning public relations specialist, including an adventurous stint for The Center for the Study of Extraterrestrial Intelligence (CSE-TI). *The Space Pen Club* is based, in part, on that period.

Made in the USA
Columbia, SC
31 July 2021